THE EY EXHIBITION

THE WORLD GOES POP

Edited by
Jessica Morgan and Flavia Frigeri

With contributions by
Elsa Coustou, David Crowley,
Lina Džuverović, Flavia Frigeri,
Sofia Gotti, Giulia Lamoni,
Kalliopi Minioudaki, Jessica Morgan,
Reiko Tomii, Mercedes Trelles-Hernández,
Sarah Wilson

Tate Publishing

First published 2015 by
order of the Tate Trustees
by Tate Publishing, a division
of Tate Enterprises Ltd,
Millbank, London SW1P 4RG
www.tate.org.uk/publishing

on the occasion of
*The EY Exhibition
The World Goes Pop*
The Eyal Ofer Galleries,
Tate Modern, London
17 September 2015 –
24 January 2016

EY

Building a better
working world

The EY Tate
Arts Partnership

*The EY Exhibition
The World Goes Pop* is part of
The EY Tate Arts Partnership

Supported by *The World Goes
Pop* Exhibition Supporters
Group: Irene Panagopoulos,
Ghazwa and Walid Abu-Suud,
and Eykyn Maclean; and Tate
International Council

A catalogue record for
this book is available
from the British Library

ISBN 978 1 84976 346 2
(hardback)
ISBN 978 1 84976 270 0
(paperback)

Designed by
Micha Weidmann Studio
Colour reproduction by
DL Imaging Ltd, London
Printed by
Graphicom SPA, Italy

Cover: Ushio Shinohara,
Doll Festival 1966
(detail of no.83)

Measurements of artworks
are given in centimetres,
height before width

FSC
www.fsc.org
MIX
Paper from
responsible sources
FSC® C013123

CONTENTS

2
Marisol
My Mum and I 1968
Painted bronze and aluminium
185.4×142.2×142.2

EY'S FOREWORD

EY is very excited to present, in conjunction with Tate Modern, *The EY Exhibition: The World Goes Pop.*

This exhibition opens our eyes to the extraordinary reach of pop art – a movement traditionally focused on only a few, high profile, western artists. *The EY Exhibition: The World Goes Pop* makes it clear for the first time that pop art actually exploded around the world, unleashing new talent and fresh ideas and also occasionally striking frissons of alarm in repressive regimes of the time. New and fascinating stories emerge of protest and challenge, with the artists involved often showing real courage. In this way, pop art was part of the challenge to the old order that helped shape the modern world.

In short, this 'EY Exhibition' sets pop art in a new and more significant light showcasing a broad range of diversity and talent which is something we also celebrate and embrace at EY. The exhibition is part of our EY Tate Arts Partnership, now in its third year. We are proud that this arts partnership supports ground-breaking exhibitions that re-examine and re-define significant artists and movements and in the process help 'Build a Better Working World'.

Martin Cook,
Managing Partner – Commercial, EY

3
Joe Tilson
Page 18 Muhammad Speaks 1969–70
Screenprint and oil paint on canvas
on wood relief
186.7×125

DIRECTOR'S FOREWORD

In 1957, Richard Hamilton famously defined pop art as 'Popular, Transient, Expendable, Low cost, Mass produced, Young, Witty, Sexy, Gimmicky, Glamorous, Big business.' Pop art was all of this, but was also a global movement, with artists from many different regions joining in, creating a political, feminist, subversive, language of protest, as well as a reflection on a shifting societal order and a combined rejection and idolatry of mass consumption and so on. *The EY Exhibition: The World Goes Pop* brings these lesser-known shades of pop to the fore. Asserting the political nature of pop art, it shows how a language of bright colours and recognisable motifs (often borrowed from mainstream media) can be put to use by artists in order to critique the established socio-political order. In doing so, the exhibition reveals the global nature of pop art, which was not solely an Anglo-American product, but emerged simultaneously in virtually every corner of the world.

By drawing attention to a cohort of artists working in a pop language outside the canonical remit of pop art, this exhibition reflects Tate's objective to acquire and exhibit works by artists from regions beyond the Western ones. The activities of the regional acquisition committees have fostered this impetus and thanks to them we were able to acquire works by Beatriz González and Parviz Tanavoli, which are included in the show. *The EY Exhibition: The World Goes Pop* also reflects Tate's ambition to rethink key art historical movements of the twentieth century, such as pop art. Thanks to the support of Irene Panagopolous, we were able to host a two-day symposium on global pop art which greatly informed our initial rethinking of the movement. This very timely exhibition was conceived by Jessica Morgan, former Daskalopoulos Curator, International Art at Tate Modern and now Director of Dia Art Foundation, New York. Upon Morgan's departure co-curator Flavia Frigeri, Curator, International Art took on the perfect delivery of the exhibition and publication, assisted by Elsa Coustou, Assistant Curator.

This is the fourth in the series of exhibitions sponsored by EY and we are grateful for their continuous and enthusiastic support, without which ambitious exhibitions like *The EY Exhibition: The World Goes Pop* would not exist. Additional support has been provided by those individuals who have joined us as part of our *The World Goes Pop* Exhibition Supporters Group and to whom we are most grateful, including Irene Panagopoulos, Ghazwa and Walid Abu-Suud and Chris Eykyn and Nicholas Maclean of Eykyn Maclean. Additionally I would like to acknowledge the support of Tate International Council.

This exhibition has been made possible by the provision of insurance through the Government Indemnity Scheme. Tate Modern would like to thank HM Government for providing Government Indemnity and the Department for Culture, Media and Sport and Arts Council England for arranging the indemnity.

Chris Dercon,
Director – Tate Modern

4
Mario Schifano
Comrades comrades 1968
Enamel and spray paint
on canvas and Perspex
140 × 140

ACKNOWLEDGEMENTS

The EY Exhibition: The World Goes Pop, has taken us on a journey across the globe and through the complex world of pop art. During this journey we have learnt that there is no single strand of pop art, and even more importantly that not all roads lead back to the most renowned American pop. The many pops we have encountered are each complex and rich in their own right. Subversive, political, feminist, commercially aware pop art is a language that thrived globally in the 1960s and early 1970s. Over four years ago we embarked on a journey to capture the spirit anew, this time looking beyond the boundaries of an accepted map of pop. The efforts of the many who contributed were sizeable, but the outcome we hope will open the doors to a new understanding of one of twentieth century's most important movements.

All of this would have not been possible without the artists. From Brazil, to Spain, passing through Argentina, Peru, Germany, France, Slovakia, Japan and further afield, many of them have opened the doors to their homes and studios, letting us into their archives of pop art and records of a significant time. Their memories were invaluable and their enthusiastic support of the project has not ceased to impress us. Without their help and the assistance of their many supporters *The EY Exhibition: The World Goes Pop* would not have been possible and our own understanding of what pop art is would, as a consequence, be much narrower. Thus our gratitude goes first and foremost to this group of exceptional artists: Evelyne Axell, Joav BarEl, Thomas Bayrle, Renate Bertlmann, Cornel Brudaşcu, Boris Bućan, Teresa Burga, Delia Cancela, Rafael Canogar, Judy Chicago, Mari Chordà, Raymundo Colares, Equipo Crónica, Henri Cueco, Antonio Dias, Romanita Disconzi, Wesley Duke Lee, Erró, Marisol Escobar, Öyvind Fahlström, Ruth Francken, Gérard Fromanger, Ángela García, Beatriz González, Eulàlia Grau, Sanja Iveković, Jozef Jankovič, Kiki Kogelnik, Komar and Melamid, Nicola L, Uwe Lausen, Natalia LL, Sergio Lombardo, Anna Maria Maiolino, Raúl Martínez, Toshio Matsumoto, Marta Minujín, Marcello Nitsche, Isabel Oliver, Dušan Otašević, Ulrike Ottinger, Joe Overstreet, Maria Pinińska-Bereś, Joan Rabascall, Bernard Rancillac, Equipo Realidad, Raimo Reinikainen, Glauco Rodrigues, Peter Roehr, Martha Rosler, Mario Schifano, Colin Self, Dorothée Selz, Ushio Shinohara, Teresinha Soares, Shinkichi Tajiri, Keiichi Tanaami, Parviz Tanavoli, Joe Tilson, Claudio Tozzi, Chryssa Vardea, Tadanori Yokoo, Jana Želibská and Jerzy Ryszard 'Jurry' Zieliński.

We are extremely grateful to the artists, private collectors, museums and galleries who have lent works from their collections, allowing us to bring global pop art to Tate Modern. Among the private collectors, we would like to thank Atlantic Grupa, Philippe Axell, The Boxer Collection, Philippe Decelle, Francisco Fandos, Xavier Gellier, Mauro Herlitzka, Eduardo Hochschild, Anke Kempkes, Marie-Claude Rancillac, Marinko Sudac, The Linea Collection, The Roger Wright Collection and all those who wish to remain anonymous.

Among the institutional collections and commercial galleries we are indebted to the following: Henri Simons and Arnaud Bozzini, Atomium, Bruxelles; Fernando Mencarelli and Rodrigo Vivas, Conservatório UFMG, Belo Horizonte; Agostinho Cordeiro and Ana Brütt, Cordeiros Galeria, Porto; Gerard Meulensteen and Martina Polakovičová, Danubiana Meulensteen Art Museum, Bratislava; Birgit Loeffler and Edzard Kreipe, DASMAXIMUM KunstGegenwart, Traunreut; Mira Bernabeu and Sandra Moros, espaivisior, Valencia; Ronald Feldman and Marco Nocella, Ronald Feldman Fine Arts, New York; Giorgio Marconi and Gina Abbati, Fondazione Marconi, Milan; Sharon Avery-Fahlström, The Öyvind-Fahlström Foundation, Barcelona; Maija Tanninen-Mattila and Tuija Kuutii, Helsinki City Art Museum; Yutaka Mino and Ayako Kawada, The Hyōgo Prefectural Museum of Art; Leevi Haapala and Kristina von Knorring, Kiasma – Museum of Contemporary Art, Helsinki; Mono Schwarz Kogelnik and Tatjana Okserek, Kiki Kogelnik Foundation, Vienna/New York; Agnieszka Rayzacher, lokal_30, Warsaw; Geoffrey Parton and Will Wright, Marlborough Fine Art, London; Alexandra Alexopoulou and Anna Ewa Dyrko, Galerie Mehdi Chouakri, Berlin; Josef Helfenstein and Heather Schweikhardt, The Menil Collection, Houston; Guy Tosatto and Isabelle Varloteaux, Musée de Grenoble; Luiz Guilherme Vergara and Marcia Muller, MAC – Museu de Arte Contemporânea de Niterói; Antònia Maria Perelló, Teresa Grandas and Patricia Sarroche, MACBA – Museu d'Art Contemporani de Barcelona; Milú Villela, Felipe Chaimovich, Cristiane Gonçalves and Cecilia Zuchi, MAM – Museu de Arte Moderna de São Paulo; Carlos Alberto Gouvêa Chateaubriand, Luiz Schymura, Luiz Camillo Osorio, Veronica Cavalcante and Cátia Louredo, Gilberto Chateaubriand Collection, MAM – Museu de Arte Moderna do Rio de Janeiro; Manuel Borja-Villel and Victoria Fernández-Layos Moro, Museo Nacional Centro de Arte Reina Sofía; Paulo César Brasil do Amaral and Raul Silva, Museu de Arte do Rio Grande do Sul – MARGS, Porto Alegre; Ana Lucía Llano Domínguez, Carolina Cubillos Muñoz and Ayda Cristina Garzón Solarte, Museo La Tertulia, Cali; Karola Kraus, Katharina Schendel, Naoko Kaltschmidt and Sophie Haaser, mumok – museum moderner kunst stiftung ludwig wien, Vienna; Ana María Cortés Solano, Maria Victoria de Robayo, Fernando López Barbosa and Adriana Patricia Nieto Triviño, Museo Nacional de Colombia, Bogotá; Philip Van den Bossche, Barbara de Jong and Huguette Devriendt, Mu.Zee, Oostende; Ivana Jankovic, Martina Munivrana and Snježana Pintarić, Muzej suvremene umjetnosti, Museum of Contemporary Art, Zagreb; Ana Cristina Perera, Corina Matamoros and Herberto Rodríguez Pérez, Museo Nacional de Bellas Artes de La Habana; Marijke Brouwer, Frank van de Schoor and Tosca Philipsen, Museum Het Valkhof, Nijmegen; Piotr Oszczanowski, Barbara Ilkosz and Jolanta Krzywka, Muzeum Narodowe we Wrocławiu, Wroclaw; Jose M. Berardo, Isabel Soares Alves and Rita Lougares, Museu Coleção Berardo, Lisbon; Milan Mazúr, Museum of Art Žilina; Dan Basarab Nanu and Simona Biris, Muzeul de Artă Vizuală Galati; Lucian Nastasa Kovacs and Alexandra Sârbu, The Art Museum of Cluj-Napoca, Romania; Saskia Draxler and Denise Moser, Galerie Nagel-Draxler, Berlin; Shinji Nanzuka and Yuki Itaya, Nanzuka, Tokyo; Piotr Nowicki and Agata Wóznica, Piotr Nowicki Gallery, Warsaw; Tadeu Chiarelli, Natasha Barzaghi Geenen, Valeria Piccoli, Fernanda D'Agostino and Keiko Nishie, Pinacoteca do Estado de São Paulo; Tot Taylor, Riflemaker, London; Alexandra Kusá, Maria Bohumelova and Lucia Gregorová Stachová, Slovenská národná galéria, Bratislava; Giulio Tega, Galleria Tega, Milano; Kari Immonen and Christian Hoffmann, Turku Art Museum, Turku.

A special note of gratitude goes to those individuals who over the years have been exceedingly cooperative in helping us to research the exhibition, contributing to its language, parameters, inclusions and exclusions, and the search for specific works. They have graciously responded to myriad queries and generally helped us navigate the complex meanders of global pop art. We would like to thank in particular Roxana Afshar, Rodrigo Alonso, João Luiz de Amuedo Avelar, Assumpta Bassas, Ana Maria Belluzzo, Bettina Bereś, Margrit Brehm, Carlos Brillembourg, Florence Bonnefous, Anton Bućan, Mary Carpenter, Paola Chieregato, Analivia Cordeiro, David Cueco, Philippe Decelle, Jeffrey Deitch, Martin van Dijk, Paulo Sergio Duarte, Maryam Eisler, Gaudêncio Fidelis, Dorotea Fotivec, Antonio Geusa, Edgardo Giménez, Lívia Gonzaga Bertuzzi, Maria Jose Gonzalez, Sonia Grosso, Axel Heil, Maria Jose Herrera, Agata Jakubowska, Sabina Jankovicova, Corinne Jennings, Roupen Kalfayan, Marco Livingstone, Patricia Lee, Sharon Lerner, Miguel López, Alma Luxembourg, Alberto Magnan, Melanie Martin, Ivo Mesquita, Teresa Millet, Samuel Monier, Shinji Nanzuka, Selima Niggl, Tania Ørum, Djohar Rancillac, José Roca, Norma Rodrigues, Marina Pacini, Adriano Pedrosa, Giovanna Pennacchi, Harald Pridgar, Guillaume Rouchon, Maria Rus Bojan, Hirofumi Sakamoto, Roberta Saraiva Coutinho, Andrea Simon, Aurel Scheibler,

Monica Schifano, Noriko Shinohara, Simone Subal, Florin Ştefan, Marta Tarabula, Cacilda Texeira da Costa, Barbara Thumm, Mimi Trujillo, Rosa Valdes, Timo Valjakka, Leslie Waddington, Kim Williams, the Argentinean Embassy in London and Air Europa. We are especially grateful to Pauli Sivonen for generously supporting the loan of Raimo Reinikainen's works.

This catalogue would not be what it is without the insightful contributions of our essayists. Their texts provide welcome routes through the unfamiliar terrain of global pop. Our thanks to David Crowley, Giulia Lamoni, Kalliopi Minioudaki, Reiko Tomii, Mercedes Trelles-Hernández and Sarah Wilson. Enhancing the essays are the biographies authored by Elsa Coustou, Lina Džuverović and Sofia Gotti. Lina and Sofia, the recipients of a collaborative doctoral award, have enthusiastically supported us in many different ways over the past three years and for this we commend them.

As part of our research endeavours we were able to host a two-day symposium at Tate Modern in 2013, which provided us with fresh insights into global pop. We would like to thank the key note speaker Walter Grasskamp as well as speakers Monia Abdallah, Michael Asbury, Liam Considine, David Crowley, Katarzyna Cytlak, Andrea Euringer-Bátorova, Dávid Fehér, Marko Ilic, Rachel Jans, Anna Kolos, Giulia Lamoni, Fernanda Lopes Torres, Elize Mazadiego, Teresa Millet, Kalliopi Minioudaki, Zheng Shengtian, Reiko Tomii, Mercedes Trelles-Hernández, Syrago Tsiara. Our learning colleagues Marko Daniel and Sandra Sykorova enthusiastically helped us brainstorm and co-ordinate the symposium, which was made possible thanks to the remarkable support of Irene Panagopoulos. Building on the outcome of the 2013 symposium, Sandra Sykorova and Anna Murray have tirelessly worked on a public programme to coincide with the exhibition.

We are also indebted to numerous colleagues at Tate who have lent their support at different junctures. Our biggest thanks goes to Elsa Coustou, Assistant Curator, who has brought great organization skills and enormous enthusiasm to this monumental project. She has been of invaluable assistance in the preparation of both the exhibition and the catalogue. Her calm and cheerful nature made her the perfect companion on this pop adventure. We were also extremely fortunate to have Caroline McCarthy, Registrar and Lucy Fisher, Assistant Registrar, complete our pop core team. With subtle diplomacy and humour they have deftly managed many sensitive and complex negotiations, the outcome of which was essential to the project. Within the curatorial department we are also thankful to Achim Borchardt-Hume, Director of Exhibitions, Helen Sainsbury, Head of Programme Realisation, Rachel Kent, Programme Manager and Neil Casey, Administration Manager who have supported us in other important ways. Lena Fritsch, Assistant Curator, Julia Bailey, Assistant Curator and Justina Budd, Administrator, have provided valuable research assistance, as did our former curatorial interns Alicia Knock, Ana Ballesteros Sierra and Micola Clara Brambilla. Phil Monk has led the art installation team with support from Rhona O'Brien, while Alex Maroon has ably overseen the art handling team. We would also like to thank colleagues in Archive and Library, Communications, Conservation, Development, Front of House, Learning, Legal, Media, Press and External Relations.

Tate's publishing department, led by Jacky Klein, worked diligently to accomplish the successful realisation of this catalogue. Alice Chasey, project editor, has been instrumental in providing essential editorial oversight and together with her colleagues Deborah Metherell and Emma Woodiwiss, she has effortlessly coordinated all aspects of the catalogue's production. Micha Weidmann, with the assistance of Dean Pauley, ably captured the essence of the exhibition, and sensitively translated it into the book's design.

The exhibition design has greatly benefitted from the imagination and sensitivity of architect Nikolai Delvendahl of Delvendahl Martin. We are greatly indebted to him and his assistants Max Gelibter and Finbarr O'Dempsey, for helping us think through the challenges of such a complicated show.

Finally, we must acknowledge EY for enabling us to bring this re-assessment of pop art to the large audience that Tate Modern commands. We thank also those individuals who have joined us as part of our *The World Goes Pop* Exhibition Supporters Group and to whom we are most grateful, including Irene Panagopoulous, Walid and Ghazwa Abu-Suud, Chris Eykyn and Nicholas Maclean, and Tate International Council.

Jessica Morgan – Director, Dia Art Foundation
Flavia Frigeri – Curator, International Art, Tate Modern

5
Antonio Dias
Note on the Unforeseen Death 1965
Acrylic paint on wood, padded fabric,
Plexiglass and Duratex
195 × 176 × 63

14

POLITICAL POP: AN INTRODUCTION

Jessica Morgan

Pop Art serves to remind us ... that we have fashioned for ourselves a world of artefacts and images that are intended not to train perception or awareness but to insist that we merge with them as the primitive man merges with his environment. The world of modern advertising is a magical environment constructed to produce effects for the total economy but not designed to increase human awareness. ... Pop Art is the product of drawing attention to some object in our own daily environment as if it were anti-environmental.
Marshall McLuhan, 'The Relation of Environment to Anti-Environment'[1]

It is difficult to exaggerate the invasion of commercial brands, billboards, photographs, magazines and packaging designs that overwhelmed culture beginning in the 1960s. Advertising and its viral propagation on the street, in the home, through print and celluloid, presented an unprecedented aesthetic challenge, marked by its proliferation around the world. If consumer culture was branded quintessentially American, it was in fact indelibly global. While Marcel Duchamp had responded to the explosive production of materiality in the latter stages of the industrial revolution with the readymade, the next generation of artists had to contend with not just the object but a whole environment. Pop art, we know, was an inevitable rejoinder to the flow and dissemination of *images* of products (as much as the objects themselves). These images were no longer created after reality, but after icons pre-coded by the media.

Ever prescient, Marshall McLuhan identified in 1966 how pop, in contrast to the 'disinterest' expressed by Duchamp's readymade, contended directly with the product or image and expressed an active interest in breaking through its passive consumer landscape, advertising attention to that very place from which it was born. Post-readymade, but pre-simulacra, pop was still concrete. It built its desired socio-economic and commercial meaning into the figuration of the object in a manner reminiscent of Roland Barthes's famous formulation, in *Mythologies* (1957), of the sign that flickers between signifier and signified, so that the image or text, icon or logo denotes a real object but also stands as a simultaneous representation of a code. Whether that code was complicit or critical has been the story of pop art's reception and, in particular, that of its

first generation of US-based artists. But that very question meant different things in different contexts.

***

Thus far, the history of pop has reaffirmed the notion of its dissemination from founding hubs in New York and London to other parts of the world. Arriving in the wake of a socially and politically revised global landscape that placed the USA in a central position, pop was of course irrevocably associated with the emerging dominance of America. Due largely to its commercial appeal and success, pop's narrative was subject to a forceful, gallery-driven marketing that resulted in narrow parameters being set from its first appearance, and the consequent exclusion of numerous, mostly female, artists from entering the arena in the USA.[2] Simultaneously, a (largely New York-based) pop history was being written in John Rublowsky's *Pop Art* (1965), Mario Amaya's *Pop as Art* (1966) and Lucy Lippard's *Pop Art* (1966), and through dealers such as Leo Castelli and curators such as Lawrence Alloway. This was a process that edited out alternative pops – and pop in other places – before they were even understood to exist. Indeed, this process of exclusion can be read as a direct or deliberate echo of the convergence of critics, market and exhibitions that established abstract expressionism as the dominant art movement in the postwar USA.

Yet around the world, 'pop' did not just signify North American popular culture. Pop arose in singular forms and designations, but in no singular lineage. Many pops emerged simultaneously, and often imbued with an ambivalence, if not outright hostility, to the notion of American economic (and implicitly artistic) dominance. While television, newspapers and magazines proved efficient conduits for transmitting the product of American culture globally, US-branded advertising was still largely absent in many regions of the world where such goods were not imported at all, or were too expensive. Instead, regional pop and film stars, local fashion houses and car manufacturers were dominant, and other home-grown visual messaging such as street signage, comics, banners and posters provided alternative inspiration and platforms for pop activity. This was global yet specific pop.

***

What do we talk about when we talk about pop? For one, pop style or a pop spirit encompassed graphic techniques that mimicked popular, commercial and media art, with flattened, simplified and cut away imagery, bright artificial colours, and the combination of text with image. Achieved through projecting an image onto a flat surface and tracing it, or through various types of printing processes – although serigraphy was not always available – the resulting abridged figuration also drew from street signs a universal and yet localised language. Mass media, desire, culture: the most iconic terms associated with pop art must be reconsidered in its global contexts, where 'the masses' and 'culture' had no single hegemonic definition.

Many pop artists, not just in the USA but all over the world, emerged from a design background, and the convergence in pop of graphics, design, architecture and art is a direct result of this crossover. The emerging force of media – television, photojournalism and a new culture of 'breaking news' – drew pop artists to bold forms used for laconic effect: re-appropriating (in many instances illicitly) the plates or moulds from printing presses and the photography commissioned for journalism. In locations where censorship was editorial policy, artists were acutely aware of the potential in disrupting intended meaning. The desire for an immediacy of impact was often directed towards political rather than profitable ends in global pop, where serial imagery and duplication became central for the production of an easily distributable mass art form comparable to popular printmaking (operating outside of a commercial context) rather than limited to a commentary on commercial practices.[3] Pop style also appropriated the advertised object itself through sculpture, often made with new consumer materials: inflatables, malleable soft sculptures and brightly coloured plastics, which offered human associations tinged with the sinister threat of the unnatural, or even, in the omnipresent shadow of war, dismemberment.

Just as 'pop style' encompasses various strategies of composition and process, so there is not one universal pop art but rather hundreds of iterations around the globe that share a populist concern. Numerous artists and movements with a pop strategy developed, including nouveau réalisme, neo-dada, Otra and Nueva Figuración, Saqqakhaneh or Spiritual Pop, and Equipo Crónica, as well as such singular figures as Öyvind Fahlström, Keiichi Tanaami and Erró. These tendencies differed from one another due to their origins in countries as various as Argentina, Brazil, France, Iceland, Japan, Peru, Poland and Spain, and were necessarily informed by their respective traditions and socio-political situations. Countering the mainstream impression that pop art operated as a simple adaptation of the techniques and images of consumer culture, global pop mined the media as a critical, material source for artists investigating the effects of everyday culture. Pop – and this can of course also be said of the more ambivalent work of Roy Lichtenstein, Robert Rauschenberg and Andy Warhol too – was rarely just an affirmative aestheticisation of commodity culture or consumer behaviour but employed the language of advertisements and marketing, the language of the magical commercial environment as identified by McLuhan, to turn established communication strategies into political opposition, satiric critique, subversive appropriation, and utopic explorations of collective and individual identity. Nowhere was this more apparent than in the multiple global permutations of pop. Tactics of pop appropriation could be made to have completely different meanings. Anti-imperialist critique clothed itself in the signifiers of dominant commercial ideology in order to outstrip it, while situating itself firmly and joyously within contemporary culture.

Given that global pop was largely a response to diverse strains of local and international commercial media rather than specifically American pop art, and reflected a desire to create a truly populist art form, it is unsurprising that its many manifestations, even in adjacent countries, could be developed in relative isolation. Despite this lack of transnational communication or dissemination, shared themes and concerns can be observed across the globe, indicative of contemporary socio-economic realities, but also an understanding of the operations of mass media itself. In particular ways, pop iterations throughout the world deformed, extended or inverted certain strategies of American pop, and developed tactics wholly different from American pop, in dialogue with specifically vernacular consumer environments.

What became of subject formation under this advertising invasion, particularly as the individual was both mass media's prize possession and its victim? While pop's canon replicated the image of the isolated consumer, reinforcing the hyper-individualisation under capitalism that burgeoned in the second half

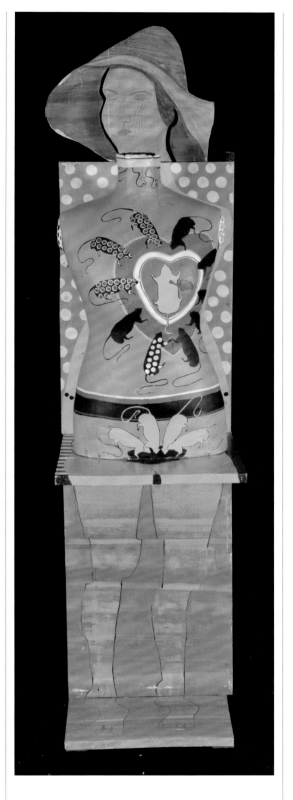

6
(Opposite)
Henri Cueco
Large Protest 1969
Iron tube structure,
8 cut up plywood
figures, enamel paint
400 × 600 × 400

Installation views
at ARC, Musée d'Art,
Moderne de la ville
de Paris, 1970

7
(Right)
Ulrike Ottinger
*Female Mannequin
– Legs Under
Water* 1966
Mannequin, wood
and acrylic paint
180 × 42 × 62

8
Jana Želibská
Kandarya-Mahadeva 1969 / 2010–12
Environment, mixed media,
plastic, mirrors, paper, neon lights
Dimensions variable
Installation view at Slovak National Gallery,
Bratislava 2012–13

9
Jana Želibská
Kandarya-Mahadeva 1969
Installation view at V. Špála Gallery,
Prague, 1969

19

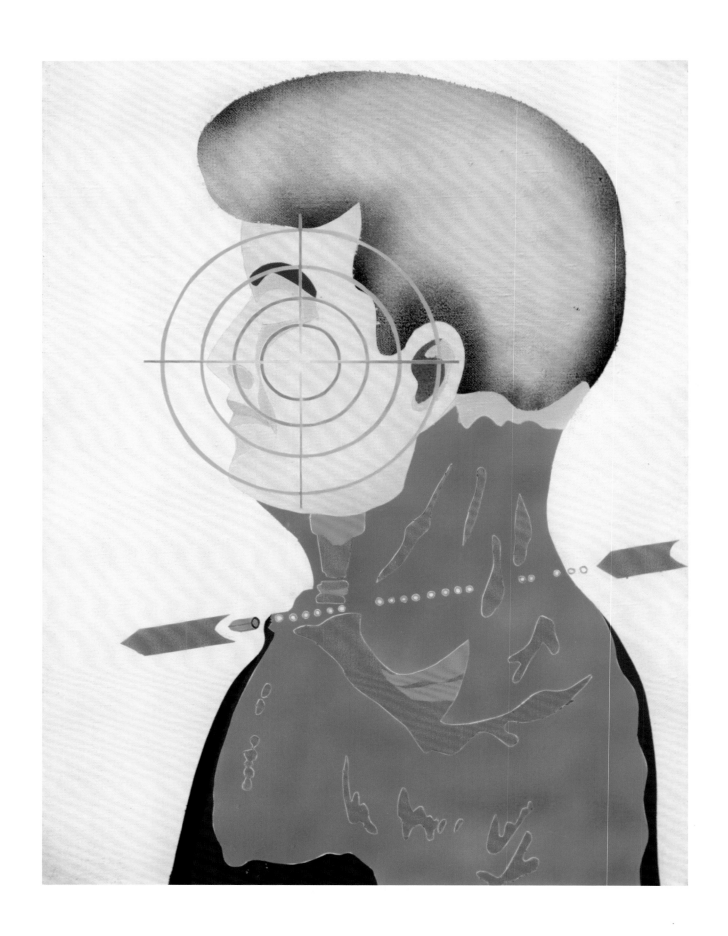

20

of the twentieth century, global pop artists brought the crowd crashing back into the living room, bursting from the contained safety of the television screen and disrupting the hygienic atmosphere of the singular figure or discreet shopper. Think of Erró's *American Interiors* (nos. 100, 130, 131) from 1968, with its globally diverse crowd of proletarians, culled from socialist realist Chinese artwork, who appear to be invading with intent bourgeois interiors collaged from a household magazine. The demonstration or crowd provided fertile terrain for a miscellaneous group of artists and artists' collectives who recognised and hijacked the image of the masses, which stood for, on the one hand, the hidden populace that made possible the consumer society being sold through an apparently subjective, individual appeal, and on the other, an assembled, and on occasion underground, political opposition to the status quo. Within the graphic arts – arguably one of the most media-appropriate realms for pop – 'pop'-style was marshalled productively for political posters from the Situationists to the Black Panthers, Sister Corita and the Viet Cong. Representations of mass events – Claudio Tozzi's *Multitude* 1968 (no.42), Gérard Fromanger's *Album The Red* 1968–70 (no.139), Henri Cueco's *The Red Men, bas-relief* 1969 (no.106), and Equipo Crónica's *Concentration or Quantity becomes Quality* 1966 (no.39) – reassert collective action and communality, in opposition to such remote pop icons as Marilyn or Elvis, based on publicity stills. Whether left-leaning graphic poster production (including the work of Paris-based New Figuration artists for the 1968 protests) or artist-designed flags for the demonstrations in São Paulo and Rio that same year (made by Nelson Leirner, Tozzi, Rubens Gerchman, Carmela Gross, Hélio Oiticica and Antonio Manuel among others), collaborative, public production aimed to bring pop-influenced work into the realm of art made for mass consumption, if not agitation. Global pop represented and framed the crowd, while also orchestrating and unifying it.

At the same time, global pop was also instrumental in representing individual subjectivity, even if only to emphasise its erosion and loss under tabloid conditions. Just as in Warhol's work, this led to image manipulations that denote celebrity or popularity, but also the traces of defamation that linger even in the most apparently elevated portrait.[4] For example, Raúl Martínez's numerous laudatory images of Fidel Castro (*Listen America* c.1967, no.105) and Evelyne

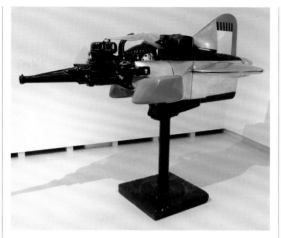

10
(Opposite)
Joav BarEl
Kennedy Assassination 1968
Acrylic paint on canvas
80 × 60

11
Shinkichi Tajiri
Machine No.7
1967–8
Steel, aluminium, Plexiglas and chromed iron
175 × 225 × 78

12
Cornel Brudaşcu
Guitarist 1970
Oil paint on canvas
130×93

13
Cornel Brudaşcu
Portrait (Ion Munteanu) 1970
Oil paint on canvas
120×91

14
Kiki Kogelnik
Bombs in Love 1962
Mixed media with Plexiglas and acrylic
paint on bomb casings
122 × 63 × 25

Axell's portrait of the astronaut Valentina Tereshkova (no.35), the ambiguous portrait of Robert Kennedy by Joav BarEl (no.10), and Dušan Otaševíc's portrait of General Tito, which was intended as a congratulatory laudation but was severely received by the Communist party of Yugoslavia as an unauthorised portrait of the leader.[5] We see the illicit instrumentalising of pop's effect by Cornel Brudaşcu in his portraits of friends and artists in Cluj, Romania, whose visages are transposed onto the appropriated pop bodies of figures that the artist extracted from imported Western magazines featuring album covers by bands such as The Doors. Understanding the elevating effect of the brightly coloured airbrushed effect but knowing nothing of the music or context for this pop culture, Brudaşcu manipulated the icon-effect to celebrate friends such as a recently deceased fellow artist in *Guitarist* 1970 (no.12).

Elsewhere, artists deployed a kind of ironic mimicry in order to address the forms of mass media as a specifically imperialist, capitalist, foreign structure. Take, for instance, Öyvind Fahlström's *Mao-Hope March* 1966 (no.40), a fake demonstration humorously and irrationally linking Bob Hope (the comedic star of US film and television) with the Chairman of the Communist Party of China (leader of the 'Long March', whose image reproduction and distribution outdid any Hollywood star or corporate logo). Recorded as a faux-documentary in which participants/demonstrators answer questions in a manner directly recalling the recent and ongoing civil rights marches or the demonstrations orchestrated against the Vietnam War, Fahlström's work reshoots the latest televisual motifs and vacuous *vox populi* commentary for a distinctly non-didactic, anarchic critique of news-lite coverage. Similarly, in Eastern Europe, the delayed arrival of consumer culture was highly fraught, and met with suspicion as both a 'liberator' from and similar continuation of older systems of mass information as disseminated by the state. Poland's relatively open economy (especially after 1972) allowed for greater access to foreign goods and exposure to advertising, both of which are critically deconstructed in such works as the film *Rewizja Osobista Personal Search* (1972) by Witold Leszczynski and Adrjez Kostenko. Actual advertisements are collaged into a story of a family's failed attempt to import European goods to Poland from Switzerland; the absurdity of the aspirational fantasy – symbolised throughout the film by a mountain of packaging with its accompanying labels and logos – is set in contrast to the final moments in which the border guard and the matriarch of the family revert to nostalgic recollections of their youthful political commitment while the teenage son sets fire to the (imported) Fiat car and its contents in a conflagration of melting products. Natalia LL's *Consumer Art* of 1972, 1974, 1975 (no.24) similarly suggests a withering send-up of the excesses of sexualised marketing: her best known work in the series is a video in which a model provocatively consumes a banana (itself a rare import in Poland in the 1970s).

***

Earth was not pop's only frontier: space exploration from the late 1950s brought the possibility and fantasy of new utopias. Interest was not confined to those countries with space programmes. The world was drawn along ideological lines: Sputnik versus Armstrong. The Cold War space race, the presence of female astronauts beginning in the 1960s, the notion of a territory unbounded by the strictures of daily life, and a fascination with cutting edge technology and materials, resulted in a profusion of pop art around the planet that utilised the metaphors of space travel to explore novel realms of national and personal identity. Sculpture materialised these interests in aggressive, alien, robot-weaponry, among them the massive-scaled *Machine No.7* 1967–8 by Shinkichi Tajiri (no.11), constructed from steel, Plexiglas and aluminium, which made evident the underlying tensions – erotic, military and technological – within competitive space exploration. Taking a different perspective, numerous women artists, attracted by the lure of a radically equal society and by the androgynous clothing – helmets and space suits – explored space imagery within their pop works. Austrian Kiki Kogelnik frequently depicted herself and others in flat outline falling through space (no.57), and Nicola L devised oversized space costumes as sexless soft sculptures, both also offering an alternative to the hyper-sexualised female space traveller *Barbarella* in the comics of J.C. Forest and the subsequent eponymous 1968 film by Roger Vadim.

If space travel offered the body a weightless, genderless existence, artists also explored its abject potential, wrested free from advertising's airbrush. The body in parts, dismembered and disembowelled, is a recurring motif among women artists' work, such as Anna Maria Maiolino's *Glu Glu Glu* 1966 (no.36), a soft sculptural relief of the featureless (with the exception of the mouth) upper body and digestive organs using a bright pop palette, and Delia Cancela's painting *Broken Heart* 1964 (no.91), in which missing parts cut from a heart hang suspended below the canvas. For artists of both genders, the pronounced representation of desire was often commingled with political radicality, as well as an uncertainty with regard to the outcome of the seismic changes taking place in the gendered social order. Antonio Dias's remarkable works, for example *Note on the Unforeseen Death* 1965 (no.5), bring together soft sculptural relief elements that combine erotic impulses with a dark militaristic imagery, the environmental painting-sculpture of Wesley Duke Lee's *Trapeze or a Confession* 1966 (no.15) suggests both a male celebration of liberated female sexuality and the conflicting desire for a coexistence of traditional domestic life.

While lowbrow culture provided global pop with its most direct and obvious source, art's own image archive was prime material for recoding history to the

25

15
Wesley Duke Lee
Trapeze or a Confession 1966
One panel in aluminium, cloth and plastic;
two panels in aluminium and plastic;
four paintings in graphite and oil paint
on canvas; steel cable and cloth rope
Each panel 200 × 200

contemporary moment. 'Pop-ing' art history was a comparatively rarefied if resonant gesture around the world. Parroting the conservative criticism that pop style was superficial and commercial, artists used pop to debase or de-throne the artistic hierarchy or heritage from which they had emerged. Equipo Crónica, a group formed in Spain in 1964 by Manolo Valdés, Rafael Solbes and Juan Antonio Toledo, made frequent use of Pablo Picasso as a national myth, in particular applying a pop style to works such as *Guernica* 1937. The artists' work of the same title from 1971 features a close-cropped image of the famous horse from Picasso's mural exploded by Lichtenstein's eponymous *Whaam!*. Equipo Crónica's work politicises Picasso through its ambiguous connection to American popular culture's iteration of violence while suggesting the ideological critique of the '*cultura de la evasión*' that existed during Francisco Franco's regime. Their collective stance was staked out in opposition to the notion of the individual genius or artwork; indeed, many of their works point to the ricocheting connections and dependencies between generations of artists. Elsewhere, both national and foreign heritage was also called into question. In Japan, Ushio Shinohara, following the visit to Japan of Robert Rauschenberg, began his *Imitation Art* series producing multiple duplicates of the artist's *Coca-Cola Plan* 1958, and thereby mass-producing the handmade pop of Rauschenberg. Shinohara's later *Oiran* series (including *Doll Festival* 1966, no.83) was based on images of geishas from Edo-period woodblock prints. These fluorescent pop works used plastics as well as paint (flat cut-out figures against empty backgrounds) and transformed traditional prints into garish, faceless travesties of taste.

***

Pop's criticality was often misconstrued as it was first developing, and the critique employed by its many artists seen as positively embracing US-influenced commercial media or indeed as an all too simplistic *détournement*. This is particularly true of women pop artists, who withstood the double exclusion of the movement's almost exclusively male terrain and a rejection by other women artists for working in a mode that appeared contrary to feminism's concerns. [6] The dialectic of pop – its immersion into a commodified environment while at the same time providing a language of mass appeal with which to critique and negate it – was felt by contemporary observers to be complicit with dominant power structures, despite that very dialectic. It is true, of course, that pop art, even in its most politically utopic iterations, was necessarily cannibalistic, a kind of ouroboros, feeding off and destroying itself. Pop carried within it what Jürgen Habermas called a 'performative contradiction' (which, ironically, he also observed in the Frankfurt School critique of the culture industry): that the denunciation of an ideology employs in its critique the very language of that ideological power. For pop,

this meant a dissolution of its own language and ethos within the banality of the everyday, an environment from which it could not always extract itself to mount a sustained critique. The negative conundrum implicit in this performative contradiction was turned into a methodological opportunity in global pop, to simultaneously champion populist expressions and disavow the media's ideological coinage.

While the past few decades have witnessed a thorough re-examination of the role of global conceptual art, and a history of postwar abstraction beyond the parameters of the USA and Europe, pop's intentionally equivocal position internationally has largely been passed over and dismissed as an (often belated) artistic influence rather than as a complex, ambiguous and self-reflexive response to contemporary culture. Pop's compound relationship to conceptual practice must be mapped more definitively, as we gradually free ourselves from the convenient monikers that have proved to be ready accomplices in a linear continuum of Western art history.

As exhibitions on pop at the Fundación Proa in Buenos Aires and the Museum Het Valkhov in Belgium, as well as the solo exhibitions of work by Axell and Kogelnik demonstrate, any effort now to redress history's imbalance of global pop coverage necessarily has to first perform acts of retrieval, followed by a consequent process of remapping its definition and potential. McLuhan's argument in 1966, ascribing to pop the capacity to act as an 'anti-environment' and provide a critical enquiry into the image saturation of twentieth-century life, attains further relevance in a contemporary moment in which this condition has increased a hundredfold. While conceptual art's ongoing significance is widely accepted, pop's varied past, particularly outside of the Western canon, needs to be reassessed and its meaning as an agitator and disassembler recognised. We should, in other words, pay attention to what pop in its global context brings to our attention.

16
Komar and Melamid
Post Art No 1 (Warhol) 1973
Oil paint on canvas
121.92×91.44

POP EFFECTS IN EASTERN EUROPE UNDER COMMUNIST RULE

David Crowley

In September 1974 Vitaly Komar and Alexander Melamid exhibited four works at an exhibition of nonconformist art in Moscow which had been reluctantly permitted by the authorities. Two weeks earlier, the artists had had an artwork – a double self-portrait as Vladimir Lenin and Joseph Stalin – destroyed in the notorious demolition of the 'Bulldozer Exhibition', another open-air display of nonconformist art.[1] The state-sponsored violence (conducted by loyal workers outraged at the anti-Soviet art, according to unconvincing official reports) had caused a storm of international protest and so a second exhibition was organised hastily. Komar and Melamid's canvases in this second show appeared to be heavily damaged showpieces of pop art: they included versions of one of Andy Warhol's *32 Campbell's Soup Cans* 1962 (see no.16) and Robert Indiana's *The Confederacy: Alabama* 1965 (see no.18). Works from their *Post Art* series, the canvases appeared as if they had been salvaged by citizens of the Soviet Union from some kind of catastrophe that had befallen capitalist America. Interpreted in these eschatological terms, Komar and Melamid's works could be aligned with official analyses of history in the Soviet Union. In the early 1970s, Nikita Khrushchev's 1961 ringing promise to 'catch up and overtake the West' was still being repeated by the Kremlin (even when it was widely known that the Soviet Union was dependent on importing US food stuffs and machinery).[2] Nevertheless, Komar and Melamid's *Post Art* hardly represented orthodoxy: art in the Soviet Union during the Leonid Brezhnev era (1964–82) was to provide ringing, uplifting images of Soviet progress.

Pop art was an unmistakably foreign phenomenon to both its champions and enemies in Eastern Europe during the Cold War. A number of Soviet commentators – including prominent aestheticians – wrote studies of pop art in the 1960s and early 1970s.[3] Their objection to pop art belonged to a broader critique of what ideologues called the 'decadence' of the West, a word that signalled the abandonment of the uplifting role of culture in favour of base and selfish pleasures. As such, pop art presented a pronounced version of what Soviet critics detected more generally in modernism. Their high-minded critiques were also underscored by deep-set anxiety about the effects of mass culture in the Soviet Union. As the state invested in television, pop music and limited forms of consumerism to satisfy the growing expectations of Soviet citizens, patrician ideologues worried about what they saw as their pernicious effects.

Even if the Soviet engagement with pop art was predominately antagonistic, it testifies to the fact that the works of Andy Warhol or Robert Rauschenberg as well as pop art from Western Europe were known, at least indirectly, through their reproduction in books and magazines. These materials often arrived 'off set', via the 'fraternal' nations of the Eastern Bloc where, by comparison, more liberal cultural policies were in place. Many Soviet artists and critics testify to having read illustrated magazines such as *Projekt* (Poland) and *Umění* (Czechoslovakia) to extract information about developments in the West.[4] Well-travelled and well-informed writers like Jindřich Chalupecký in (former) Czechoslovakia and Urszula Czartoryska in Poland wrote articles and books on contemporary art that detailed the activities of the Independent Group in London or the Sonnabend Gallery in New York.[5] Their analyses were remarkably free of the heavy hand of official ideology and might even be read indirectly as a critique of Soviet culture. In his 1965 book, *Umění dnes* (Art Today), Chalupecký, for instance, characterised pop as social critique, writing:

> Too often art disguises the truth: here, instead, it is revealed. This is the theory and the practice of anti-art. (Daniel) Spoerri only fixes a random piece of ordinary reality in his 'snare pictures' (a table with the dishes after a meal, a shelf with spices); Wolf Vostell uses the direct methods of Pop Art – such as reproduction of news photographs – to make a shocking critique of modern society.[6]

Czech readers may well have interpreted Chalupecký's words as a rebuttal of the seemingly unshakeable Soviet tenet of realism in the arts.

Opportunities for the citizens of Moscow's satellites in Eastern Europe and former Yugoslavia to see works of art by Western pop artists first hand also occurred, albeit

17
Komar and Melamid
Post Art No 2 (Lichtenstein) 1973
Oil paint on canvas
107 × 107

30

18
Komar and Melamid
Post Art No 3 (Indiana) 1973
Oil paint on canvas
107 × 107

19
(Top)
Tomislav Gotovac
My Jazz Day 1964
Printed photographs,
newspapers, painted
paper, cigarette
butts, razors, glue
on hardboard
48.3 × 75.6

20
Ilya Kabakov
*Pipe, Stick, Ball
and Fly* 1966
Ceramic, textile
reliefs, enamel and
oil paint on plywood
130 × 180 × 20

infrequently. The first exhibition of pop art in the region, featuring screenprints by Jim Dine, Allen Jones and Andy Warhol among others, was held in Belgrade and Zagreb (both in Yugoslavia) in 1966 with sponsorship by tobacco concern, Philip Morris International.[7] Three years later the Smithsonian Institution organised a larger touring show of American art after 1945 entitled *The Disappearance and the Reappearance of the Image*, which featured works by Warhol, Roy Lichtenstein, Rauschenberg and Claes Oldenburg. It travelled to various Eastern European cities including Prague (Czechoslovakia) (remarkably, twelve months after Warsaw Pact forces repressed the reform movement there). These US displays belong to the long and well-recorded history of attempts to use modern art and design to broadcast 'American values' during the Cold War.[8] Interest in pop in Eastern Europe also took in its Western European variants. Strong French connections in Poland brought the works of Alain Jacquet, a representative of nouveau réalisme, to the Muzeum Sztuki in Łódź, Poland, where he had a solo exhibition in May–June 1969, and to the Foksal Gallery in Warsaw, where he arranged a performance of 'Le Tricot de Varsovie', which involved the production of a large soft sculpture *in situ*.

The effect of these various encounters with spectacular works of pop art on artists from Eastern Europe is clear. A number of young artists went through a pop phase. Hungarian painter László Lakner, for instance, who has admitted a debt to Rauschenberg, started doubling and fragmenting his careful renderings of documentary photographs and masterpieces of art history.[9] Instead of using the mechanical process of screen printing, Lakner painted these photographic details by hand. Later, in the 1970s, he was to extend his interest in documents in conceptual and photorealist works. In Yugoslavia, Tomislav Gotovac – later well known as a performance artist and filmmaker – made numerous collage works throughout the 1960s using advertisements, packaging and pages from magazines from the West and, as Yugoslavia underwent its own consumer revolution, from local sources too (no.19). Leonhard Lapin, the central figure in nonconformist art in the former Estonian Soviet Socialist Republic, was one of the founders of a short-lived pop alliance called 'Soup 69' (another reference to Warhol) at the end of the 1960s.[10] For these and other artists, pop was often a brief experiment in careers that were later made in performance, conceptual art, experimental film or other artistic practices that established deeper footings in the artistic cultures of Eastern Europe in the 1970s. Pop provided an introduction to the practice of appropriation, a rebuttal of the shibboleths of modernist art: self-expression, originality and individuality. This was what made this embryonic and fleeting engagement with pop at the end of the 1960s an important watershed: the revival of modern art, and of abstract painting in particular, after the death of Stalin and the so called 'Thaw' of the mid-1950s had been strongly motivated by humanist principles, not least intellectual and artistic freedom.[11] Ten years later new questions about the effects of the mass media image seemed to press on the minds of artists in Eastern Europe.

This interest ran through happenings, performances, environments and experimental films as well as early forms of conceptual art in Eastern Europe.[12] In fact, those categories that have been used to describe art in the West – such as pop art – have often been rejected by both artists and critics in Eastern Europe as inadequate and distorting labels. In 1971 János Major made a conceptual artwork in which he combined a small photograph of the tombstone of an otherwise forgotten man called Lajos Kubista (Lajos Cubist), with 17-point text that begins:

1. Cubist Lajos was interred at the
   Farkasrét Cemetery in Budapest
2. Cubism was born in Budapest
3. No ism was born in Budapest
4. Victor Vasarely was born in Hungary
5. Op-art was not born in Hungary
6. Nicolas Schöffer was born in Kalocsa
7. Kinetic art was not born in Kalocsa
8. Theodore Herzl was born in Budapest
9. Zionism was not born in Budapest
10. The father of the nuclear bomb, Leó Szilárd
    was born in Hungary, died in the USA
11. Pop-art was born in the USA, its influence
    extended to Hungary ...[13]

Major's doleful text emphasised the alienness of many international currents in modernism, even those that had Hungarian-born pioneers. His point could be extended to other Eastern Bloc cultures too. Moreover, critics – particularly those writing about the Soviet Union – have often denied the existence of pop art in Eastern Europe under Communist rule because consumerism never succeeded there. Of the brilliant early works by Russian artist Ilya Kabakov, which feature casts of mundane objects from Soviet life seemingly set into blank surfaces (such as *Pipe, Stick, Ball and Fly* 1966, no.20), Matthew Jesse Jackson writes, they 'resembled constructions such as Warhol's Brillo Boxes: ambiguous, three-dimensional eruptions that coalesced with their surroundings whilst remaining tenuously distinct from them ... This work has nothing in common with films, advertisements, magazine covers, television programs, and comic books – the raw

material of Western pop art – but a great deal to do with the desolate Soviet consumerscape.'[14]

The fact that Eastern European citizens confronted shortages and queues in their daily lives is undeniable,[15] but that does not mean that they were unaware of the existence of consumer goods. In Eastern Europe under Communist rule, this knowledge could be both a matter of fantasy and of frustration. Consumer goods and images acquired from the West – particularly clothes, cosmetics, foodstuffs and LP records – gained special significance. Mundane in their original, capitalist context, such things came to carry a heightened importance not only because of their rarity but also because the unfamiliar materials and seductive forms of Western consumer goods could trigger fantasies about capitalist civilisation. Gotovac's early pop collages – featuring pin-ups and branded goods from the West – are full of libidinal desire. Frustration that was felt strongly by many citizens in Yugoslavia and the Eastern Bloc was the product of the gap between expectation (opened up by Soviet promises to 'catch up and overtake the West') and experience. In fact, many countries in Eastern Europe underwent their own consumer revolutions at the end of the 1960s in which 'soft sell' advertising, brightly packaged and branded consumer goods, new kinds of shops such as supermarkets and fashion boutiques as well as 'lifestyle' magazines promised 'socialist consumerism'. In the recursive fashion characteristic of pop in the West too, many film posters, magazine covers and LP sleeves featured serial images that were dressed in the flattened forms and bright colours of pop art.

The response to the spread of commodity aesthetics across what Polish art historian Mieczysław Porębski called the 'ikonosfera' (iconosphere) was not uncritical.[16] Feminist artist Natalia LL in Poland produced a body of works that she called 'Sztuka Konsumpcyjna' (*Consumer Art* 1972–5, no.24) – films and photographic series in which a model toyed with a hot dog, a banana and a runny pudding in a highly sexual manner, exaggerating the techniques of arousal employed in advertising. In Yugoslavia, Sanja Iveković addressed the way in which the authorities sought to balance socialist politics with free-market economics. The 'Ekonomsko Propagandni Program' (Economic Propaganda Programme) broadcast daily on Radiotelevizija Zagreb was, in effect, state-sponsored advertising of domestic and, sometimes, international products. In *Sweet Violence* 1974 (no.23) Iveković recorded one of these broadcasts on a television overpainted with black bars, a simple gesture that alluded to illusory freedoms offered by consumerism. Both Iveković and Natalia LL were preoccupied with the effects of the media – the Polish artist being interested in distinguishing authentic sexuality from its reified forms and Iveković in understanding how private life is haunted by the commercial image. Such differences aside, these works belong to a New Left critique made on both sides of the Iron Curtain, namely that East and West were coming increasingly to resemble each other. A few years

21
Cover of March 1967
issue of *Ty i Ja*
(*You and I*)
magazine published
in Poland.
Artwork by
Roman Cieslewicz

22
(Opposite)
Sándor Pinczehelyi
*Sickle and
Hammer* 1973
Screenprint on paper
60 × 49

earlier Raoul Vaneigem had written in his book,
The Revolution of Everyday Life (1967):

> The cultural détente between east and west is not
> accidental! On the one hand, *homo consomator*
> buys a bottle of whiskey and as a free gift the lie
> that accompanies it. On the other, Communist man
> buys ideology and gets as a free gift a bottle of
> vodka. Paradoxically, Soviet and capitalist regimes
> are taking a common path, the first thanks to their
> economy of production, the second thanks to their
> economy of consumption.[17]

So was there a distinctly Eastern European pop art?
Can the phenomenon only be understood as ripples
of what Czartoryska called a 'wave', which originated in
the West?[18] Pop was, as she observed in 1965, a form of art
that in its original setting passed comment on the incessant
demands of mass media images on their audiences not
through direct and explicit critique but through repetition,
multiplication and concentration ('their creativity is a kind
of dramatic intensification of sensation'[19]). Viewed in these
terms, the chief claim on the title of Eastern Bloc pop
must surely belong to Sots-art. A compression of two terms
(Sotsrealism/pop art), Sots-art was coined by the Russian
duo Komar and Melamid to describe their own artworks
in 1972. In this year they began creating works that treated
the mass slogans and political images which formed a
ubiquitous backdrop to life in the Soviet Union as art.
Early Sots-art works included *Our Goal-Communism*
1972, a plain red banner painted with a slogan in white
block letters and signed by the artists. Another in the
series, entitled *Quotation* 1972, simply replaced the letters
with tidy white blocks arranged in a grid bracketed with
quotation marks. This was a code, seemingly without a
message. Nevertheless, it made a point that was articulated
a few years later by the Czech dissident writer Václav
Havel describing a Communist Party poster: 'The real
meaning of the ... slogan has nothing to do with what the
text of the slogan actually says. Even so, this real meaning
is quite clear and generally comprehensible because the
code is so familiar.'[20] Other Komar and Melamid works
approached ideology as a commodity, as if illustrating
Vaneigem's words above. In 1974 the duo created a series
of ersatz products: hamburgers ground from a copy of
Pravda; and *Leo Tolstoy* and *Maxim Gorky Flavoured
Vodka* (the latter featuring Isaak Brodsky's 1936 much-
reproduced portrait of the Soviet writer on the label).
Alongside the painter Eric Bulatov, Komar and Melamid
were the first artists to rework the codes and symbols of
Soviet propaganda. Often exercises in appropriation, their
early works have a kind of cool, ironic tone that is lacking
in the sardonic combinations of Western adspeak and
Soviet imagery characteristic of much later Sots-art.

Sots-art was not exclusively a Soviet phenomenon
(although it was longest lived there). In Hungary in 1973
Sándor Pinczehelyi created *Sickle and Hammer*,
a self-portrait holding the central symbol of Soviet

authority (and, as the tools of the workers, its claim on legitimacy) (see no.22). Some versions are overprinted in a wash of red. Aleš Erjavec has described this work as an attempt at demystification: 'The Hammer and Sickle have lost their original meaning as mere tools and have been completely appropriated by the symbolic universe of political ideology. It is now up to the artist to revert them back to their non-symbolic, quotidian reality, producing by this procedure an artistic effect.'[21] Pinczehelyi's straight-faced stance was read as both loyalty and dissent: 'Everyone sensed irony at that time', recalled critic László Beke, 'a man positioned in a heroic stance with a hammer and sickle, yet the police were unable to accuse him of subversive activity.'[22]

The ambivalence of irony has allowed critics to read other works produced in Eastern Europe as critical commentaries on power. Young Yugoslav artist Dušan Otašević's triptych *Towards Communism on Lenin's Course* 1967 (no.112) featuring the Bolshevik leader is a case in point. Lenin gestures to a five-point red star on the left-hand panel while another, on the right, has a traffic sign marked with the symbol for 'no right turn'. Produced in the year when much of the world was reflecting – often critically – on the fiftieth anniversary of the October Revolution and Lenin's image was being widely reproduced, Otašević's telegraphic aesthetic perhaps alluded to the enervation of the revolutionary spirit. Other works of this period include his *Comrade Tito, White Violet, Our Youth Loves You* 1969, a combine (or mixed-media piece) made from timber and aluminium panels with a vividly-coloured portrait of the Yugoslav leader as a Second World War partisan, under an 'empty' red star. Kitsch, and seemingly composed in the manner of amateur propaganda displays, Otašević's portrait lacked the aura of heroism and ideological sanctity that characterised almost all Yugoslav representations of Tito. Weighing up the political character of these and other works by Otašević, Branislav Dimitrijević has characterised them as ambivalent reactions to the ways in which socialist ideology and Western consumer culture were becoming entwined.[23]

The extent to which pop art in the West constituted a critical practice has preoccupied many critics and historians. Although pop works produced in Britain and the USA in the 1960s once seemed to have critical and anti-authoritarian potential, they were subsumed easily within the gallery system. Writing of the work of celebrity artists such as Warhol, Jean Baudrillard in 1970 made his reading of pop and consumption clear: it was the end of the modernist avant-garde, a 'total integration' of the artwork into the political economy of the commodity-sign'.[24] Sots-art used many of the same procedures as pop, not least the appropriation of the official imagery that was central to the propaganda apparatus. Yet such works could hardly be absorbed in the same manner. Those made by Komar and Melamid, Pinczehelyi and Otašević maintained a cool distance when power required eagerness, and offered ambivalence when official culture called for commitment.

23
(Opposite)
Sanja Iveković
Sweet Violence 1974
Video, black
and white, sound
5 min 39 sec

24
Natalia LL
*Consumer Art,
excerpts* 1972,
1974, 1975
16mm film,
digitalised
15 min 47 sec

25
Jerzy Ryszard 'Jurry' Zieliński
The Smile, or Thirty Years,
Ha, Ha, Ha 1974
Oil paint on canvas
58.5 × 70

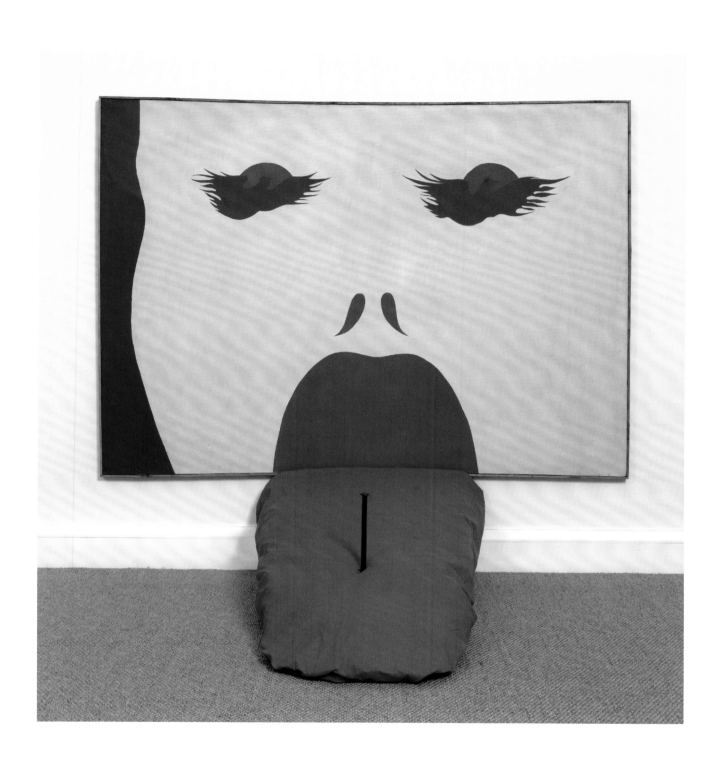

26
Jerzy Ryszard 'Jurry' Zieliński
Without Rebellion 1970
Oil paint on canvas with
pillow, fabric and nail
Canvas 150×200;
Tongue approx. 45×80×130

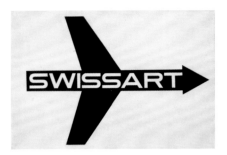

27
Boris Bućan
Bucan Art 1972
All acrylic paint on canvas
50 × 70

A
Bucan Art
(according to Swissair)

B
Bucan Art
(according to Pepsi)

C
Bucan Art
(according to Avis)

D
Bucan Art
(according to JAT)

E
Bucan Art
(according to Pan Am)

F
Bucan Art
(according to Dunhill)

G
Bucan Art
(according to KLM)

H
Bucan Art
(according to Coca-Cola)

I
Bucan Art
(according to IBM)

J
Bucan Art
(according to ELF)

N
Bucan Art
(according to ESSO)

K
Bucan Art
(according to Nivea)

O
Bucan Art
(according to Life Magazine)

R
Bucan Art
(according to INA)

L
Bucan Art
(according to a No Parking traffic sign)

P
Bucan Art
(according to Agfa)

S
Bucan Art
(according to a 500m traffic sign)

M
Bucan Art
(according to Marlboro)

Q
Bucan Art
(according to Polydor)

T
Bucan Art
(according to BMW)

28
Bernard Rancillac
At Last, a Silhouette
Slimmed to the Waist 1966
Vinyl paint on canvas
195×130

1966 IN THE WORLD OF POP

Flavia Frigeri

'Since Pop Art has suffered from critical banalities often more appalling than the visual clichés from which it departs, this varied attack seemed valuable.'[1] Critical banalities, visual clichés and varied attacks were the ingredients used to map the rise and spread of pop art by Lucy Lippard in her seminal study on pop. Published in 1966, Lippard's was one of the first attempts to weave a cohesive historiography of pop, while simultaneously disentangling its many strands. Pop art was young, it was instantaneously hot and cool, it was parodical, it raised many eyebrows, it undermined the throne of abstract expressionism, it was complacent yet ironical of consumer society, it thrived in the 'discotheque' era, it was condemned for its de-personalisation, it was optimistic and yet it was deeply pessimistic.

Pop art was a minefield; intrinsically ambivalent, it encompassed many extremes. Lippard – with the aid of Lawrence Alloway, Nancy Marmer and Nicolas Calas – attempted to navigate this complex landscape. Although prevalently focused on American and British pop art, Lippard conceded – albeit reluctantly – the existence of 'other pops'. The final chapter of the book is in fact dedicated to 'Europe and Canada', but Lippard's approach here is dismissive rather than celebratory. Treating 'other pops' as a footnote at the most to the more widely acclaimed American movement, Lippard systematically undermines their relevance and strategically redeploys their 'flaws' to celebrate Anglo-American hegemony in the field. As she sums it up: 'The further in spirit the cultural heritage of a country is from that of America, the more tenuous is the bond between Pop Art and related manifestations in that country.'[2]

Tenuous at the most was the bond that emerges from Lippard's study, and while undoubtedly New York was perceived as a centre from which pop art radiated, it omits the possibility for alternative pops to exist independently of the Anglo-American axis. However, pop art not only existed but thrived outside of the official pop hemisphere. Distinctly and critically removed from American cultural heritage, global pop artists had little interest in Andy Warhol's feats, or those of his companions: they pursued pop as a device to reflect on current events and voice their social and political convictions, of which America was often the target. History, politics and societal shifts were global pop's daily bread and while the visual language – garish colours and bold images – showed some affinities with mainstream pop, the subject matter clearly stirred away from it.

With political subversion and social empathy high up the global pop agenda, artists were outward-looking attempting to surreptitiously capture, challenge and comment on current events. Many of these have acquired with time legendary tones, but in those days they were pressing matters in need of urgent attention and resolution. Women's emancipation together with countercultural movements, for instance, were key among the societal shifts redefining not only the traditional familial structure but also society as a whole. The space and nuclear races, the two biggest by-products of the USA-USSR Cold War match, and the Vietnam War with its twenty-year string of atrocities, were the source of ongoing debate. Dictatorial regimes, from Francisco Franco's in Spain to the succession of military dictatorships in Brazil and Argentina, curtailed freedom and replaced it with fear. And in the midst of all of this many followed with alarm or trepidation the rise of consumer culture. National events of course also played a role but those events that made headlines internationally were at the fore of global pop's concerns.

History thus offers a simple way to enter the labyrinthine world of pop, and the year 1966 – when Lippard published her survey – is a device to uncover relationships and discrepancies across pop hemispheres. From Brazil to Spain, passing through Iran, France, Japan, Sweden, Belgium, Finland and Germany, pop art was thriving. While Lippard was setting the canon of Anglo-American pop art a global contingent of artists were engaged with the social and political turmoil of the 1960s.

Despite not being the most emblematic year of the 1960s, 1966 had nonetheless its own share of historically significant events. The Vietnam War saw the dreaded B-52 first entering into action in North Vietnam on 12 April. Chinese leader Mao Tse-tung initiated a radical upheaval of Chinese society through the Cultural Revolution. France withdrew from NATO's command structure and LSD was withdrawn from the market after widespread misuse. Major civil rights rallies sprung across the USA, from Jackson (Mississippi) to Chicago, San Francisco and further afield. Organised movements including the Black Panthers, the militant

29
Raimo Reinikainen
Sketch 1 for the U.S. Flag 1966
Oil paint on paper with
newspaper, collage
36×65

30
Raimo Reinikainen
Sketch 3 for the U.S. Flag 1966
Oil paint on canvas with
newspaper, collage
40×65

31	32
Raimo Reinikainen	**Raimo Reinikainen**
Sketch 2 for the U.S. Flag 1966	*Sketch 4 for the U.S. Flag* 1966
Oil paint on canvas with	Oil paint on canvas with
newspaper, collage	newspaper, collage
40×65	40×65

33
Marcello Nitsche
I Want You 1966
Cotton padded plastic and
acrylic paint on PVC
127×106×11.6

African-American paramilitary and the National Organization of Women (NOW) founded by the feminist Betty Friedan were taking their first steps in the public arena. Britain and France agreed plans for the Channel tunnel, and England was protagonist as host nation and winner of the soccer World Cup beating West Germany. In the world of popular culture, Batman, Star Trek and Dr Seuss's *How the Grinch Stole Christmas* first made their appearance on TV screens. Simon and Garfunkel's 'The Sound of Silence' hit number one on American song charts. Walt Disney died aged sixty-five and John Lennon audaciously stated that the Beatles were more popular than Jesus Christ.

Although a hot topic of the day, and ostensibly one of the most pop-related events listed above, the Beatles' daring claims to fame were far from global pop's concerns, which hinged instead on tangible social shifts and political struggles. French artist Bernard Rancillac, for instance, set out to chronicle 1966's key events through a series of paintings. A pseudo-almanac, Rancillac's compilation draws on the inexhaustible reservoir of news and advertisements offered by the printed media. In *At Last, a Silhouette Slimmed to the Waist* 1966 (no.28) he juxtaposes US soldiers torturing Vietnamese prisoners with an advertisement for female underwear. A seemingly incongruous pairing, it mimics the non-hierarchical relationship promoted by newspapers, where politics and commerce can share the same spread. Significantly the issue of *Life* magazine from 11 February 1966, which featured two wounded GI's on the cover, contained an extensive report on the Vietnam War alongside lifestyle and fashion advertisements. In Rancillac's work the union is reinforced through the shared title (originally accompanying the lingerie advertisement alone), which reads 'finally figure refined to size'. The constricting yet embellishing corset is associated with the gory efforts to overtake the North Vietnamese population under American attack. Ultimately torture is a double-edged sword: both the tool of political hegemony and a source of beauty.

Similarly enticed by newspaper headlines is Finnish artist Reimo Reinikainen. His proposals for a new US flag – in the form of four painted sketches (nos. 29, 30, 31, 32) – replace the traditional fifty stars symbolic of the fifty American states with images of the Vietnam War. The sepia coloured snapshots bring the atrocity of the war to the fore, while the white and red stripes are traded for a rainbow-like set of stripes. Despite the vivacity of the new flag the anti-war sentiment is clear, and the project as a whole seems to ironically respond to President Lyndon Johnson's call – on 23 April 1966 – for 'more flags' (i.e. more nations) to join their cause in Vietnam.

Along with the Vietnam War another hot topic of the day was women's global struggle for emancipation. One key aspect of this movement that was not only aimed at changing woman's position in society, but also at redefining conventional familial structures, is a newfound sense of control over one's own body, offered by the legalisation of the contraceptive pill. *Pilules Capsules Conciliabules* (no.37), another of Rancillac's topical 1966 paintings, responds to this shift, but cunningly does so without drawing the pill itself into the work. An absent protagonist, the pill is both the trigger of the girls' conspiratorial gossip, as well as the antagonist to the uterus floating away into space. At one remove from the female body and venturing into unknown territories, the unborn child is like an alien evocative of a new civilisation, the product of imminent societal shifts.

Space, the womb hosting Rancillac's uterus, was in the 1960s the locus where fantasy, politics and dreams of escapism conflated. In quick succession, objects, dogs and humans had attempted to conquer this remote universe leaving millions seduced by these ambitious journeys. Either rooting for the USSR or the USA, space was one of the Cold War's most competitive battlefields. In the minds of many, especially those living under the Iron Curtain, it became an emblem of freedom from the harshness of daily reality. To Evelyne Axell, a Belgian artist who gave up a successful acting career to become an artist and changed her name to the gender neutral Axell – to avoid dismissive comments from her male counterparts – space represented an emancipatory site for women. Axell selected as the emblem of her cause the Soviet cosmonaut Valentina Tereshkova. An idealised silhouette projecting from a gilded background, Axell's *Valentine* 1966 (no.35) is both a feminist heroine and a monument to female eroticism. The cosmonaut can be zipped and unzipped at the viewer's leisure, while a toy helmet (courtesy of Axell's son Philippe) is playfully associated with the sexy figurine. Influential critic of the time Pierre Restany described Axell's paintings as a 'sexual revolution in art', a revolution linking woman's emancipation with female eroticism.

Similarly seeking to vindicate women's rights through the depiction of the female body is the oeuvre of Spanish artist Mari Chordà. Chordà, a Catalan native working during Francisco Franco's regime, experienced a social and political climate very different from Axell's liberal context. As contemporary artist Ángela García recalled, in Franco's days women went from their fathers to their husband's protection with no freedom in between, a legacy sanctioned by traditionalist Catholic values. Chordà herself married young and relocated with her husband to Paris where under the aegis of the Spanish Communist Party she was involved in cultural activities organised by the party. Her involvement was suddenly curtailed on the day when she was found out to be pregnant. Forced to stay at home and 'take care of herself' Chordà embarked on a process of self-introspection, which led to the creation of a series of works in which she unveiled her own body. *The Great Vagina* 1966 (no.133), an enlarged close-up of female genitalia, is the largest of this group of works, which challenge conventional notions of femininity through the exploration of tabooed body parts. The body, in its most visceral and fragmented state, is a subject matter widely redeployed by female pop artists globally

34
Parviz Tanavoli
The Poet and the Beloved
of the King 1964–6
Wood, tin-plate, copper, steel,
fluorescent light, Perspex and oil paint
189.7 × 108 × 107

48

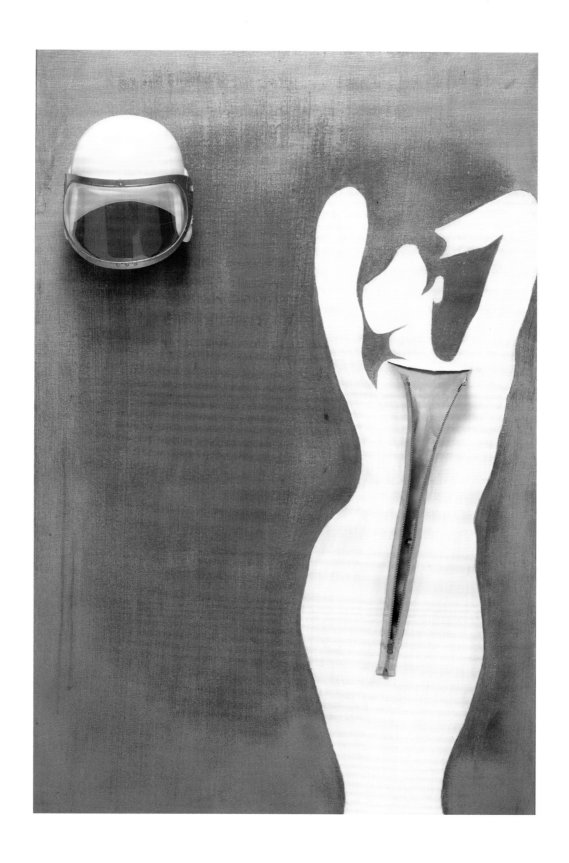

35
Evelyne Axell
Valentine 1966
Oil paint on canvas,
zipper and helmet
133×83

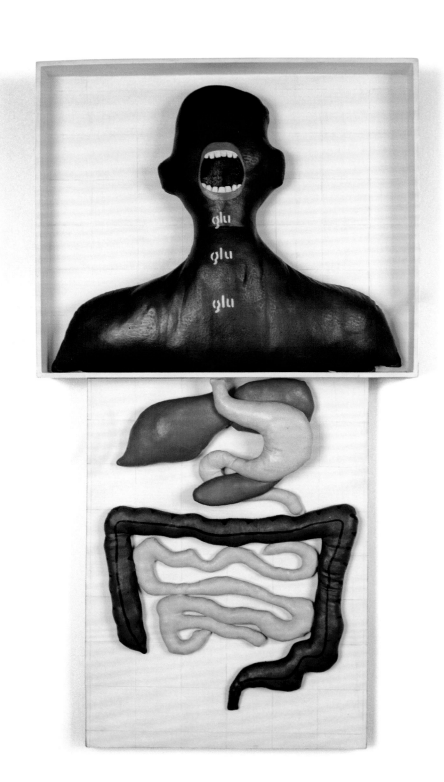

36
Anna Maria Maiolino
Glu Glu Glu 1966
Acrylic paint on quilted fabric
110 × 59 × 13

37
Bernard Rancillac
Pilules Capsules
Conciliabules 1966
Vinyl paint on canvas
146×228

as a means to reflect upon women's condition. Growing control – even visually – over one's body was conceived in fact as a step towards emancipation.

The body as the locus where rights could be voiced is also the site where private and public spheres coalesce. Brazilian artist Anna Maria Maiolino, in *Glu Glu Glu* 1966 (no.36) – a visceral rendering of the digestive apparatus – conflates the intimate bodily functions with the military repression that had seeped into Brazil's everyday life imposing a regulatory apparatus not dissimilar from the digestive one evoked here. Looking back on this work Maiolino claimed: 'it's the hunger of my childhood, of Brazil, of the whole world.'[5] Hunger was at one and the same time a personal affliction and a universal condition Maiolino tells us. The switch between in-dividual and universal symbols is a trait that runs through pop art generally and global pop specifically.

The commercial and socio-political nature of the motifs borrowed by pop enhances their legibility, making them accessible to a wide range of audiences and nationalities. Exemplary of this transliteration is Marcello Nitsche's *I Want You* 1966 (no.33), which takes the widely recognisable pointing finger of US military recruitment advertising campaigns and enhances it with a stuffed blood drop. Roy Lichtenstein had appropriated the same pointing finger a few years earlier and revisited it through his traditional dot technique. The result was a tamed finger falling under the spell of pop art. In contrast, with Nitsche the bluntness of the juxtaposition between finger and blood was revelatory of a deep-seated critique literally pointing to the consequences of US imperialism on Brazilian and Vietnamese soil and far beyond. Both artists embrace pop as a means to rethink the US military campaigns. However, while Lichtenstein uses pop to overtake the subject matter, Nitsche does the exact opposite. Pop in his hands is a mere tool, a language that can be understood by many and as such can be redeployed to lift the veil on US foreign policies. Overtly political and plainly aesthetic come head to head in the rendering of this recruitment campaign, which calls for political awakening on the one hand and popular subjugation on the other.

More than anything, what unites disparate types of pop art produced all over the world is the use of a shared yet un-prescriptive language. Bold colours, hard-edged lines and appropriation of images produced by the mass media are all common traits of this idiom,

which is globally understood yet remains individually practised, in many cases with little or no knowledge of other practitioners. As such, pop is developed by independent agents and in response to specific social and political conditions. For instance, Iranian artist Parviz Tanavoli's desire to bring pop to Iran had to be filtered through popular symbols and traditional handicraft. Hustling century-old bazaars, rather than slick shopping malls, provided an inexhaustible source of inspiration. Moreover the lack of a sculptural legacy in Iran made it all the more challenging for Tanavoli to develop three-dimensional pop works while keeping with tradition. The answer came in the guise of folk pop, a marriage of pop with traditional handicraft. Locks, birdcages, ladders, grills, the simplest objects found in every household provided an inexhaustible source of inspiration, which as in *The Poet and the Beloved of the King* 1964–6 (no.34) could be removed from their original context and usage and in-corporated in a robot-like figure celebrating the heroic poet of tradition.

The union of pop and tradition, which Tanavoli seeks and achieves, seems a counterintuitive partnership, one that runs counter to pop's association with novelty and immediacy. While Rancillac and Reinikainen, but also Axell and Chordà, had elected pop as a means to bring to the fore current events, Tanavoli and the Japanese artist Ushio Shinohara found in pop a device to actualise tradition. Popular handicrafts rather than newspapers provided Tanavoli with his source material and, similarly, fifteenth-century Japanese ido prints gave Shinohara the impetus for his *Oiran* series. Through fluorescent paint, plastic and aluminium sheets warriors in traditional attire were 'popped', showing how also 'art history' had fallen under the spell of pop. Moving from a fascination with American pop, which had led Shinohara to create his spoof-tribute to Robert Rauschenberg in the form of *Coca-Cola Plan* 1964, the Japanese artist soon abandoned American-inspired motifs to look at his own historical legacy through the lens of pop. *Doll Festival* 1966 (no.83), one of the largest panels produced as part of the *Oiran* series, juxtaposes the garish colours and the shiny material with the violence of the depicted scene. The faceless warriors embrace the arms but lose their facial connotations in the midst.

The loss of facial traits is not something that Shinohara alone promulgates, but it is a widespread symptom of the new consumer-driven society where individualism is often subsumed into collectivity. Pop mirrors this condition in the abundance of images where the faceless and standardised mass overtakes the individual sphere. The individual is the victim of this phenomenon, but also acquires strength through the unity with others. With the proliferation of protests, from those in the name of student rights, to civil rights rallies, and protests against the Vietnam War, dictatorships and so forth, the 1960s saw a critical mass taking over the streets of the globe. As Spanish collective Equipo Crónica tells us, 'concentration or quantity is turned into quality'. In its manifesto-like painting *Concentration or Quantity becomes Quality* 1966 (no.39), the faceless mass gradually assembles, from three lost souls in the upper left corner to hundreds in the lower right. The last square of this grid-like graph is filled to the brim, showing how both concentration and quality have been fulfilled. But why was concentration in the face of loss of individualism so desirable? In an oppressive culture spearheaded by the Spanish dictator Francisco Franco, collective gatherings represented one of the biggest threats to his reign of controlled repression, thus the power of the individual rested in the collectivity.

While Equipo Crónica celebrated the mass, German artist Uwe Lausen mourned the helplessness of the individual in the wake of recent historical events. Born and raised in the aftermath of the Second World War, Lausen – like many artists of his generation – was seeking to come to terms with the atrocities perpetrated by Nazism. In a move to renegotiate this cumbersome legacy, Lausen turned to pop. However, his visual output was tragically tainted; carcasses, headless bodies, blood and exposed flesh were regular features of his paintings. Set against brightly coloured backdrops, Lausen's deteriorating bodies merged pop with human violence. Out of this dark mood – in Lausen's case enhanced by the regular use of LSD – emerges *Pilot* 1966 (no.38), a headless near life-size statue (one of the few in the artist's primarily pictorial oeuvre) of a standing pilot. With no facial traits left to indicate age or personality, the pilot becomes a stand-in for all unnamed losses, as well as providing an insight into the psychedelic effects of LSD. Almost entirely dedicated to the rise, spread and frenzy around LSD the issue of *Life* from 25 March 1966 mapped 'the exploding threat of the mind drug that got out of control'. Trips into worlds of serenity and terror were amongst the many reactions to this drug that by 1966 had reached a peak in consumption. Lausen's *Pilot* with his brightly coloured suit seems to be returning from an LSD induced trip, one which has left him headless.

Lausen's head-deprived *Pilot* stands in stark contrast with the 'head inflation' concocted by Swedish artist Öyvind Fahlström. Unlike Lausen, Fahlström discards the body and retains only the head of two widely dissimilar characters: American actor Bob Hope and Chinese leader Mao Tse-tung. Reproduced on picket posters, this unlikely pairing are the protagonists of a fake demonstration. In a decade ravaged by real demonstrations of all kinds, Fahlström orchestrates his own personal manifestation.

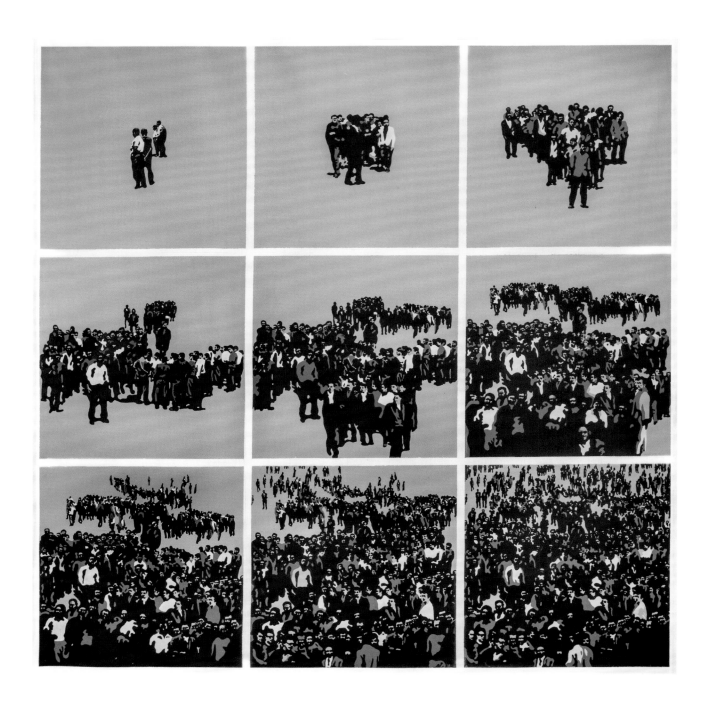

54

A project conceived as part of the piece *Kisses Sweeter Than Wine*, his *Mao-Hope March* 1966 (no.40) sees a small group of people carrying portraits of Mao and Hope around the streets of New York. As a backdrop to Fahlström's fake protesters' wanderings is radio personality Bob Fass asking people 'Are you happy?' Happiness as the range of comments demonstrates is inextricably tied to the socio-political en-vironment of the 1960s. The contrast between true happiness, fake protest, showbiz and political domination is ironically blurred in Fahlström's *Mao-Hope March*.

Also blurring the line between reality and mockery are artists Vitaly Komar and Alex Melamid. Based in the USSR at one remove from mainstream pop art, Komar and Melamid encountered pop art through Lucy Lippard's 1966 survey. 'A priceless gift from an American student friend', Lippard's book, with its coloured reproductions of iconic pop works, soon became a critical source of inspiration for their *Post Art* series.[4] A group of 'post-nuclear' survivors, the *Post Art* works are archaeological artefacts. Warhol's Campbell soup can, Lichtenstein's comic strip and Indiana's target are scarred, marked by the nuclear tragedy, which has swept away the glossy patina endemic to pop art (nos. 16, 17, 18). Pop is under siege in Komar and Melamid's caustic renderings of iconic American pop works, and the biggest irony is that Lippard's celebratory survey of pop art is the main source for its demise. Lippard's structured endeavour to canonize pop art as a quintessential American movement is emblematically undone by Komar and Melamid. Pop in its post-nuclear guise proves that the spirit and socio-political circumstances of different cultures can inflect pop art in different ways, and that each manifestation deserves to be acknowledged regardless of its relationship to America.

39
(Opposite)
Equipo Crónica
Concentration or Quantity becomes Quality 1966
Acrylic paint on canvas
160 × 160

40
Öyvind Fahlström
Mao-Hope March 1966
16mm film, digitalised, black and white, sound
4 min 30 sec

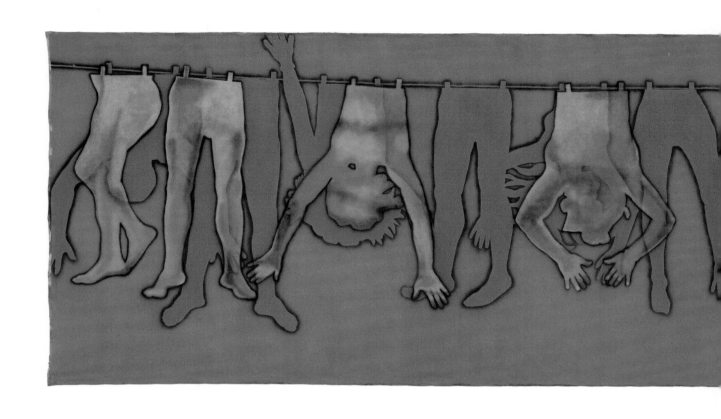

41
Kiki Kogelnik
Friends 1971
Oil paint and acrylic paint
on canvas
170 × 680 × 4.3

56

42
Claudio Tozzi
Multitude 1968
Acrylic paint on agglomerate
199×120

UNFOLDING THE 'PRESENT': SOME NOTES ON BRAZILIAN 'POP'

Giulia Lamoni

'A formidable disaster'

'A formidable disaster',[1] 'a true invasion of barbarians',[2] these are some of the phrases used by art critic Mário Pedrosa in 1967 to describe, not without humour, the Brazilian section at the 9th São Paulo Biennial. Pedrosa referred, more specifically, to the significant role attributed to the participation of the audience in many artworks by Brazilian artists displayed at the Biennial. This radical and collective experience with participation eventually led, as observed by the critic, to the destruction of many of the artworks presented,[3] as leaving a 'contemplative attitude'[4] often translated into a behaviour that was 'a bit too impetuous'.[5]

The 9th São Paulo Biennial, with its striking presentation of North-American pop art,[6] also stimulated a lively debate in the media concerning the wide selection of artists in the Brazilian section and the heterogeneous quality of their work.[7] Critical voices tended to converge in characterising this section as 'chaotic',[8] babelic, 'vibrant'[9] and 'explosive'.[10] In this sense, critics such as Mário Schenberg – also a member of the jury – and Mário Pedrosa articulated views that connected the diversity of the Brazilian works, and in some cases the 'inexperience' of young artists and the poor execution of some pieces, to the definition of a specific moment of crisis, renewal and experimentation in the context of artistic practices and art criticism in Brazil.

It was a 'revolutionary moment'[11] for Schenberg, and for Pedrosa, 'a sort of general anarchy, the mark of a transition, of a phase of transition'.[12] Representation of the USA, in contrast, with its exhibition *Ambiente USA: 1957–1967* showing pop art, and a solo show by Edward Hopper, was significantly described as 'well assembled',[13] and indicated as the highlight of the Biennial because of the strong quality of the artworks on display.[14] Other differences emerged though: according to critic Frederico Morais, the participation of female artists in the Brazilian section was remarkable, whereas in the representation of the 'great countries', among them the USA, no artworks by women were to be found.[15]

Through the sharing of the same institutional space, the 9th São Paulo Biennial marked the physical encounter of North-American pop art with the Brazilian realist currents of the 1960s, thus constituting a privileged stage for the unfolding of a network of relations between different forms of realism, as well as between what were then perceived as central and peripheral artistic languages. In the 9th Biennial, the chaotic and participatory space defined by Brazilian artists materialised in a way that was radically different from that of the North-American pop exhibition.[16] At the same time, one cannot avoid acknowledging the discussion of lines of connection and comparison – often expressed in terms of imitation[17] or singularity[18] – that were articulated then in Brazil regarding pop art and European figurative and realist currents, as well as the frequent reception of pop produced in the USA in terms of lack of a critical and political dimension.[19] Considering the interweaving of these transnational relations, can the term 'pop' be charged with such a complexity of meanings and diversity of perspectives? Would it be more fruitful to submit the word 'pop' to a process of differentiation in order to speak of a Brazilian 'pop', or to use other terms that emerged in the Brazilian context of the 1960s, such as 'new realism'[20] or 'critical realism'?[21]

Certainly, if the challenge proposed by art historian Sônia Salzstein is to be accepted – that is 'to speak of "pop" from a Brazilian point of view, or one that foregrounds the relevance of a local contribution in the understanding of pop as an international phenomenon, where local and global are strangely hybridised without being ostracised from the game of mutual tensions that nourishes them'[22] – the term 'pop' itself will have to be envisioned here as a site of encounter, thus opening possibilities for dialogue as well as for diverging views and conflicting practices and discourses.

'New objectivity'

Between 1964 and the end of 1968 – between the military coup that overthrew President João Goulart and the establishment of the Institutional Act No.5, with the hardening of oppressive policies – the Brazilian artistic scene was characterised by an atmosphere of strong effervescence involving the visual arts as well as theatre and cinema. In this context, artistic practices were often associated with the creation of spaces of resistance as well as with the discussion of the relation between the artist and the public and its reconceptualisation in terms of participation. Although foreign artists affiliated to new realist and figurative trends had been exhibited in Rio de Janeiro since 1963,[23] it was in 1965 that two important events contributed to the opening of a space for Brazilian

43
Glauco Rodrigues
The Song of Solomon –
Concha Shell 1967,
from the series *Concha Shell*
Ink self-propelled on acrylic paint
and 3D glasses
127 × 136 × 16

44
Raymundo Colares
Untitled 1969
Enamel paint on folded
aluminium plate
100×231×15

practices engaged in a critical apprehension of reality to be exhibited and discussed.[24]

The exhibition *Opinião 65*,[25] organised by Ceres Franco and Jean Boghici at the Museum of Modern Art in Rio de Janeiro, gathered works by foreign artists such as Antonio Berni, Juan Genovés and Alain Jacquet, and a group of Brazilian artists including Hélio Oiticica, António Dias, Rubens Gerchman, Carlos Vergara and Vilma Pasqualini. Described by Franco as a 'rupture with the art of the past',[26] the exhibition borrowed its title from the popular theatre show *Opinião*,[27] and presented works that were critically committed to the representation of reality in what was, in political terms, a particularly sombre time.[28] The experience of this exhibition was re-enacted, although in a different way, at the Fundação Armando Álvarez Penteado in São Paulo, where *Proposta 65* took place in December of the same year.

These exhibitions certainly manifested a significant turn in the panorama of Brazilian art, one that led from languages of abstraction to a renewed interest in reality – the everyday life of the city and the suburbs and the languages of the media – while making possible a series of heterogeneous dialogues between the two.[29] As for the articulation between these new realist perspectives and international trends such as pop, different positionings materialised among artists[30] as well as among critics.[31] Mário Schenberg, for instance, in his influential text 'Um novo realismo', regarded Brazilian practices gathered under the umbrella of 'new realism' as somehow connected to a wider international neo-realist movement while having specific characteristics linked to the economic, social and cultural conditions of the country.[32]

In 1966, Hélio Oiticica used, in a seminar at *Proposta 66*, the term 'new objectivity' to qualify the current state of Brazilian vanguard art, while stressing the urgency of 'defining a specific position'[33] for this vanguard, separated from that of pop and European realisms. While acknowledging the existence of a link, Oiticica clearly stated: 'As an artist integrating this Brazilian vanguard, and a theoretician, I say that the collection that we can call Brazilian vanguard art, is a new phenomenon in the international panorama, independent from typically American or European manifestations'.[34] Along with the assertion of the need to negotiate with these central and dominant 'models', Oiticica's intervention identified, in the tendency towards the creation of objects and in the 'delocalization of what is called art',[35] singular features of Brazilian vanguard art.[36] In two articles of the same year, Morais, while quoting the term 'new objectivity', described the relation with foreign cultural models by referring to Oswald de Andrade's idea of anthropophagy – their assimilation and transformation in local terms[37]– and insisted on the importance of taking into account Brazil's oppressive situation in order to comprehend the vanguard's engagement with political and social questions.[38]

In 1967, 'new objectivity' became the title of a groundbreaking exhibition of Brazilian vanguard art that took place at the Museum of Modern Art in Rio de Janeiro. As explained by Oiticica in the text in the catalogue, 'new objectivity' as a grouping of various tendencies of Brazilian vanguard art did not aspire to unity but was explicitly heterogeneous.[39] Among the specific features explored by Oiticica, the disposition to create objects while abandoning canvas painting, the participation of the spectator – both somehow related to the neo-concrete experience – and the fact of 'taking a position regarding political, social and ethical problems'[40] were key to new objectivity's formulation, along with the desire to shape collective projects.[41]

'Pop', popular and public space

When, in 1965, at the opening of *Opinião 65*, Hélio Oiticica arrived at the Museum of Modern Art in Rio with several samba dancers from the Mangueira dressed in his parangolé capes – artworks to be worn and activated by participants – the group was denied access.[42] As a result, the parangolé were presented outside. This episode somehow illustrates the tensions between public space and institutional space that would inhabit, in the following years, vanguard artistic practices and discourses in Brazil. It also mobilised the idea of the 'popular',[43] with all its polysemic charge, as explored in the Brazilian art of the 1960s and, in particular, in its realist currents. In fact, as recalled by artist Gerchman, 'it was the first time that the people entered the museum'.[44]

In a 1966 short film by António Carlos Fontoura, *Ver Ouvir*,[45] young 'pop' artists Roberto Magalhães, Dias and Gerchman were often shot while traversing public spaces: walking in an amusement park, on a beach in Rio de Janeiro, riding a bus or passing along urban streets, mingling with the city crowd.[46] In the film, Gerchman's paintings and objects in particular were brought to the street, and made available to the gazes and comments of passers-by. This radical immersion in public space is not surprising as it is precisely in a dialogue with the city itself, with its anonymity and violence, its social myths and popular aesthetics, that these pieces seem to have been created. In the midst of a group of people in the city stood a 1966 painting by Gerchman entitled *Os desaparecidos 2*. It realistically depicts, one above the other, the faces of a man and a woman, in the style of photographs for identification cards. At the top are the words 'os desaparecidos "2"', a reminder of the brutality of the military regime, while their common names 'Teresinha Maria' and 'Paulo da Silva' simultaneously identify the individuals and signify the ordinariness of their story.

The shared interest in confronting public space, the city streets and urban popular culture characterised some of these realist practices.[47] It is in this way that the specific concern with the multitude can be comprehended: the crowd at political gatherings, as in *Multitude* 1968[48] (no.42) by Claudio Tozzi, as well as the masses attending national popular spectacles such as beauty contests and football games in Gerchman's

45
Antonio Dias
Accident at the Game 1964
Acrylic paint, oil paint and vinyl
on wood, and padded fabric
103 × 77 × 55

63

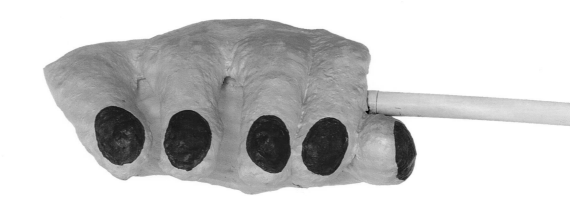

46
Marcello Nitsche
Kill Fly 1967
Plastic pipe, paint on polystyrene
and paint on fibreglass and resin
68.5 × 312.5 × 58.7

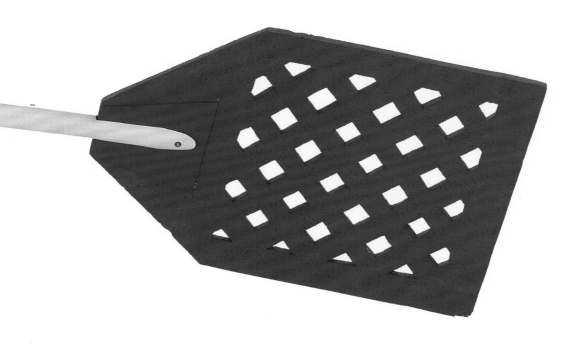

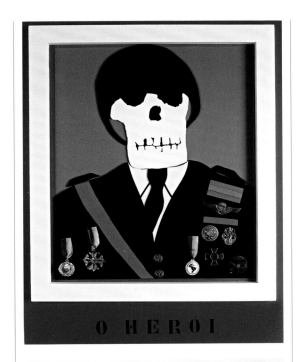

Concurso de miss 1965[49] and *Palmeira 2×0
Flamengo* 1965. At the same time, artists also
intended to encounter people and stimulate
participation. In this regard, two significant
happenings took place in 1966 and 1967, at
the G-4 gallery in Rio de Janeiro[50] and at the
Rex gallery in São Paulo respectively. The first
involved artists Gerchman, Vergara, Dias,
Oiticica and Pedro Escosteguy. The second,
organised by the Rex Group on the occasion
of an exhibition by Nelson Leirner, ironically
entitled *Exposição não exposição*,[51] allowed
the audience to freely take possession of the
objects exhibited. In both cases the reaction
of the public was particularly strong and
resulted in some sort of depredation,[52] a
behaviour that anticipated, although in a
much more radical way, the events of the
9th Biennial.

Furthermore, in this context of radical
experimentation, many artists challenged the
institutional space of the museum and
eventually brought, created or sold their work
outside, in a more 'popular' environment, on
the streets.[53] Whereas actions such as *Arte no
aterro*, organised in Rio de Janeiro in July 1968,
included happenings by artists in public spaces
and during art or art history courses,[54] other
more commercial events in the city, like
Supermercado 66 at the Relevo gallery[55] in
1966 and the 1st Rio de Janeiro Art Fair, which
took place outside the Museum of Modern
Art in September 1968, promoted the selling
of artworks at accessible prices. One of the
most iconic events in this sense was the one
that became known as the *Domingo das
Bandeiras*.[56] In December 1967, artists Nelson
Leirner and Flávio Motta created a series of
silkscreen flags with north-eastern popular
iconography and urban themes, and
'improvised'[57] an exhibition on the street, in
São Paulo.[58] The police apprehended the flags,
however, claiming that the artists lacked the
necessary licence. As a result, on Sunday 18
February 1968, a similar event was organised
in Rio de Janeiro, with the artists from São
Paulo along with others such as Anna Maria
Maiolino, Vergara, Oiticica and Escosteguy.[59]
In a festive atmosphere, with the participation
of the samba school of Mangueira and the
Jaguar band, flags were exhibited and sold
to the public.[60]

These experiences tend to show that the
heterogeneous mobilisation of the 'popular'
in Brazilian art of the 1960s can hardly be
envisioned as disconnected from the definition
of critical positions regarding art institutions,
art criticism and the negotiation with foreign

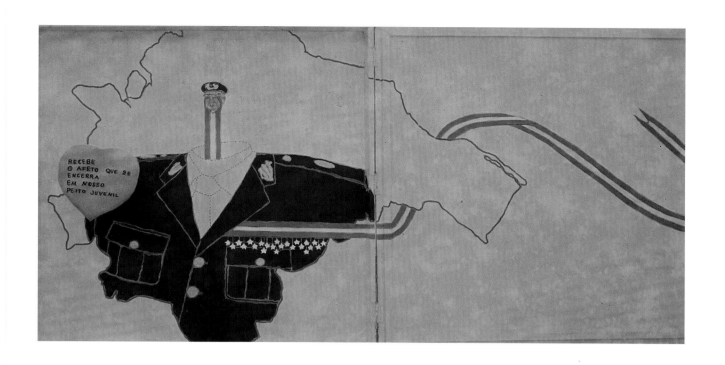

50
Teresinha Soares
*So Many Men Die and I Am
Here So Lonely* 1968,
from the series *Vietnam*
Mixed media
117.5×152.5

51
Teresinha Soares
Die Wearing the Legitimate
Espadrille 1968,
from the series *Vietnam*
Mixed media
116×153.8

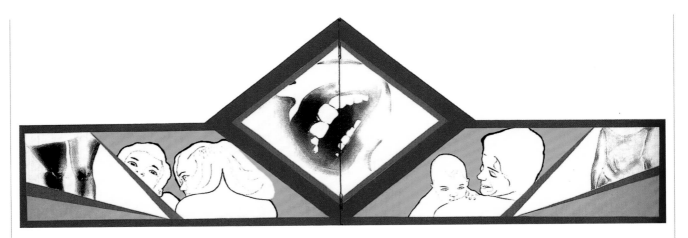

cultural models. Inflammatory actions were developed in this sense. In 1967, Leirner sent to the jury of the IV Salão of Modern Art in Brasilia a stuffed pig – an ironic challenge to the system of the salons and to art criticism – and succeeded in generating much public controversy.[61] Also in 1967, Lygia Pape exhibited *Caixa de baratas*,[62] a box containing a number of cockroaches, displayed in a systematic order, at the show *Nova Objectividade Brasileira*. In the artist's words, the box 'represented dead art in museums, or mummified collections'.[63]

Women in 'pop'[64]

In 1967, Maiolino created a woodcut engraving titled *The Baby* (no.48). As in comic strips, the work is articulated in three juxtaposed images, all depicting domestic family life. The first shows a couple with a baby, whereas in the two following scenes the baby pronounces the word 'mãe' – 'mother' in Portuguese – then the mother holds, or bathes, the baby. The colours are simple, black and white with the addition of red, and the technique evokes local popular traditions, and in particular the woodcut illustrations in north-eastern *Cordel* literature.[65] 'For us, approaching the popular meant looking for our roots',[66] said Maiolino in a recent interview. On the one hand, this work resonates with those of other Brazilian artists who were drawn to the use of techniques and images from popular culture while articulating a 'pop' aesthetic. Artist Lotus Lobo, for instance, created a series of engraving works, in the late 1960s and early 1970s, using industrial lithography from old brands, such as for butter and biscuits, from the state of Minas Gerais.[67] On the other hand, Maiolino's work proposed a significant exploration of women's experience in the domestic realm.

In 1965, when asked by a journalist why she included only one female artist, Vilma

52
Maria do Carmo Secco
Scenes from a Marriage (*Cenas de um casamento*) 1967
Vinyl paint, enamel and collage on Duratex
31×240

Pasqualini, in the *Opinião 65* show, Ceres Franco answered that at that moment the women whose artistic practice matched a contemporary aesthetic were very rare.[68] Interestingly, a few years later, commenting on the significant presence of Brazilian female artists at the 1967 Biennial,[69] Frederico Morais observed that through their work these women were 'considering themselves as a theme, questioning themselves'.[70] This process of questioning possibly began a few years before as, in 1965, one of the texts published in the catalogue of the key exhibition *Proposta 65* – written by artist Mona Gorovitz and entitled 'Why the feminine' – had already attempted to establish a network of relations between female artists working in a realist vein in Europe, the USA and Latin America, such as Niki de Saint Phalle, Marisol, Dalila Puzzovio, Celia Barbosa and Marta Minujín.

At the 1967 Biennial, young artist Cybèle Varela exhibited an object entitled *O presente*[71] (no.49): a box representing a gift that, when opened by the public, revealed a colourful caricature of a soldier placed within a map of Brazil and a pop-up heart with the words of a military hymn.[72] The work, considered offensive, was withdrawn by the police.[73] Besides the relevance of this episode of censorship (one of many) Varela's playful piece resonates – by its political dimension of protest imbued with humour, its comic strips iconography, garish colours, and three-dimensional quality – with other works of this period, such as Maiolino's portrait of a decorated general, with its head replaced by a skull and ironically titled *The Hero* 1966[74] (no.47),and Maria do Carmo Secco's painting *Senhores* 1966,[75] also associating the military with the map of Brazil. During the same period, though, Varela – as were Maiolino and Secco – was also producing works that explored gendered subjectivity. The triptych

Of All That Could Be And Was Not 1967
(no.53),[76] for instance, ironically points to
shifting social codes and gender relations by
depicting a virtual exchange of clothing on
a city street between women in miniskirts and
nuns. Secco often represented, in her folding
canvases, scenes from women's lives, too
– exploring for instance marriage dynamics
and sexual pleasure – the folding evoking
cinematic language.

The multi-focus work of these artists
inhabits a zone of tension between the
questioning of gender relations and female
subjectivities, the will to take a position as
to the country's political situation and
international conflicts – often through humour
and parody – and a critical appropriation of
a variety of languages as those of the media
– especially cinema, television and comic
strips – along with those of Brazilian concrete
and neo-concrete art.

At the 1967 Biennial, artist Teresinha Soares
displayed an object entitled *Caixa de fazer
amor*[77] as part of her exploration of eroticism
from a female perspective. The following year,
she created her *Vietnam* series (nos. 50, 51),
in which she combined a vision of the Vietnam
War as seen from a Brazilian point of view with
references to cinema and photography. Other
artists, such as Regina Vater,[78] Mona Gorovitz
and Sonia von Brusky, also created works in
the mid- and late 1960s that engaged, although
in different ways, with this multi-faceted
approach. By interplaying with an incipient
social and symbolic re-conceptualisation of
gender relations in Brazil,[79] the development
of a 'pop' aesthetic – with its focus on everyday
urban life, local popular culture, representation
by the media, and national and international
politics – possibly opened a critical space
for some Brazilian female artists to express
their multiple positions as women in the
symbolic and socio-political fields.

In Letícia Parente's 1975 video work *Marca
Registada*[80] the artist embroidered the words
'Made in Brasil' directly onto the sole of her

53
Cybèle Varela
*Of All That Could
Be And Was Not
(De tudo aquilo
que poderia ter sido
e que não foi)* 1967
Industrial painting
on wood
Each 65 × 81

foot, thus leaving a powerful, violent, mark
of belonging on her skin. In 1977, Lygia Pape
developed a research project entitled
'The Woman in Mass Iconography',[81] which
was connected to her 1976 installation *Eat me
– a gula ou a luxúria?*[82] The project, which
was financed by Funarte, aimed to constitute a
'visual archive' of women in mass iconography,
critically examining the way this image was
constructed and 'consumed'.[83] As with the
relationship between concrete art, neo-
concretism and 'pop' experiences – whose
differences do not exclude lines of continuity
and hybrid practices – we could possibly
envision the articulation of critical positions
regarding the country's political situation, art
institutions, criticism and cultural imperialism
as potential lines of connection between 'pop'
and post-1968 artistic practices. At the same
time, we can imagine that the work of some
female Brazilian 'pop' artists somehow
anticipated feminist positionings articulated
in Brazil in the late 1970s, creating, in difficult
times, a fertile ground on which projects such
as Pape's could bloom.

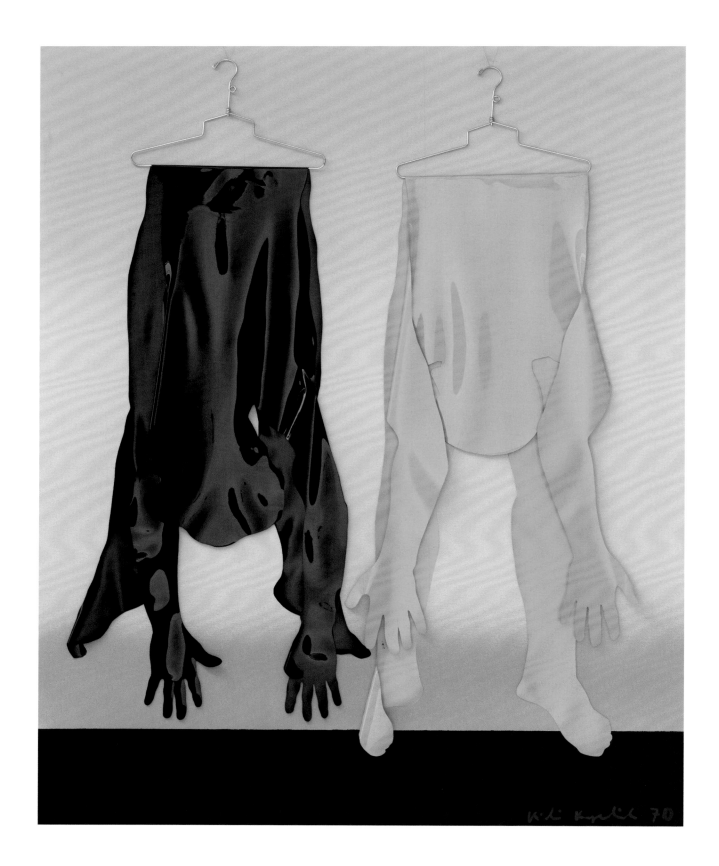

54
Kiki Kogelnik
Hanging 1970
Mixed media with acrylic paint,
sheet vinyl and hangers on canvas
168×137

FEMINIST ERUPTIONS IN POP, BEYOND BORDERS

Kalliopi Minioudaki

I want to create disposable images that are able to reflect all sorts of desire, with a brilliance that whets the appetite of the masses. My dream: … A factory at the service of imagination, fantasy, eroticism …
Evelyne Axell[1]

What interested me about pop was it was directly engaging with the imagery … I saw it as critical.
Martha Rosler[2]

How do I as a woman and an artist work within the society of spectacle while residing within it?
Barbara Kruger[3]

Since the 1970s, female artists have played leading roles in contemporary art with multifariously subversive explorations of mass culture. Deconstruction and feminism, whose premises are often (mis)distinguished from those of pop art, have sanctioned the critical valence of their practices. Yet it is in the context of pop that female artists pioneered subversive dialogues with mass and consumer culture that produced diverse feminist, in essence deconstructive effects that fracture the narratives of postwar art. Indeed many female artists participated in the multifaceted return to reality in postwar art that can be identified with pop art by embracing mass and common culture in a variety of ways (personal, impersonal, parodic, critical, celebratory, etc.) that allowed them to voice female subjectivity, while critically positioning themselves in the society of spectacle. Presaging the 'theoretical' and the 'bad' girls as their nominal foremothers, they often radically intervened in pop, whether by exposing mass culture's patriarchal pitfalls for women, or/and by strategically transvaluating pop pleasures to articulate a variety of transgressive feminist concerns – the most prominent being the retrieval of female sexuality and pleasure from its silencing in Western culture.[4]

Lifting the Borders Among the 'Women' of Pop
Only five years ago, two exhibitions highlighted the eclipse of female artists from the canons of pop art, bringing to light a great number of its contributors.[5] The marginalisation of 'women pop artists' is largely symptomatic of the early critical (mis)construction of pop as an American art movement of commercial subject matter, reproductive techniques and an apolitical coolness

that has left an indelible imprint on pop art's reception and revisions.[6] Resuming thus the diversity of women's contributions to pop, in its contingency and dissonance from its distinct formation in each context, enriches the understanding of pop in its national and transnational dimensions. Lifting, however, the geocultural and chronological borders among the women of pop offers a unique opportunity for what Marsha Meskimmon has described as a 'spatialized engagement' with feminist practices beyond borders yet in the context of pop.[7]

Mapping women's pop with due attention to its locational and gender specificities can unveil important transnational feminist affinities that in all their diversity underpin the radical intersections of women and pop across its centres and peripheries. For example, the early work of Judy Chicago in California (*Flight Hood, Bigamy Hood, Birth Hood* 1965/2011, nos. 56, 115, 116) and Mari Chordà in Catalonia (*The Great Vagina* 1966, no.133), who both explore female experience and the body with an abstract vocabulary variously informed by pop aesthetics. Moreover a 'spatialised' engagement reveals alternative pop scenes and paths of cross-cultural exchange, which undermine widespread misperceptions about the colonising transference of Anglo-American pop and the isolation of women artists in the 1960s. Given the invisibility of its female participants, pop art was perceived even by women as an art of male artists and desires. Martha Rosler's *Pop Art, or Wallpaper* c.1966–72 from the series *Body Beautiful, or Beauty Knows No Pain* (no.125) and Chordà's *Coitus Pop* 1968 (no.132) reflect pop art's fetishistic colonisation of female bodies and the phallocentricism of pop eroticism, the eclipse of female subjectivity in pop, against which many female artists reacted with their work. Yet the international success of Niki de Saint Phalle's celebration of femininity with the grotesque yet pop bodies of her *Nanas* provided an inspirational paradigm of feminist perspective in pop. This is perhaps suggested by the exploration of the female body by Evelyne Axell, who befriended her in Paris, and the environmental erotic nudes of Jana Želibská (*Object II* 1967, no.75), who was in contact with the Parisian scene in the late 1960s.[8]

Despite the sociopolitical and economic disparities of the Cold War era summoned in this exhibition, shared historic circumstances shaped everyday anxieties and hopes in the 1960s due to the globalising media and the

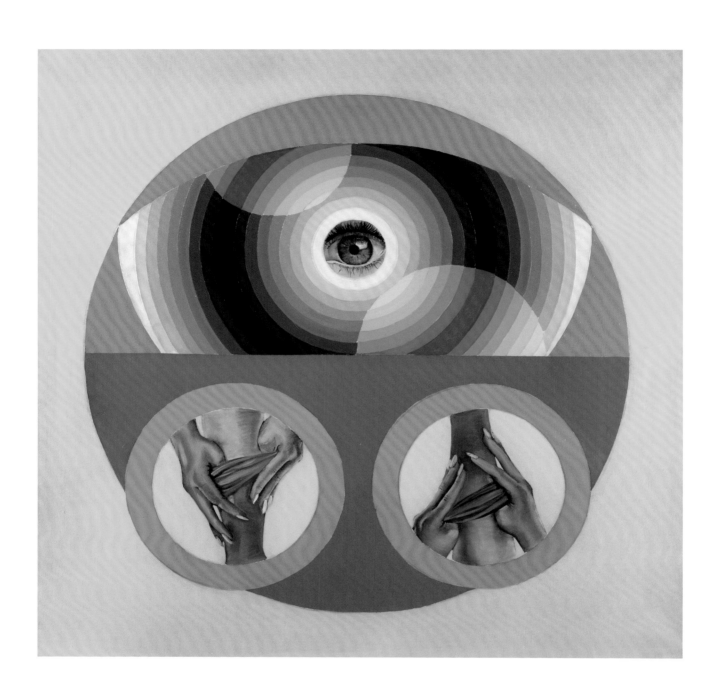

55
Evelyne Axell
Licensed in Both Ways 1965
Oil paint on canvas
120×120

74

56
Judy Chicago
Flight Hood 1965/2011
Sprayed automotive
lacquer on car hood
109×109×10.9

57
Kiki Kogelnik
Fallout c.1964
Mixed media with oil paint
and acrylic paint and
sheet vinyl on canvas
137×183

58
Evelyne Axell
The Pretty Month of May 1970
Triptych, enamel paint on Plexiglas
245.5 × 344.5 × 4.5

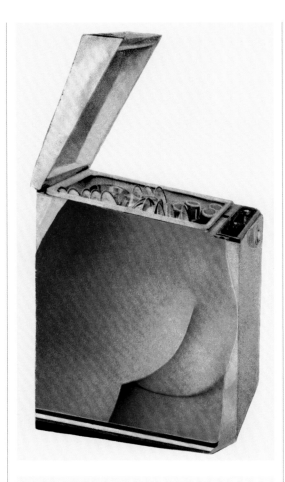

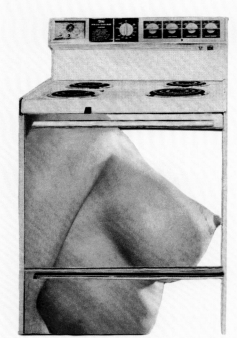

59
(Top)
Martha Rosler
Damp Meat
c.1966–72, from
the series *Body
Beautiful, or Beauty
Knows No Pain*
Photomontage

60
(Bottom)
Martha Rosler
*Kitchen I, or Hot
Meat* c.1966–72,
from the series *Body
Beautiful, or Beauty
Knows No Pain*
Photomontage

infiltration of the free market. The space race, for instance, marked by the exhilaration of technological progress and space conquest rather than its threatening face often conjured in pop, resurfaces in the work of Axell, Delia Cancela, and Kiki Kogelnik (*Fallout* c.1964, no.57) in contexts as far apart as Brussels, Buenos Aires and New York. Divergences, however, in the treatment of common subjects, capture the irreducible diversity of pop and feminist positioning within it. In the work of Cancela (and of Pablo Mesejean), astronaut costumes transform international stars and couples into liberating models of modern subjectivity and love.[9] For Kogelnik and Axell, outer space provides a utopian arena of liberated sexuality. Yet the fragmented humanoid silhouettes of Kogelnik often evoke radically genderless cyborgian hybrids, while the space flights of Axell's nudes celebrate femininity and female sexuality, as does her portrayal of the first female astronaut – Valentina Tereshkova – as a stylised nude (*Valentine* 1966, no.35).

Telling of the diversity of pop's own critical ends is also the difference between Kogelnik's and Nicola L's plastic 'skins'. The evacuation of subjectivity in Kogelnik's depersonalised portrayals of friends or everyday people with her 'hangings' (*Hanging* 1970, no.54) (whether vinyl or painted cut-out silhouettes) resonates with the postwar anxiety about the 'loss of self' that underpins the effects of capitalism, corporatism, consumerism and the media in various pop evocations of the mass subject. Conversely, Nicola L's performative and wearable sculptures – especially her *Red Coat* 1969 (no.153) – provide remedial unisex costumes that heal the one-dimensionality of the mass subject by embracing difference and activating libidinal embodiment, intersubjectivity and togetherness, in line with the politicisation of the body and love in the countercultural milieux she straddled in the late 1960s.[10]

Had it not been men who first pillaged the domestic domain, pop art would have never left the kitchen, feminist critic Lucy Lippard has said in a rare comment on the masculinism of the pop canon that she had nonetheless helped to shape as editor of one of the first books on the subject.[11] With hindsight, it can also be observed that feminist criticism has not let pre-feminist explorations of the home be seen through the frame of pop. Yet the home, along with the representation of the female body and the commodity, offers a rich terrain in which to map the critical attitudes of women in pop. Despite societal changes in the democratic West and the egalitarianism of socialist countries, in the 1960s the domestic domain was still the privileged yet restrictive territory of women and a primary target of everyday consumerism and patriarchal fictions. It is as a chief and gendered Cold War commodity, if not weapon, signifying the American way of life that Rosler reveals the suburban home as complicit with US imperialism and the atrocities of the Vietnam War in *House Beautiful: Bringing the War Home* 1967–72. While several artists focused on the repressive effect of the upgraded pop kingdom of women on their agency and sexuality, home was materially or iconographically evoked by others as a liberating site of female creativity and sexuality.[12]

The juxtaposition of incongruous everyday realities, culled from the mass media, that underpins the collage aesthetics of some pop manifestations, gave female artists an invaluable tool to unmask the gap between women's experience at home and the ideological grip of consumerism and media culture on their lives – albeit in societies of differing degrees of patriarchy and implementation of free-market economy. In her early 1970s painting collage series *Misses and Embroideries* (*Composition* 1974, no.65) Ángela García intermeshes cut-outs of beauty queens with comic book heroines or insignia of women's work at home, such as embroidery patterns. García's attention to the artistic properties of women's work honours the home as a space of female creativity. Her juxtaposition of pop heroines, however, criticises the legalised inferiority of women in General Franco's Spain. Women were educated to their delimiting roles – as mothers and slaves in the homes, and beauty objects in public – as much by propagandistic institutions, such as the fascist party's department of women's affairs (the Feminine Section), which taught Spanish women their feminine skills, as by the comic-book heroines and beauty queens that updated the vision of ideal womanhood during the modernisation of Franco's regime.

The distantiating effect produced by the juxtaposition of unaltered found fragments of women's mediated reality is systematically explored by artists such as Eulàlia Grau, Sanja Iveković and Rosler in combined critiques of patriarchy, consumerism, national ideology, and the sexism of mass culture. The bars that Iveković pasted on a television monitor to film the propagandistic programme featured in *Sweet Violence* 1974 (no.23) literalise the disruption of the real and its media fictions

61
(Top)
Martha Rosler
Cold Meat I
c.1966–72, from the series *Body Beautiful, or Beauty Knows No Pain*
Photomontage

62
(Bottom)
Martha Rosler
Cold Meat II, or Kitchen II
c.1966–72, from the series *Body Beautiful, or Beauty Knows No Pain*
Photomontage

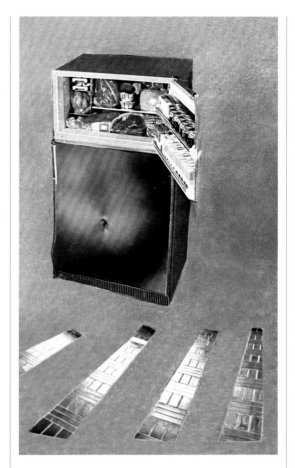

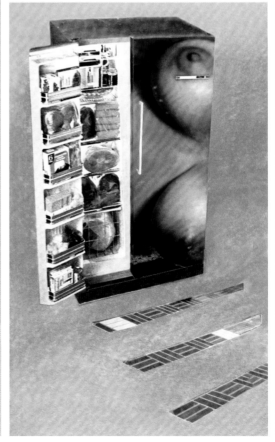

63
Martha Rosler
Woman With Vacuum,
or Vacuuming Pop Art c.1966–72,
from the series *Body Beautiful,*
or Beauty Knows No Pain
Photomontage

80

64
Isabel Oliver
The Family 1970–3,
from the series *The Woman*
Acrylic paint on canvas
98×98

to critique the agency and sexism of mass-media representation of women and Tito's 'Third Way'. Interlaced in this work is also a critique of the beauty industry that cuts through the rest of Iveković's work in the 1970s, as it does in that of many other artists, such as Isabel Oliver (*Beauty Products* 1970–3 from the series *The Woman* no.69). Iveković often intervenes in the media narratives juxtaposing idols of femininity from magazines with photographic self-portraits from her private archive. Rosler, instead, in her celebrated series *Body Beautiful, or Beauty Knows No Pain* c.1966–72, disrupts the pop ideals of beauty from further distance, with resignifying displacement of beauty and fashion advertisements or incongruous collaging of naked body parts onto them. Rosler's conflated indictment of patriarchy, commodity and media culture in the latter series converges also with Grau's and her feminist anti-commodities. Foregrounding the home as a target of gendered consumerism and patriarchal ideology, in *Vacuum Cleaner (Ethnography)* 1973 (no.73) a vacuum cleaner sucks a bridal model, while a refrigerator, an oven and a washing machine are plastered by Rosler (nos.59–62) with cut-outs of female 'meat' from the latest pornographic magazines such as *Playboy*. Here Rosler exposes the mediated fictions of domesticity and the pornographic fetishisation of the female body as the two sides of the same ideological coin servicing patriarchal culture.

Maria Pinińska-Bereś has also framed the tools of feminine beauty as fetishistic commodities in the service of phallocentric desire, through the sexy underwear or bathing suit of *Is a Woman a Human Being?* 1972 (no.74). Displayed as a product with an expiration-date tag, this work comments on the commodification of the female body in a socialist society that briefly espoused consumerism.

Patriarchy is revealed by such works as the only situation commonly shared by women in the variegated spectrum of societies that this exhibition brings together. Yet Pinińska-Bereś's outfit, unlike other pop lingerie that variously celebrates femininity or exposes its predicament,[13] updates her long preoccupation with corsets as culturally inflicted shackles of female sexuality characterising the ultra-Catholic and conservative patriarchal milieu in which she was raised even though in socialist Poland.[14] As such it reminds us of the plurality of female subjectivities inscribed in pop, shaped by locational, cultural and sociopolitical specificities as well by gender differentials (such as age, religion, ethnicity, class and sexuality). This urges us to apprehend the global through the local in order to prevent the polemic insistence on the study of 'women's' work from erasing the multiplicity in difference that it strives to unveil.

It is thus worth scrutinising the inscription of difference in the series *The Suicides of Sisga* 1965 (nos. 78, 79, 80) by Beatriz González. González's predilection for local idioms and culturally resignified Western images shaped a pop vocabulary resistant to the internationalisation driving the modernisation of

Colombian art in the 1960s, and spoke eloquently about Colombian society and the class role of taste within it. The artist established her pop reputation with the scandalous *The Suicides of Sisga I*, based on a photograph published in a tabloid newspaper featuring a couple drowned in Lake Sisga in redemption of their sin of deflowerment. In its reprographic focus on love and death, the series resonates with many pop manifestations, from Andy Warhol's *Death and Disaster* series to the cinematic couples of Rosalyn Drexler that unveil violence and subjugation as the predicament of woman in love in Western society. Though also punished for love, González's heroine shares little with Drexler's desiring urban subjects (*Kiss Me, Stupid* 1964, no.68). The scarf of González's protagonist – a signifier of low-class and Catholic mores – hints at the many underprivileged Colombian girls migrating from the country to urban centres in search of a better life during Colombia's postwar industrialisation. Virginity for proletarian women was not only a moral virtue defined by Marianismo, but a treasured social and economic capital.[15] It is through such classed and gendered evocations of the drama of Colombian modernisation that the Sisga suicide series acknowledges the constraints of female desire in patriarchal society from a feminist point of view. Foregrounding religion, class and ethnicity as modifying difference in pop, it highlights not only the sociocultural factors that diversified womanhood across borders in the 1960s – from the sexually liberated 'Swinging London' to a violently changing Colombia – but also the concomitant diversity of feminist politics produced in pop.

Whose Politics? Whose Pleasure?
For their public debut in Barcelona in 1973, Grau introduced her *Ethnographies* with a collage comprised of a self-portrait surrounded by advertisements targeting women – of sweet delicacies and beauty products, for instance – and a biographic list of sins. The latter included trespasses she had committed against the Catholic Church, while the former admitted the seductive snares of the capitalist system to which she had herself fallen prey. Grau's confession foregrounds the crucial dilemma that – as implied by Barbara Kruger at the beginning of this essay – is faced by women artists as producers and consumers and is diversely dealt with in pop: the critical negotiation of women's oppressive yet pleasurable symbiosis with mass culture.[16]

65
(Opposite Top)
Ángela García
Composition
1974, from the series *Misses and Embroideries*
Collage and acrylic on canvas
150×150

66
(Opposite Bottom)
Delia Cancela and Pablo Mesejean
Love and Life 1965
Industrial acrylic paint on canvas, wood, paper, tarlatan fabric
Installation view at Lirolay Gallery, Buenos Aires

67
(Top)
Evelyne Axell
Erotomobile 1966
Oil paint on canvas with painted tyre
150×150

68
(Bottom)
Rosalyn Drexler
Kiss Me, Stupid 1964
Acrylic paint and paper collage on canvas
50.8×61

69
Isabel Oliver
Beauty Products 1970–3,
from the series *The Woman*
Acrylic paint on canvas
98×98

84

70
Isabel Oliver
Surgery 1970–3,
from the series *The Woman*
Acrylic paint on canvas
98×98

85

71
Isabel Oliver
It is a Girl 1970–3,
from the series *The Woman*
Acrylic paint on canvas
98×98

72
Isabel Oliver
Happy Reunion 1970–3,
from the series *The Woman*
Acrylic paint on canvas
98×98

87

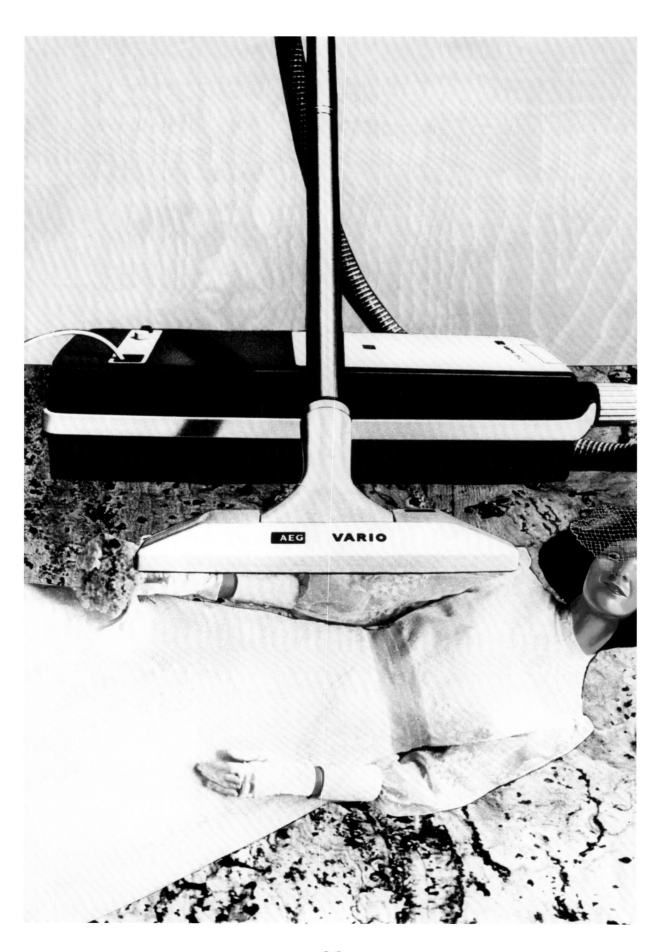

It is the strategic embrace of such guilty consumptive pleasures, whether of products or images, that distinguishes the less explicitly critical paths through pop followed by artists such as Axell. In the process of fashioning what can be claimed as a feminist pop erotica, Axell utilised consumer goods and key tropes of pop culture's representation of female sexuality – the pin-up and the pornographic nude – as an empowering tactic to advocate female desire. Erotically coupling ice creams and automobile parts with the female body (*Erotomobile* 1966, no.67), she radicalised pop's fetishistic fascination with consumer objects, producing feminist fantasies of erotic consumption and bachelor machines for women.

Unlike artists who invented new languages exploring the female body – whether abstract such as Chicago or figurative such as Saint Phalle – Axell adopted an established sexist language. Yet she radically repurposed it in order to rewrite female desire and pleasure in Western visual culture, transgressively advocating their autonomy and activeness by emphasising their homo – and autoerotic manifestations. As an ex-actress and an artist Axell was well aware of the gendered cultural divide of high and low and the objectification of women in visual culture, including the endangerment of the radicality of her nudes under the male gaze. This is true, too, of Jana Želibska, whose celebration of female sexuality and eroticism was accompanied by a critical solicitation and sabotaging of voyeurism, through the systematic replacement of the sex of her nudes by mirrors (*Kandarya-Mahadeva* 1969/2010–12, no.8).

Axell has in fact prefigured both the feminist theorisation of the 'male gaze' and problematising of the images of women.[17] In an interview, she spoke critically of the 'traditional role of the nude as prey' in Edouard Manet's *Le Déjeuner sur l'herbe*, explaining the 'allergy of the fair sex' to the nude in a manner that pre-empts the feminist unpalatability of her work.[18] The triptych *The Pretty Month of May* 1970 (no.58) – a doctored commemoration of May 1968 as the pinnacle of the sexual revolution in the form of a love sit-in by libidinal creatures of indeterminate gender – is framed by a nude self-portrait and a portrait of the critic Pierre Restany as evangelists of the sexual revolution. Yet Axell usually portrayed male critics and their gaze as threats to her nudes. In fact she variously circumvented the threat of the 'male gaze' whether by usurping its scopophilic pleasures, supplanting them by those of touch – as manifested in *Licensed in Both Ways* 1965 (no.55) – or by displacing it, locking female bodies in homo/autoerotic doubles that prefigure the Irigarayan 'love of the same'.

It is by performatively enacting mass culture's immanent position of woman as image that Axell tackled 'the problem' with the images of women.[19] Complementing her depiction of the sexual/ised female body in pop culture and art by performatively enacting it – by reiterating staple poses of femininity with what Amelia Jones has described as radical narcissism – Axell grafted her mind and her body in her art, effectively exposing and

73
(Opposite)
Eulàlia Grau
*Vaccum Cleaner
(Ethnography)* 1973
Photographic
emulsion and
paint on canvas
164×110

74
(Top)
**Maria
Pinińska-Bereś**
*Is a Woman a
Human Being?* 1972
Plywood, glass,
papier mâché,
acrylic paint
102.5×58.5×38

75
(Bottom)
Jana Želibská
Object II 1967
Mixed media,
glass, metal pelmet,
textiles, lace, wood
148×70×50

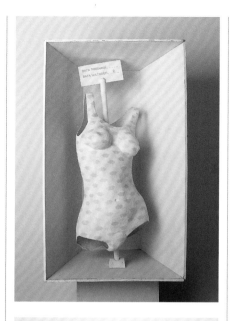

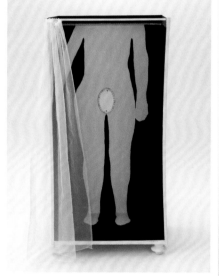

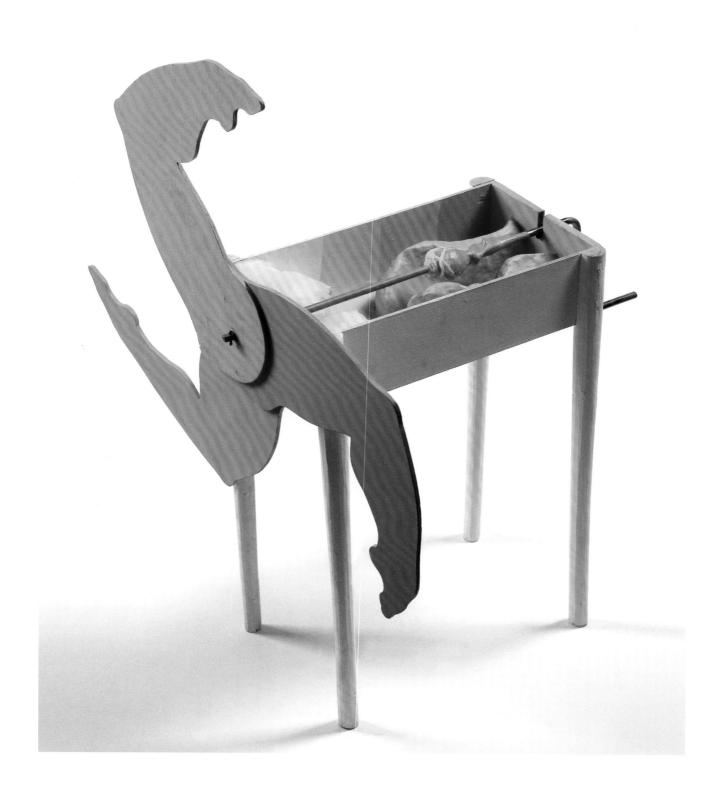

76
Maria Pinińska-Bereś
Love Machine 1969
Wood, plywood, papier mâché,
metal handle, tempera, assemblage
94×63.5×71

90

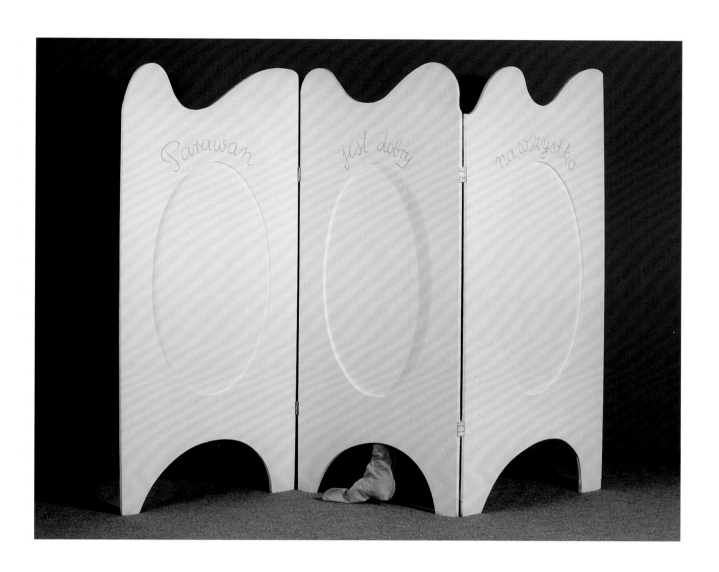

77
Maria Pinińska-Bereś
Screen 1973
Plywood, canvas,
tempera, assemblage
194×132×63

78
(Top)
Beatriz González
*The Suicides of
Sisga I* 1965
Oil paint on canvas
120×100

79
(Middle)
Beatriz González
*The Suicides of
Sisga II* 1965
Oil paint on canvas
120×100

80
(Bottom)
Beatriz González
*The Suicides of
Sisga III* 1965
Oil paint on canvas
100×80

81
(Opposite)
Ruth Francken
Man Chair 1971
Polyurethane
foam, white
lacquered epoxy
102.5

exploding the logic of the male gaze.[20] Moreover, she deconstructed femininity itself, by exposing the performativity of gender through the parodic nature of her mimicries. This resonates with Dorotheé Selz's humorous debunking of pop pornography in her series *Relative Mimetism* 1973 (nos. 127, 128, 129). Yet Axell's radical narcissism also reinforced her belief in the erotic female body as an instrument of women's liberation and claimed women's right to look at the female body, represent it and depict its pleasures.

So did a number of what I have called pop's 'bad girls', whose strategic embrace of pop culture, as well as visual and sexual pleasure, has been often treated at best with feminist suspicion and at worse with aggression or neglect.[21] I have already argued elsewhere that the prolonged indifference to and the critical contours of the feminist reframing of some of pop's feminists as counter-pop show that feminism's critique of pop culture and art left no space for the female pop artist in early feminist art discourse. Moreover, dominant feminist views about women's relation to popular culture and the feminist potential of the representation of the female body have disfavoured the 'seductive subversions' of artists who knowingly embraced pop and explored the female body to feminist ends. The asymmetry of the feminist celebration of those who concentrated on the critique of pop culture and its representation of women suggests that explicit critique was privileged as the only radical position for women until feminist practices and shifts in feminist thinking have discursively allowed the critical subversiveness of pleasure to hesitantly resurface since the 1990s. Tellingly, Natalia LL's early reputation as a pioneer of feminist art in Poland, where feminism yet had no foothold in the 1970s, has overshadowed the subversive pleasures lurking in her pornographic photographic installations and her series *Consumer Art* 1972, 1974, 1975 (no.24), predicated instead upon their interpretation as critiques of the objectification of the female body by feminists outside the Iron Curtain with few recent exceptions.[22]

The feminist dilemma – critique or pleasure – that underpins the feminist reception of women in pop, echoes the conundrum – critique or affirmation – that has haunted the most vexed question of pop's discourse: pop's politics. While a global view of pop enriches its political aspects, it remains true that the complicity with the culture that fuels its pleasures in fact delimits its politics, whether pop is seen as the last realist language of modernity or as a critical meta-language of its ruinous transformations under the reign of consumerism and the simulacrum. Added, however, to the gendered critique of the system, the radical pleasures promulgated and performed by many female artists in pop complement a landscape of subversiveness that in its feminist radicality and diversity unfolds a truly avant-garde side in the heart of pop, and an early chapter of the essential plurality of feminist politics in the arts.

82
Toshio Matsumoto
Mona Lisa 1973
16mm film transferred
to digital file
3 min 50 sec

94

OIRAN GOES POP: CONTEMPORARY JAPANESE ARTISTS REINVENTING ICONS

Reiko Tomii

Proto-Pop and Pop in Japan

Japan in the 1960s is a paradigmatic site of world art history. With its phenomenal experimentalism and innovations, it offers many exciting avenues of investigation for transnationality and 'international contemporaneity' (*kokusaiteki dōjisei*)[1] in a non-Western locale. For the past two decades, scholarly and museological attention has focused on the study of conceptualism and postminimalism in Japan, with the latter mostly concentrating on the Mono-ha group of artists (School of Things).[2] Pop art has somehow been overlooked until recently, mainly because globalised re-examination was somewhat discouraged by the unmistakable association of Pop art with the USA and, to some extent, the UK. In Japan, such disregard has persisted since the 1960s, when, for example, even the *Oiran* series by Shinohara Ushio, the most evidently Pop-inspired work on this East Asian archipelago, was barely discussed within the concept of Pop at the time. 'Pop in Japan' has long been an elusive category, frequently subsumed into other practices, especially the dominant vanguard movement of Anti-Art (*Han-geijutsu*), which endeavoured to dismantle the modern construct of Art (*geijutsu*) with a capital 'A'.[3]

In retrospect, it is not an overstatement to say that the introduction of American Pop jump-started Japanese Pop.[4] The country was potentially a fertile ground in which American-style Pop could develop, given its saturation with American culture as a result of the seven-year American Occupation that followed Japan's defeat in the Second World War. Yet, Japanese artists did not merely follow the imported model; they inventively adapted the Pop strategies, such as appropriation of popular and cultural motifs, use of commercial art techniques, and replication and multiplication among others, while tapping into the rich indigenous tradition of pop culture, both pre-modern and modern. The local pop cultures, which engendered what can be understood as the 'proto-Pop' practices, made the American strategies not entirely alien, thereby facilitating the intelligent retooling of proto-Pop into the distinctly Japanese version of Pop.

Japan's proto-Pop existed in many ways. Japan was, indeed, a land of proto-Pop, with its strong graphic culture and its tendency to mix and equalise high and low. Most notably, *ukiyo-e* woodblock from the late seventeenth to the nineteenth centuries featured actors and beautiful women as well as scenic sites, offering inexpensive pictorial enjoyment to lowly townsfolk and exalted samurai alike in the thriving economy of Edo Japan (1603–1868). *Ukiyo-e*, however, is but one example among many instances of proto-Pop. Limited space here does not allow further discussion, but suffice it to say that *ukiyo-e* constitute a fundamental aspect of Japan's cultural genes that informed the work of Pop in Japan in various ways. This short text explores the emergence of Pop in Japan through the lens of proto-Pop in a selection of important examples.

Shinohara's Oiran as a Pop Icon

No other artist better exemplifies the essence of Pop in Japan than Ushio Shinohara. A leading member of the Tokyo-based vanguard collective Neo Dada (act. 1960), Shinohara is one of the central figures of Anti-Art, who devised his first signature series, *Boxing Painting*, in 1960. In 1963, he launched the *Imitation Art* series, stimulated by American Pop, and then moved on to devise another series, *Oiran*, by reinventing an old icon of *ukiyo-e*: high-ranking courtesans à la Pop.[5]

The news of American Pop art came to Japan almost contemporaneously. Ground Zero of New York Pop, the Sidney Janis Gallery in New York organised the seminal exhibition *The New Realists* in October 1962; the January 1963 issue of *Art International* that carried a special feature on it reached Japan by April 1963. After studying the article enthusiastically, Shinohara came to two contradictory conclusions: while he wanted to keep up with the latest New York trend, he reckoned that the Americans were too original to emulate. He soon intuited that the very core of Pop lay in its criticality: 'If Pop Art has any substance, that's intellectual paradox, which is to say, parody.'[6] Thus was his *Imitation Art* series born, for which he first created hybrid imitations by combining a few artists' signature motifs (for example, George Segal's plaster body and Jasper Johns's flag (*Drink More*

83
Ushio Shinohara
Doll Festival 1966
Fluorescent paint, oil paint,
plastic board on plywood
196.1 × 399.7

1964, no.84) and subsequently re-created such masterpieces as Robert Rauschenberg's *Coca-Cola Plan* 1958 (only two of ten pieces he made being extant) and Johns's *Three Flags* 1958 (now lost).[7] His sources were frequently monochrome reproductions found in art magazines, and his imagination supplied any missing information – hence his use of fluorescent paint, a novel material typically evocative of Pop's industrial-age design aesthetics. His work questioned the ingrained modernist idea of originality and constituted an almost self-mocking commentary on the fundamental dilemma of Japan as a latecomer to modernism, which suffered the perception of lacking originality due to its unavoidable need to catch up with the West by imitating the imported examples.

On the Pop front, the *Imitation Art* series helped Shinohara to expand his technical skills, including airbrushing fluorescent paint and using such precision tools as stencils and masking tape. A chance discovery of some nineteenth-century *ukiyo-e* woodblock prints with the themes of sex and violence opened his eyes to Japan's proto-Pop tradition, which he appropriated to devise the *Oiran* series in 1965 by using his newly acquired mechanical techniques to maximum effect. A genuine attempt at Japanese Pop, Shinohara's *Oiran* bloomed into a variety of manifestations for his first solo exhibition at a commercial venue in 1966, filling the entire space of the Tokyo Gallery, from the floor to the walls to the ceiling (no.85) The exhibition title, *Doll Festival*, referred in an oblique manner to the traditional annual celebration of the future happiness and well-being of female children. Instead of the customary representation of the empress or other courtly women, Shinohara featured *oiran*, high-class courtesans whose beauty was their ultimate weapon for success in the cruel sex trade.[8] His depictions show his *oiran* garishly coiffed with *kanzashi* hairpins, together with a variety of other female types (for example, a princess and townswomen), looking into mirrors, holding fans, making love, or even being murdered.

Only a few canvases have survived from this exhibition, which gained him some critical attention but no commercial success. Among them are the three-panel *Doll Festival* 1966 (no.83) and the six-panel folding screen *Kanzashi* 1966. They escaped destruction, unlike much of his 1960s oeuvre, because a friend took the latter and used it as a headboard, while the artist surrendered the former to the gallery to cover the exhibition expenses. (A hard fact of life was that there was little demand for Japanese contemporary art, Pop or otherwise, at this time, in marked contrast to that for American art.) The exceptionally cheerful *Doll Festival* reveals Shinohara's hybrid narrative strategy and technical sophistication.

In a tight composition, under cherry blossoms, five figures congregate – from left to right, a parade leader, a townswoman with her hair down, a man with a bowler hat, a young male prostitute (*wakashū*) and an *oiran*. They are culled from different *ukiyo-e* sources, one of which was an early Meiji print depicting how the city of Tokyo was being changed through the brisk Westernisation begun in the mid-nineteenth century. This image, which Shinohara saw in a newspaper, showed some Japanese people wearing Western clothes and others dressed in Japanese kimono, giving a 'sense of mismatch'.[9] His painting captures this feeling well, with the *oiran* in a kimono and the Japanese man with the hat in chic Western clothing. The situation was not so different in Japan during the Occupation and the ensuing postwar period, when the young Shinohara experienced at first hand the rapid Americanisation. The sense of mismatch is accentuated by the acrylic sheets, custom-cut by a professional fabricator, which he used to portray, for example, the gaudy *kanzashi* that adorn the *oiran* – the transparent fluorescent orange acrylic is skilfully layered over the painted hairpins. Such small details as two chrysanthemums (a typically Japanese flower) on the man's hat and two Japanese flags on his breast emphasise the incongruity of this man's Western attire. Indeed, this is a pictorial narrative of *ukiyo-e* updated with contemporary sensibility and materiality. By 1968, Shinohara distilled his fascination with *oiran* into an iconic head shot, thus recasting his various women into *Oiran*, a personification of the female archetype of old Japan and an authentic counterpart to Andy Warhol's *Marilyn* 1962 (no.86). A surprise source for this head shot was a reproduction of Van Gogh's *The Courtesan (after Eisen)* of 1887 that he happened to see. He faithfully copied all details, including the number and composition of hairpins, but gave her a crisp Pop physiognomy.[10] When he moved to the USA in 1969 on a grant from the JDR 3rd Fund, Shinohara took his idea of *Oiran* with him. She kept him company, so to speak, until he identified a new icon that encapsulated his experience of pop culture in New York: the motorcycle.

Shinohara's Pop Peers
Shinohara was not the only Japanese artist to have a dialogue with American Pop or to engage with Japanese proto-Pop. Having studied commercial design at college, Tiger (né Kōichi) Tateishi was obsessed with Mount Fuji, a ubiquitous and potent icon of Japan since ancient times. Intent on giving it a truly modern expression, the budding artist decided to make a neon Fuji. He was so determined to do this that, upon graduation from college in 1963, he took a job at a neon factory in order to learn the trade. Unfortunately, it

84
(Opposite)
Ushio Shinohara
Drink More 1964
Fluorescent paint, oil paint, plaster, and Coca-Cola bottle on canvas
46.4 × 35.6 × 16.5

85
(Top)
Installation view of *Doll Festival* at Tokyo Gallery, February 1966

86
(Bottom)
Ushio Shinohara
Oiran 1971/2014
Acrylic paint on canvas
213.4 × 213.4

87
Tadanori Yokoo
KISS KISS KISS
1964
Animation film
2 min 5 sec

88
(Opposite)
Kishin Shinoyama
*Yokoo Tadanori
and Mishima
Yukio* 1968
Gelatin silver print

was too costly to realise his vision in the scale of a mural. However, his job had unexpected perks: he received training in airbrushing and had ready access to a blueprint facility (which was indispensable for producing life-size plans for neon fabrication).[11] Fuji continued to appear in his paintings as well as in the blueprint posters and fliers that he created by commandeering the factory's equipment and which he distributed at art venues in order to promote himself as an artist. Airbrushing was useful when he consciously worked against American Pop art and French Nouveau Réalisme by incorporating the 'radiating rising sun' (*kyūjitsu*) motif in his paintings, both large and small, in 1963 and 1964.[12] Notable among them is a brief series of gouache on paper that combines the motif of solar beams, word play exploiting the ideographic nature of Chinese characters, and what can be called 'bulked up' characters.[13] (*Hi* 1964, no.90). The solar motif dates back to his memory of seeing a radiating rising sun painted on an exterior wall of a large shop near a railway station in his neighbourhood at the age of nine; the thick characters, which somewhat resonate with those of Edward Ruscha, derived from the logo of a film company (20th Century Fox), with which he was familiar from avidly viewing American films since he was five. Born and raised in a thriving coalmining town in Kyūshū, he was extensively exposed to Hollywood and Disney films as well as manga and other Japanese popular entertainments, which in combination contributed to Tateishi's superb graphic sensibility.[14] After a brief experiment with the indigenous mode of Pop, he moved on to Salvador Dalí-inflected paintings and nonsense manga, but he never lost the spirit of populism in his work.

Born and raised in Tokyo, Tanaami Keiichi has a vivid visual memory of the American firebombing during the Second World War, which became *the* defining moment of his life. A graphic designer by profession, he sought non-commercial creative outlets in the areas of animation, experimental film, collage and artist's books, while, in his words, 'editing memories' and 'traveling through memories' in them.[15] His fearful wartime memory was complicated by the subsequent exposure to and enthralment with American popular culture. In adulthood, like his good friend Shinohara, he was also a serious student of American Pop art and this interest further nuanced his engagement with memory. As art historian Hiroko Ikegami has noted, Tanaami's work is marked by his ambivalent feelings towards

89
Keiichi Tanaami
Crayon Angel 1975
Animation film,
2 min 50 sec

90
(Opposite)
**Tiger (Kōichi)
Tateishi**
Hi 1964
Gouache on paper
64.4 × 44.3

the USA that was both 'destroyer' and 'seducer'.[16] Perhaps the most straightforward reflection on his war memories is *Crayon Angel* 1975 (no.89).[17] In this short animation, his hand-drawn images are intercut with documentary photographs and film footage of the Pacific War, many tinted ominously orange, the colour of firebombing in his memory. The menacing and recurring appearance of a rooster with a flaming cockscomb, taken from the package design of an anti-mosquito incense, symbolises the American bomber plane. A woman with equally bright blond hair is in fact Japanese, with her black hair illuminated by the firebombing to appear golden. The threatening feelings suggested by these visual elements are accentuated by pounding sounds, echoing sirens and the memorable groans borrowed from Led Zeppelin's *Whole Lotta Love*. Various photographs from his childhood in the film, often featuring himself with his mother, point to the innocence that the war destroyed.[18]

Known for his technological innovations in experimental film and video art, Matsumoto Toshio has a far more jaded view of popular culture and Pop art than any of the other artists discussed here. When he took on the ultimate icon of art history, the *Mona Lisa* (no.82), in 1973, it was not because he wanted to pay homage to the eternal beauty created by Leonardo da Vinci, but because he needed to 'mentally steel himself against the eager anticipation for the visit of Mona Lisa to Japan',[19] that is, the blockbuster *Mona Lisa* exhibition which opened in April 1974 at the National Museum of Tokyo. With Marcel Duchamp's *L.H.O.O.Q.* 1919 in mind, he 'forced her into the world of schizophrenia' through a novel image-synthesising technology called Scanimate. The resulting video exquisitely dialogues with Duchamp's descendant, that is, Warhol's *Mona Lisa* 1963: just as Warhol commented on the reproducibility of icons of the information society through the rudimentary technology of silkscreen, Matsumoto further compounded their mutability and fluidity by deploying a sophisticated transmedia technology. In 1974, when Warhol visited Japan for the first time, Matsumoto gave a cinematic treatment to the international celebrity by 'expos(ing) the crime of Warhol through double and triple reproduction and multiplication' in his film *Warhol: Re-Reproduction*.[20]

In a sense, Warhol himself became a veritable icon of contemporary culture – that is, for more than his much-quoted '15 minutes of fame'. It is tempting to ask whether there was a Warholian counterpart in Japan. The most promising candidate is Yokoo Tadanori, a multi-talented and prolific graphic designer whose Pop-influenced posters have been highly appreciated worldwide since the 1960s. In 1968, to capitalise on his pop-star status, a magazine editor hatched a photobook project titled *My Idols*, wherein the designer would get 'two shots' taken with famous figures that he idolised, ranging from actors and sports stars to novelists. The young photographer assigned to the project was Shinoyama Kishin, who was as hot as Yokoo and was making a quick ascendance on the cultural scene.[21]

The first celebrity approached for the project was the novelist Mishima Yukio. He posed naked except for a loincloth, with a gigantic *hinomaru* national flag as a backdrop and with the head of Yokoo, who was dressed in an old-fashioned school uniform, tightly locked in his muscular right arm (no.88). Due to various circumstances, the photobook was not published for another 25 years, but soon after the shoot Mishima authored a short essay for Yokoo's graphic works, which he perceptively observed 'connect with a straight line the sorrow of Japanese local customs (*dozoku*) and the idiotic and daylight nihilism of American Pop art.'[22]

***

These works of Pop in Japan constitute a dynamic transnational episode of postwar art history. American Pop art frequently offered inspiration, but Pop in Japan was more than a story of transmission because of the pre-modern and modern tradition of proto-Pop, which was ripe for retooling as full-fledged Pop. In this sense, American Pop provided reinforcements to the already existing and developing experiments. Beyond the engagement with cultural and social icons, there are various strains of Pop in Japan; some of them took populist approaches in bringing art to a wider audience, which form a separate topic for discussion. It must be remembered, however, that, taken together, the practitioners of Pop in Japan ingeniously realised many possibilities inherent in American Pop art. This aligns them with the broader circle of global Pop that developed contemporaneously in other parts of the world.

91
Delia Cancela
Broken Heart 1964
Oil paint on canvas, lace
and painted wood panels
150×100

POP ART IN ARGENTINA

Mercedes Trelles-Hernández

For how to speak of Pop without reflecting on the correlation between the visual arts and the modern extension of the means of information?[1]

Pop art was often discussed in Buenos Aires throughout the 1960s. Several artists associated with this movement – Carlos Squirru, Miguel A. Roldano, Dalila Puzzovio, Edgardo Giménez, Pablo Mesejean, Delia Cancela, Juan C. Stoppani, Susana Salgado and Alfredo Rodríguez Arias – featured on the cover of the widely circulating magazine *Primera Plana* in 1966, making clear that the style was a subject of extensive interest (no.92). Pop art was also frequently on view in private galleries and prestigious art venues, such as the newly formed Centro de Artes Visuales (CAV) of the Instituto Torcuato di Tella (ITDT), which played a major role in the development of Argentinean art in the 1960s.[2] Wherever pop art was shown, be it on the walls of a gallery or in a busy city street, it seemed to attract a gleeful air of scandal.

As pop became a topic of widespread interest nationally, it also captured the attention of international art critics visiting Buenos Aires as jurors of the ITDT's Annual Prize. Among these, Pierre Restany (France) and Lawrence Alloway (Great Britain) became interested in a new art that combined objects with viewer participation: Restany baptised it 'Pop lunfardo', a reference to the dialect or slang spoken in the River Plate area. In an essay titled 'Buenos Aires and the New Humanism', written after his 1963 visit, the French critic proclaimed:

> Buenos Aires is on the eve of a great organic transformation comparable to that which has made of New York an international centre for contemporary creation. On the River Plate we witness the first manifestations of this awareness. The day is not far off in which Buenos Aires will be covered by a cloud of collectors, galleries, critics, analysts and especially creators of an art 100% Argentinean.[3]

Restany's vision of Buenos Aires as a city culturally on a par with New York and Paris was a potent and particularly seductive message for Argentinean ears.

Pop art seemed to be the key to international artistic success, especially between 1963 and 1967, when Marta Minujín produced her scandalous happenings and installations, and artists such as Dalila Puzzovio, Carlos Squirru and Edgardo Giménez removed art from the galleries and placed it on the streets of Buenos Aires.

Delia Cancela's *Broken Heart*, an oil and canvas construction of 1964 (no.91), gives a good idea of how the new art that eventually became known as pop was developed by the young artists of Buenos Aires. To begin with, Cancela's starting point was painting, the primary medium of Argentinean art at the time. Yet there are several differences between this piece and those created by the reigning abstract artists – known as 'Informalistas' – or, alternatively, by those working in the recently successful 'New figuration' style (Luis Felipe Noé *Closed by Sorcery* 1963, no.93).[4] In Cancela's work there is no texture and no drama. The painting is a simple red heart on a white background: high contrast and clean silhouettes, without any hint of the dramatic or the painterly. However, the lower left-hand side of the heart is irregular and from the bottom edge of the painting hang hand-painted red canvas sacks of different shapes. These recall the undefined forms of our internal organs – heart, kidneys, stomach. They also correspond to the missing pieces of the flat, iconic heart. The naïve and sentimental effect of the heart symbol is destroyed and the medium of painting is challenged by the precarious materiality of the hand-painted canvas sacks that droop from it. The body, though not present, is strongly suggested.

Cancela's piece has not received much critical attention.[5] Up to a point, the piece is too discreet to truly exemplify Argentinean pop: there is still a frame around the canvas and there is no overt provocation of the viewing public. Yet it helps us understand Argentinean pop by showing its starting point as a rebellion against a certain type of abstraction and good taste. The challenge to reigning notions of taste is present not only in the kitschy symbol of the heart, but also in the rather unpleasant suggestion of hanging organs.

In Marta Minujín's work the body was a crucial factor from the very start. Her *Colchones* or *Mattresses* (irregular stuffed pieces), exhibited under the title *Eróticos en technicolor*, were produced between 1962 and 1964 upon her return from Paris (no.95). Like Cancela's *Broken Heart*, they were hand-sewn and hand-painted, giving them a strange, handcrafted appearance. They are not hung on a frame; instead they are meant to be manipulated, 'worn', embraced. A picture of critic Jorge Romero Brest shows him wearing one like a flotation device (no.94). Their garishly bright colours are a reference to holidays, graphic design and film. By 1964

Minujín had turned these stuffed, irregular pillows into a full-blown installation, in which viewers were expected to stand, sit or lie down, much like they would on a canopied bed. She titled this work *¡Revuélquese y Viva!* (*Roll around and live!*) and it won her the national prize at the ITDT's annual juried show.

Viewers and critics faced with these works encountered a decidedly experimental turn in Argentinean art. Yet the piece that definitively changed Argentineans' expectations of the relationship between viewer and work of art is without a doubt *La Menesunda* (no.96), a collaboration between Minujín and Rubén Santantonín, to which Pablo Suárez, David Lamelas, Rodolfo Prayon, Floreal Amor and Leopoldo Maler also contributed. A sixteen-room installation presented at the CAV in 1965, and for which an estimated 30,000 people queued for hours, *La Menesunda* created a wholly different notion of what was art and, of course, of what pop was, associating the movement not only with the experimental, but also with a sense of gleeful transgression.[6]

In *La Menesunda*'s 'flyer', written by Marta Minujín, Rubén Santantonín and Jorge Romero Brest, it is explained as follows:

'LA MENESUNDA'
is not like exhibitions
of painting or sculptures
of any sort of
IMAGE-SYMBOL things
that limit 'existence'
where though profound
the 'gaze' of the viewer
DAMAGES 'time'
…
Since this is neither
'exhibition' nor 'spectacle'
There is no 'work'
nor 'viewer' nor 'spectator'
ALTHOUGH THERE IS ART[7]

Crossing a plastic veil, the viewer entered a neon-lit tunnel and proceeded to a series of rooms at different levels. In one room there was a wall with ten TV screens with their sound blasting. After walking along a corridor accompanied by the noises of city streets, the viewer faced a man and a woman wearing pyjamas inside a re-created bedroom. In yet another room, made of gesso and shaped as a woman's head, the viewer could have a make-up artist apply beauty products to him/her. At a particular point in the installation, the viewer had to guess a code and punch it into a telephone in order to proceed. At times there was a persistent smell of fried food. In the final room, mirrors and confetti filled the space. Throughout, a subtle reminder of the urban atmosphere and its strong disjunctions was present (after all, the title of the piece comes from Buenos Aires slang and means something like 'the mix up'), but there was also a sense of play similar to that experienced at a carnival funhouse.

Considering that this vulgarly titled work could be seen at one of Buenos Aires' most prestigious art addresses, the challenges inherent in *La Menesunda* seem multiple. First and foremost, there is the artists' explicitly stated desire to transcend the act of contemplation and the discreet art object. But there was also a sense of direct provocation of notions of good taste and class embedded in a piece that chose to present shocking scenarios and situations to a well-heeled public: the domestic intimacy of a man and a woman in pyjamas inside a re-created bedroom is still evident today in the black and white pictures taken at the ITDT, while the intense accumulation of things and interest in the banal is also remarkably tangible in the pictures of the make-over room. Moreover, *La Menesunda*'s success managed to bring 'people from the street to a sphere reserved for the elite' as Marta Minujín recently recalled of the varied public that attended the show.[8] Without a doubt, *La Menesunda*'s transgressive aesthetics translated into a 'succès de scandale' that attracted unprecedented audiences, media coverage for the Argentinean avant-garde and intensified the fierce competition between artists that had already been triggered by the ITDT's annual juried prize.

In 1965, the same year that *La Menesunda* left its mark on the Argentinean art scene, Dalila Puzzovio, Carlos Squirru and Edgardo Giménez – artists who had been active in the pop scene creating installations, graphic works and paintings, as well as working in happenings called 'micro-sucesos' – rented an advertising hoarding (billboard) on a road junction in Buenos Aires: between Viamonte and Florida streets. The hoarding presented the three smiling artists, with recent examples of their works in their hands: above the image was the provocative question, *Por qué son tan geniales?* (Why are they so brilliant?) (no.98) This work, which stood in place for a month, actively challenged notions of art's traditional privilege and autonomy, bringing it into the city streets, soliciting a new public and establishing the urban environment as the correct place in which to experience art. It also exemplified the intense competition between Argentina's avant-garde artists and helps to explain how media coverage of the pop artists shaped pop itself in Argentina, by infusing it with a growing interest in media, communications and advertising.[9] Indeed, as the decade continued, Argentinean artists veered increasingly towards exploring means of mass communication, such as the use of the daily press as a forum for artworks, the creation of fashion magazines or the integration of closed circuit television into artworks. At the same time, Argentinean

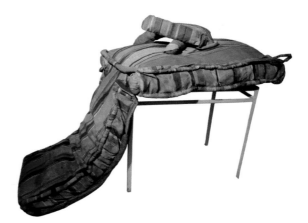

pop artists translated the radical engagement between viewer and work of art implicit in *La Menesunda* into a totally different experience: the experience of pop as a product.

Far removed from the traditional notions of art – painting, sculpture, prints – pop in Argentina continued to court the experimental and to challenge notions of good taste. In fact, by the late 1960s, the idea of pop as a consumer lifestyle had come to the fore. Pop boutiques, such as '*La Flor de San Telmo*', opened up in 1967 in two locations, selling both pop fashion and pop objects. Important personalities of the Argentinean art world, including the critic Jorge Romero Brest, the Director of the ITDT's Center for Visual Arts, commissioned artist Edgardo Giménez to decorate his Buenos Aires apartment as a pop environment. Film director Héctor Olivera also employed Giménez to create pop sets for his movies – *Psexoanálisis* (1968) and *Los neuróticos* (1971) – while Dalila Puzzovio did part of the wardrobe design. Delia Cancela and her partner, Pablo Mesejean, who had worked in wardrobe design for the ITDT's theatre, began exhibiting fashion designs and fashion editing at art venues. Susana Salgado, who had won a prize at the 1966 ITDT juried show, also began working in fashion. Giménez, in collaboration with Marta Romero Brest, opened a multiples[10] art gallery, *Fuera de Caja, Arte para consumir*, in 1969, where the relationship between the public and the work of art was transformed as the art object became more accessible and 'domestic' (no.97).

This extraordinary development – the creation of a public and an appetite for pop as a commodity – is one of the signs of pop's enormous success in Argentina. Pop fashion, pop apartments, pop crockery, pop film … all of these attest both to the Argentinean avant-garde's questioning of the discrete nature of the art object and its relation to the public, as well as to the wide acceptance and media coverage of this transgression, which made it possible for art to make its crossover into 'life'.

Yet the widespread interest and acceptance of pop did not mean its scandalous edge had been completely blunted. In fact, Dalila Puzzovio recalled the decidedly subversive effect her outfits could have on the authorities:

> The first time I went out wearing these double platform shoes was for a *vernissage* (exhibition private view), wearing golden baubles, a black velvet mini, a monkey stole, hair this big, little braids, all of them with golden coins.

96
(Opposite)
Marta Minujín
La Menesunda 1965
16mm film,
digitalised
8 min 9 sec

97
(Right)
Fuera de Caja (Out of the Box) 1970
Poster design by
Edgardo Gimenez

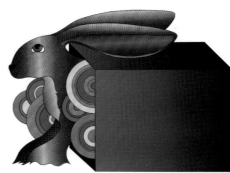

When I descended from the taxi, two cops saw me and seemed to want to arrest me, but they were afraid of me: I was a vision.[11]

After the 1966 coup d'état that would establish General Onganía in power, Argentinean society had become more repressive and pop was sometimes mistaken for revolution.

Although pop did not achieve all of its early promises – the dream of transforming Buenos Aires into a great artistic centre on a par with New York or Paris slipped as the decade drew to a close – it did bring about an experimental turn in Argentinean art, where the role of the artist as provocateur, and the role of the public in relation to the work of art, were intensely scrutinised and transformed and the field was opened up for media and conceptual art. More surprisingly, pop in Argentina also managed to transform the avant-garde, associated with elite culture, into a subject of public interest, and the work of art into a concept accessible, if not to many, at least to considerably more than before, as fashion, jewellery, multiples and prints became part of the pop arsenal at the end of the 1960s.

111

100
Erró
American Interior No 1 1968
Glycerophtalic
paint on blended fabric
130 × 162 × 2.5

CHILDREN OF MARX AND COCA-COLA: POP IN A DIVIDED WORLD

Sarah Wilson

The year 1967 marks both the apex and turning point of pop's international story. In the USSR and its satellite states, the fiftieth anniversary celebrations of the Russian Revolution in 1917 coincided with centenary celebrations of Karl Marx's *Das Kapital*. China's Cultural Revolution gathered momentum. The Icelandic painter Erró's *American Interior No 1* 1968 (no.100) shows Red Army troops from a Maoist poster bought in Paris, invading a US dream home (straight from a catalogue).[1] Pop was not just an expression of capitalist America's triumph: it contended with national variations of Communism, Marxism and Maoism in the West as well as the East, as a critical tool, a gesture of anti-Americanism or a subversive signal of the 'free West' in countries behind the Iron Curtain.

Erró's exhibition *Forty-Seven Years*, held in Milan, confronted the two Cold War enemies. His paintings were worked up from complex collages, where a postage stamp with three Soviet cosmonauts could dialogue with James Rosenquist's World's Fair mural. Ephemera from his visit to the Fair in 1964 collided with his 1965 May Day souvenirs from a trip to the USSR. Each oil painting had a triptych structure: past or contemporary works by Soviet and American painters were intercut with imagined scenes of prehistoric man.[2] He juxtaposed Roy Lichtenstein's work (already a copy of Pablo Picasso's *Seated Woman*) with Vladimir Mayakovsky's anti-alcohol posters for the Russian Telegraph Agency (ROSTA). Theorist Slavoj Žižek points to the fact that nomination alone distinguished 'mass-ideological-aesthetic experience' between right or left, capitalist or Communist.[3] These were dangerous proximities in 1967, in the wake of Adolf Eichmann's trial for Nazi crimes in Jerusalem, the context of Israel's Six-Day War and, as always, the US 'apocalypse now' in Vietnam. Yet 1967 was also lyrical: a 'summer of love' with the music of the Beatles, or the *Psychedelic Light Show UFO 1967: Soft Machine* by Mark Boyle.[4]

Two exhibitions exemplify Cold War divisions in 1967. In Montreal the mighty Expo '67 received over 50 million visitors. Buckminster Fuller's sparkling geodesic dome – the American pavilion designed with a Minirail escalator for the passage of 5,000 people an hour – boasted Apollo and Gemini space capsules suspended in the air accompanied by tapes of Cape Kennedy blast-offs. Pop art hung on a lower level: large-scale commissions by James Rosenquist, Jasper Johns, Tom Wesselmann, Claes Oldenburg and Robert Rauschenberg, among others.

In Fidel Castro's Cuba, the *Mural Cuba Colectiva*, financed on a remarkably small budget, involved artists and writers within the field of 'expanded pop' on the ideological 'other side'. Cuba looked to Paris and the Salon de Mai, founded in 1945.[5] Volunteer artists and the Salon show itself were simply flown to Havana. The *Mural Cuba Colectiva* was designed across six panels with a spiral, game-board structure and Cuban surrealist Wifredo Lam at the centre. On 17 July 1967, accompanied by a live orchestra, dancing and many TV cameras, the *Mural* was painted through the night by one hundred artists from all over the world. This televised international event affirmed Castro's Havana-Moscow axis, and offered a riposte to extensive American cultural exchange programmes.[6]

Within the spiral grid, Bernard Rancillac created a *Portrait of Che* (Guevera) with its silkscreened effect painted in acrylics; Jacques Monory and Valerio Adami signalled the presence of French narrative figuration, with Lourdes Castro the Paris-based Portuguese pop artist. The Cubans also staged the show *Guerillas y pintores* (*Guerillas and Painters*) starring Erró's *Bay of Pigs* (Castro with a cigar against a background of snouts). Subsequently, works were gifted to the Museo Nacional de Bellas Artes Havana, constituting its contemporary – anti-American – collection.

Into this situation of stand-off, another major show of 1967 must be factored: the American section at the IX São Paulo Biennial, the 'pop art biennial', held under the military government of Marshal Costa e Silva.[7] Works by Johns and Rauschenberg, Andy Warhol, Lichtenstein and Rosenquist created both a sensation and a template for contemporary responses by Marcello Nitsche and the Rex Group.[8]

Montreal, Havana, São Paolo: three points mapping certain coordinates of pop art as it expanded and was received in 'mid-career'. But what of the alternative pole, Paris, within the 'global pop' discourses of the 1960s? New York did not, of course, 'steal the idea of modern art' after 1939: artists in Latin America, fascist Spain,

Communist Poland, Czechoslovakia or in Israel had no love for capitalist America and one aim: to get to Paris. Cold War lines of force met here at the heart of the 'third way'. France's intellectual and spiritual prestige and her revolutionary tradition were seen to compensate for a diminishing political world influence – and no space programme. Huge cultural budgets were distributed under Minister for Cultural Affairs André Malraux. The irony of anti-Americanism in a country whose postwar economic recovery was entirely dependent on Marshall Aid was not lost to those on the right, or the captains of industry; while the strongest cultural force on the left – the Communist Party – had co-opted the greatest stars of art, literature, theatre and music from the 1940s onwards.[9]

Malraux's Paris Biennial, founded in 1959, welcomed forty countries from the very start, with extraordinary retrospectives and off-site events: British pop artists including Patrick Caulfield (so influential on Valerio Adami) starred at the Biennial of 1965; in 1967, the United States of America Biennial exhibition, organised by the Pasadena Art Museum, included Edward Ruscha's bare word-slogans on monochrome grounds.[10] This was the arena for artists such as Eduardo Arroyo or Equipo Crónica. Arroyo quit Spain in 1958, showing his *Four Dictators* including Franco at the 1963 Biennial. The very year Rafael Solbes, Juan Toledo and Manolo Valdés founded Equipo Crónica in Valencia, 1965, they rushed to exhibit in Paris's *Salon de la Jeune Peinture*. Peter Saul moved from his native USA to Paris in1964; violently anti-American and a 'strong Communist', he wished to escape the false anti-Semitic implications concerning his name.[11] Haitian-born Hervé Télémaque left New York in 1961 to live in Paris in part because of the racial prejudice he experienced in America (see his *My darling Clementine* 1963, with 'Banania' black doll-in-a-box).[12] Alina Szapocznikow came from Poland to Paris and studied at the Académie des Beaux-Arts from 1948 to 1950; she moved back again in 1963, her work responding to the pop art climate. Wojiech Fangor's work transformed from socialist realism (like *Korean Mother* 1951) to abstract psychedelic targets shown in Paris in 1964 and at the Grabowski Gallery, London, 1965–6. In August 1965, *Pop Por, Pop Corn, Corny* showed that Paris conceived itself as always already pop, with characters like Salvador Dalí alive and well (*Venus de Milo with Drawers*) and a transmission to new generations (Raymond Hains or John Wesley), while surrealist leader André Breton's last show, *L'écart absolu*, included Télémaque's *Confidence* (with attached white stepladder) in December.[13] François Pluchart's *Pop Art & Cie, 1960–1970*, with a bronze expansion by César oozing over the cover of the luxury version, continued this native story.[14]

But this is to avoid the drama. American pop arrived in Paris slowly. Jasper John's *Bed* was shown at *Eros*, the International Surrealist Exhibition, in 1959; his first solo show was followed by a second in 1961.

In 1962, Larry Rivers made a sculpture with Jean Tinguely called *The Turning Friendship between America and France*.[15] There were inseparable links between Johns, Rauschenberg, Niki de Saint Phalle, Elaine de Kooning and others in Paris at this time, chronicled for New York by the poet and critic John Ashbery. American neo-dada and Pierre Restany's nouveau réalisme merged in Sidney Janis's Gallery in 1962 as the *New Realists*; significantly, before 'pop' as a word went pop.

Working with Leo Castelli, her New York partner, Ileana Sonnabend stormed the Bastille. Each of her exhibitions presented an array of pop masterpieces, now in major museums and private collections all over the world.[16] At the end of 1962 Jasper Johns showed *Flag* and *Flag on Orange Field* 1957; pop drawings in 1963 in *From A–Z 1963: 31 American Painters* at the American Art Center; then Robert Rauschenberg: two shows including *Monogram* (the famous stuffed goat with tire now in Stockholm); Jim Dine; American pop art – Wesselmann, Oldenburg (*Ice Cream Cone* and *Hamburger*); Warhol (*Twenty Marilyns, Four Marilyns in Colour* and *Big Torn Campbell's Soup Can (Black Bean)*); Lee Bontecou; Rosenquist; John Chamberlain; and Lichtenstein (including his 'Picasso', *Femme dans un fauteuil*, and his works with speech bubbles, *I know how you must feel, Brad…*). In 1964, Sonnabend showed Warhol's silkscreen prints including *Pink Race Riot, Green Car Crash* and *Blue Electric Chair*; an exhibition of Rosenquist's work opened later that year. Finally, Rauschenberg's Grand Prix at the Venice Biennale wrested leadership from France, with a huge international scandal. Quantities of work shifted to Paris reappeared in the Castelli-Sonnabend pop exhibition in 1964 at the former American Consulate on the island of San Gregorio, for all the world to see.[17]

It was Bernard Rancillac with Hervé Télémaque who curated *Mythologies Quotidiennes* at the Musée de la Ville de Paris in July 1964. But the 'riposte to Venice' failed: there were far too many European artists to counter the 'Magnificent Seven' Americans. Rancillac went to London to see British pop art too at this time: the pull of pop and Carnaby Street for Parisians, a ferry journey away, must not be underestimated.[18] Rancillac's *Walt Disney* show in 1965 was acerbic: he dressed as a sheriff for the opening; it was followed by his first trip to New York, and an obligatory stay in the Chelsea Hotel. With the arrival in Paris of the epidiascope to project and draw around images, and a change to harsh acrylics imitating silkscreened effects, his production accelerated, becoming more critical. *The Year 66* at the Galerie Mommaton in February 1967 showed paintings of Vietnam, the war between Israel and the Arab states, the assassination of Che Guevara in Bolivia, the Red Guards in China, apartheid in South Africa, and legalised abortion and the contraceptive pill in the West.

At Last, a Silhouette Slimmed to the Waist 1966 (no.28) is a visual pun, to be exhibited either way up. A South Vietnamese soldier plunges a Vietcong prisoner

101
Nicola L
Woman Sofa 1968
Vinyl
31×208×85

head-first up to the waist in a cauldron of water – or, if you prefer, five models sport waist-length, stretch-nylon bras. In *Holy Mother Cow* 1966, he replaces the desert sun with 'La Vache qui rit' (Laughing Cow), a cheese spread label above a blinding desert of yellow acrylic; a veiled woman struggles with her son, mule and water-pot (an image from a tourist brochure): the Hindu cult of the sacred cow coexists with starvation. *Dinner-Party of the Head-Hunters* 1966 (no.103) is a vicious denunciation: a canvas that 'opens' via shutters to reveal three black faces. On the left, Patrice Lumumba, the Congolese Independence leader, believed to have been assassinated by the CIA with Belgian aid, rehabilitated in 1966. Opposite him (shutters open) is Frantz Fanon, revered at the time as a member of the Algerian National Liberation Front, and author of *The Wretched of the Earth*.[19] Malcolm X completes this concealed triptych: black rights leader and founder of the Organisation of Afro-American Unity, his conflictual relationship with Islam had resulted in his murder in 1965. The Parisian black tie art collectors' dinner party shows guests posing with African masks: a crude joke at the expense of their host, Tony Saulnier (professional photographer, African art collector and amateur ethnologist). Published in *Paris Match* within an article on the first World Festival of Black Arts in Dakar, the photograph was the catalyst for the first 'intellectual property' court case.[20]

Pierre Bourdieu's preface to Rancillac's show engaged with this 'art which uses the everyday language of comic strips, posters or photographs'. The comic strip, or BD (*bande dessinée*), had penetrated the avant-garde with its *détournement*: literally 'hijacking' by the lettrists and Situationist artists from the late 1950s onwards.[21] Its apotheosis came in 1967, with the exhibition *Bande dessinée et Figuration Narrative*.[22] The long history of the comic strip was juxtaposed with works by contemporary pop artists, and a range of Europeans. What of *figuration narrative* – narrative figuration? Evidently, while Lichtenstein used comics as a source, Rosenquist was a realist painter: his billboards were enlarged from photo-based material. Narrative figuration, focused in Paris, was born alongside pop and artists like Rosenquist, but was engaged with decades of debates around realism and politicised socialist realism. Its critical dimensions dialogued with the ironic self-reflection and distancing devices of the French *nouveau roman*, the *photo-roman* and New Wave cinema.[23] Narrative figuration hit

102
Erró
Big Tears for Two 1963
Oil paint on canvas
130 × 195

the public in October 1965, with a 'serial-killer' attack on Marcel Duchamp.[24] The artists Gilles Aillaud, Eduardo Arroyo and Antonio Recalcati had used a serial, narrative structure (*A passion in the desert*, recounting a Balzac novella) prior to this critical assault.[25] In François Mathey's comics show, however, the shock was total, for it housed Rosenquist's room-sized *F-111*: a depiction of the US fighter-bomber, mixed with blown-up tinned spaghetti, atom bomb mushroom clouds, and a blonde child under a metallic helmet with blow-dried Shirley Temple curls.[26] Rancillac helped to hang the approximately twenty-six-metre-long (eighty-six feet) panels, along with works by Lichtenstein and others provided by Castelli via Sonnabend. *F-111*'s European tour continued. Everywhere it was seen as pure American imperialism, yet it encouraged, one could argue, the creation in France of spectacular multipanel narrative projects, by the group *Les Malassis*, denouncing the French government, racism, sexual mores and low-cost housing policies. Their *F-111*-type size and scope – too large to display in French museums – has erased this important riposte to pop from European art history.[27]

In 1968 revolution was worldwide. The Mai Lai massacre followed the Tet Offensive in Vietnam. Rising against Soviet domination, the 'March events' in Poland involved student strikes, but also an official 'anti-Zionist' campaign, and the mass emigration of Jewish citizens; the 'Prague Spring' and occupation of Czechoslovakia by Warsaw Pact troops was a trauma for the Western Marxist left, additionally marking the end of their Cuban dream (Fidel Castro inevitably backed the harshest Soviet positions as dependent ally). The graphic power of Cuban posters now emigrated to Paris: the mobility of images and styles accelerated through the next decade.

Gérard Fromanger – 'Red' Fromanger – was at the heart of the student revolution in Paris, making posters in the occupied École des Beaux-Arts. With the new silkscreen technique imported from the US, 800,000 posters were created based on 800 designs. Fromanger's tricolour flag 'bleeding' (no.139) – the red trickling over the blue and the white – (eventually considered 'counter-revolutionary') lead to his meeting with Jean-Luc Godard, their collaborative friendship and a pioneering video version of the 'wounded' flag: *Film-tract n° : 1968* (no.140). With photographs taken on the streets in May 1968 by Elie Kagan, Fromanger created images for *Album The Red* 1968 with its anonymous red silhouettes (no.139).

103
Bernard Rancillac
*Dinner-Party of
the Head-Hunters* 1966
Vinyl paint on wood, 3 sections
170 × 150

118

Shown first in Paris's Print Biennial, *Album The Red* won the first prize at the 7th International Print Biennial in Tokyo, 1970, outclassing Warhol and Rauschenberg.[28]

Henri Cueco's great relief *The Red Men, bas-relief* (no.106) and associated paintings were begun during the summer of 1968. 'These works don't celebrate the protests ... They energetically bear witness to power on the move. Revolution, battles, are the principal theme. It's an epic ensemble; bright and terrifying ... bodies horrified and magnified by the encounter with their historic destiny.'[29]

By 1970 the climate had changed. While 1967 marked the fiftieth anniversary of the Russian Revolution, 1970 witnessed global centenary celebrations for Lenin.[30] The most political framing of pop was the touring show *Kunst und Politik*, which started in Karlsruhe.[31] Herbert Marcuse's text for *Kunst und Politik* analysed the position of art in a one-dimensional society. The hybrid 'Children of Marx and Coca-Cola' (Jean-Luc Godard's phrase) were saluted in a special issue of *Tendenzen*, 'Was Tun?' (Lenin's 'What is to be done?').[32] Here was Colin Self's scorched *The Nuclear Victim (Beach Girl)* 1966, Fromanger's *Album The Red* (no.139), Erró's *American Interiors* (nos. 100, 130, 131), Rancillac's *At Last, a Silhouette Slimmed to the Waist* (no.28), *Holy Mother Cow*, together with 1968 posters, works from the 'Red Room for Vietnam' and the 'Police and Culture' painters' Salon of 1969. There were also works relating to the division of Germany and Eduardo Arroyo's 'Miro-based' parodies of fascist Spain.[33] Everywhere old masters were present, including Equipo Crónica's most famous paintings quoting Diego Velázquez and Picasso's *Guernica* and the Art Workers' Coalition's famous anti-Vietnam poster, *Q. And babies? ... A. And babies*, which was used for the catalogue cover. The show (with its one female artist, Olimpia Hruska) toured to Frankfurt at the end of the year, and then on to Wuppertal and Basel.

Is the military background of 'hard' pop a reason for its gender inequalities? Lichtenstein and Wesselmann had done US army service; Rauschenberg had been in the navy; Johns had been stationed in Japan during the Korean War. Self's scorched and misshapen *The Nuclear Victim (Beach Girl)* and his *Nuclear Missile* 1967, both exhibited in *Kunst und Politik*, are far from the utopian blueprint of 'pop culture'. He worked, he said, retrospectively in a 'solitary state of post-nuclear non-being'; hence the irony of his *Leopardskin Nuclear Bomber No.2* 1963 (no.124), which recalls the planes made by his uncle, a grounded would-be pilot working in war-time military aviation.[34] How could pop in its 1960s context not harbour hidden memories of trauma, rekindled in the Cold War scenario of developing technologies, cybernetics, warhead stockpiling, the passionate marches and speeches for peace and nuclear disarmament?

Alina Szapocznikow's lamps of breasts and lips with their limb-like distortions and charring – like *Glowing Bust* 1967 – contain the memories of her infinitely traumatic past in a Poland of concentration camps, metamorphosing from her earlier brutalist sculpture.[35]

It was only after May 1968 that a positive women's movement acquired momentum. Hence Evelyne Axell's *The Pretty Month of May* 1970 (no.58) retrospectively takes the iconic image of Caroline de Bendern, 'Marianne' of the May 1968 revolution, and surrounds her with the Afro-haired nudes of a female rights love-in (approved by godfather art critic Pierre Restany in the left-hand panel). Later, Nicola L's all-embracing *Red Coat* 1969 (no.153) shares the same 'love-in' ideal.[36] It was only through long interviews that philosopher Jean-François Lyotard became aware that Ruth Francken, the attractive author of the emblematic *Man Chair* 1971 (no.81) – that sexualises any sitter – was a Prague-born artist-in-exile, her own painful memories sworn to a 'sear of silence'.[37]

In the retrospective exhibition *Douze ans d'art contemporain* in 1972, just two women artists represented creativity since 1960 in France – Niki de Saint Phalle and Sheila Hicks – compared with seventy men! Both women were seasoned transatlantic air travellers with global careers.[38] Less well known – as a counterpart to *Kunst und Politik* – was Myriam Bat-Josef's huge psychedelic environment, *Art Total*, at the Israel Museum, Jerusalem, in 1971, where empty aircraft petrol tanks were transformed into flying, pregnant sculptures, suspended or perched high on masts (compare Kiki Kogelnik, *Bombs in Love* 1962, no.14). In 1970, in New York, the slogan 'The Personal is Political' was coined.[39] For Bat-Josef, child of Berlin, an Israeli soldier, Parisian Beaux-Arts student, lover and wife of Erró, artist who showed with Arturo Schwarz (in 1965 and 1969, in Milan), and feminist in the Womanspace gallery on Venice Boulevard, California, the pop adventure was part of a personal adventure where the need to connect personal identity with questions of nation and Cold War politics was overriding.[40]

Looking back in 1974, the critic Jean-Clarence Lambert wrote '1967: the postmodern era has already begun.'[41] The tensions, topologies and traumas of world pop in mid-career have been discussed here, anticipating the collapse of the sustaining 'grand narratives' tracked in the mid-1970s.[42] Pop's militancy, beginning with its 'summer of love', marked the beginning of a global regime change.

104
Uwe Lausen
Geometer 1965
Acrylic paint on canvas
180.5 × 221

105
Raúl Martínez
Listen America c.1967
Oil paint on canvas
292×256

106
Henri Cueco
The Red Men, bas-relief 1969
Cold enamel glycerophtallic
paint on plywood
260 × 310 × 21

A CONVERSATION ABOUT POP: TATE ASKS THE ARTISTS

Interviews carried out in 2014–15,
organised alphabetically.

DID YOU EVER CONSIDER YOURSELF (NOW OR IN THE PAST) TO BE A POP ARTIST?

Thomas Bayrle Never one hundred per cent! I always felt I was representing a mix of several styles – as much op as pop – and already by 1966 I was working towards technologies like mapping.

Cornel Brudaşcu No, I never considered myself a pop artist until now.

Teresa Burga Ever since I started using pop imagery and iconography, I considered myself to be a pop artist.

Rafael Canogar I'm not a 'pop' artist now, but I can concede to the fact that my earlier work had some points in common with this tendency. However, this is true only if you understand the label in a much broader and universal way than how it was promoted in the USA.

Judy Chicago No.

Henri Cueco No. At its beginning, my work and that of my close friends, colleagues and artists was categorised as *nouvelle figuration* (new figuration) or *figuration critique* before being defined as *la figuration narrative* (by Gérard Gassiot-Talabot, the French art critic) in 1967.

Romanita Disconzi Not in the past, and although I know that my works share most of the same inspirational sources as pop art, I understand that pop artists are historically considered as such.

Gérard Fromanger No. I don't consider myself today, nor did I in the past, to be a pop artist. For me, between 1958 and 1964 there was no pop art in France.

Ángela García At that time I forcefully embraced this new language, exploring all the possibilities it offered, collage, aerography, photomontage … in that precise moment, in my city Valencia, we actively sought to represent the political condition of the time through plastic creation. This gave birth to many groups to

which I was connected and we redeployed this new language in its many variants. Later we realised that the same was happening across Europe.

Beatriz González No, I considered my work a provincial type of painting. I've always considered myself more of a painter and within this remit I painted the joy of the underdeveloped. For me the type of art that I was doing could only circulate internationally as a curiosity. Mine was a provincial type of art without horizons, confronting the everyday: art is international.

Sanja Iveković No, I would not consider myself a pop artist. I belong to the generation who came onto the art scene at the beginning of the 1970s. We were commonly known as the 'conceptualists'. As young artists we were eager to react to the work of the generation before us. We wanted to break with the modernist tradition, which was accepted in socialist Yugoslavia of the 1960s as 'official art'. Our main concern was the political critique of the high, elite, institutional culture. We questioned the nature and function of art itself, the 'autonomy' of the gallery-museum context, the influence of the market logic on the production of the artwork, the social and political role of artists … We shared the opinion that pop art was not radically different from abstract expressionism: the content had changed but everything else stayed the same. The artists were exhibiting in the commercial galleries, their works were quickly accepted by the market … pop art seemed to be just another product of a capitalist mainstream culture. At the time we still believed that the alternative was possible.

I was preoccupied with the question of gender identity and gender roles in society so the politics of the representation of femininity in the mass media was my favourite subject; pop art seemed to be an almost exclusively male movement so it wasn't inspiring for me.

Vitaly Komar [Komar and Melamid] Very often artists don't like it when they are attributed to one of the collective styles. I know, for instance, that in Russia and China there are artists who don't want their work to be called either pop art or Sots-art. Some works of pop art I believe to be Sots-art. When I asked Andy Warhol why he drew a hammer and sickle he answered: 'Maybe because I'm Czech.' And then with a smile he added, 'You did my soup can, and I did your hammer and sickle.' He meant our *Post Art No 1* (no.16).

In 1978, Lawrence Alloway asked me why we [Komar and Melamid] didn't call our work pop art, but instead chose Sots-art. I knew that in the mid-1950s he had coined the term pop art, but since then the value of the term had changed. Therefore I told him that our Sots-art is closer to his [Alloway's] original understanding of pop art as 'the products of the mass media'. I explained to this great critic that Sots-art is not equivalent to the later understanding of pop art as an elitist reflection on the visual imagery of popular and mass culture. The thing is that although the propaganda images of the Soviet 'mass media' surrounded us always and everywhere, they were never popular among the masses. They were imposed on the people by a totalitarian elite.

In the 1950s huge abstract expressionist canvases were hanging on the walls of museums in New York. And through the window, the streets were dominated by the commercial advertising of Coca-Cola and other popular products. In those same years, on the walls of museums in Moscow hung huge patriotic canvases depicting the heroes of labour and war. And through the window, on the streets there were eye-catching political billboards, red slogans, quotes and appeals to build Communism, to praise the Communist Party and to love the government and party leaders.

Through this comparison one can see the similarities and differences between pop art and Sots-art.

Nicola L Without knowing it, the *Sofa Foot* that I did during my first stay in New York City in 1967 was my first pop piece: made in red vinyl 5 feet 9 inches (approximately 175) long, exactly my height. I held it up, hiding myself naked behind it. I still have the photo, which was on the invitation for my exhibition at Galerie Daniel Templon in Paris in 1969.

Sergio Lombardo I consider all avant-garde paintings after 1960 as pop art, or variations of it. But there are many differences between different groups. I still consider my artistic theory, 'Eventualism' as an evolution of futurism, arte concreta, pop art, conceptual art, and new instances from scientific and mathematical fields, aiming to robotic art.

Anna Maria Maiolino No, I have never considered myself to be a pop artist.

Toshio Matsumoto I have never thought of myself as a pop artist and have never been called a pop artist. However, it is surely possible that it stimulated and inspired my work.

Alexander Melamid [Komar and Melamid] Never thought about it.

Marta Minujín Yes, of course. When I made *El Batacazo*

in 1966, I felt that I was a pop artist. Then I was interested in technological art, conceptual art, media art.

Ulrike Ottinger Yes.

Joe Overstreet No, I never considered myself to be a pop artist mainly because I never had a full understanding of its logic. My artist friends at the time talked mostly about art as needing to be politically and socially engaged. Some of them wanted no categories of any sort.

Joan Rabascall During the 1960s everything new was pop, in art, fashion and music of course.

Dorothée Selz Not really, but pop art culture influenced me. Today I can still define myself as influenced by pop art, eat art and performance. Between 1962 and 1972 I often went to London. I was fascinated by the Beatles, Rolling Stones, British rock music, the gigs at the Roundhouse, the Arts Lab created by Jim Haynes (1967), the music records' design, fashion at Biba, Twiggy's style, 'The Shrimp's' [Jean Shrimpton] style, make-up by Mary Quant, pop artists that I had seen in galleries – Peter Blake (Kasmin gallery), Richard Hamilton – and the events at the ICA [Institute of Contemporary Arts]. In London, it was mainly the radical changes in society, the socio-cultural changes, which were the most visible and palpable. I was fascinated by a part of Britain's youth. I was living and fully embracing pop culture, I wanted to be pop, whether I was or not. Inspiration was found in the streets, posters, adverts, industrialisation of the everyday life, fashion. Pop was influenced by subversive trends, which were protesting against institutions' stiffness, conservative traditions and the role of women as housewives.

Ushio Shinohara I have never thought of myself as a pop artist. At the time, I just gave up my drawing and brushstroke skills and started using a stencil method.

Teresinha Soares Yes. I consider myself to be a Brazilian artist with a pop art influence. Yet pop art in Brazil differed greatly from pop in the United States, because of its inherent questioning of social behaviour and politics in spite of the military dictatorship that governed Brazil in the 1960s and 1970s.

Parviz Tanavoli I did not, but others did. In November 1965 Karim Emami wrote an article entitled 'Tanavoli Turns Popper' (see *Kayhan International*, Tehran, 8 November 1965.

Claudio Tozzi The source of the language used in my work, appropriated from the mass media and the urban signals, created a visual similarity with international pop art. My work focused on the social and historical conditions we were going through in our country [Brazil] and my themes referred to our major concerns at the time. I was aware of the huge difference between the works of American artists, who were engaged in stressing the consumerism in their milieu and with the glamorisation of their images, and goods on the supermarket shelves. The choice of alternative

107
Rafael Canogar
The Punishment 1969
Polyester and wood
195 × 151 × 70

125

126

spaces to show our works, and the possibility of silkscreen reproductions on a massive scale, enlarged and created a new awareness in an ample and diversified population. From the point of view of image consumerism we established a close link with the proposals of pop art.

Manolo Valdés [Equipo Crónica] We never considered ourselves pop artists. The world places you in this category and you accept it, but we didn't work under the premises of this label. First there was 'new figuration,' then came 'realism,' and finally 'pop,' we didn't fit in any of these categories, we simply developed a new way of understanding figurative subject matter.

Jana Želibská I do not consider myself to be a pop artist, but in the past I have used some expressive means of pop art in my work.

WAS 'POP ART' A TERM USED BY YOURSELF OR COLLEAGUES OR WAS THERE A DIFFERENT TERMINOLOGY THAT REFERRED TO A NEW FIGURATIVE ART MOVEMENT IN THE 1960S AND EARLY 1970S?

Renate Bertlmann From the mid-1960s to the mid-1970s there existed an Austrian variant of pop art. Works by Christian Ludwig Attersee and Kiki Kogelnik were significant here, as well as the critical realism of the 'Wirklichkeiten' ['Realities'] group.

Cornel Brudaşcu The term that we were using at the time was 'hyper-realism' or 'photographic realism'. There was a figurative movement at the time, but what I was doing was more particular.

Boris Bućan My colleagues and I were informed about the term pop art, and there was not a different terminology used. This was true of all the terms of the visual arts at that time. I was at secondary school when Robert Rauschenberg was awarded the first prize at the Venice Biennale

108
(Opposite)
Ángela García
Self-Distraction
1973,
from the series
Morphologies
Acrylic paint on
canvas and wood
100 × 100

109
(Top)
Ángela García
Divertimento 1973,
from the series
Morphologies
Acrylic paint on
canvas and wood
150 × 100

110
(Bottom)
Ángela García
Breathing Out 1973,
from the series
Morphologies
Acrylic paint on
canvas and wood
165 × 110

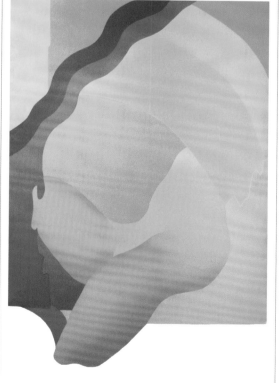

127

(1964). His victory and the scandal it generated first drew me to the world of visual art, and pop art as a consequence.

Delia Cancela Pop was a label that I accepted. But I don't like categories, neither in art nor in life.

Rafael Canogar I didn't use the term 'pop' to describe my work in those years, but I was occasionally labelled as such by critics and art journals. The terms on which I mostly relied were 'realist period' and 'chronic of reality'. I wanted to keep a distance from American pop, mainly because the Spanish social and political context was very different from the American one.

Judy Chicago I was living in Los Angeles and in graduate school at UCLA (University of California, Los Angeles) in the early 1960s. The figurative art movement that was dominant in LA at that time was certainly not 'pop'. Rather, it was a tradition that emanated from the artist Rico Lebrun, and the colour palette favoured tended towards earth colours. My own colour sense leaned towards the pastel, which was completely unacceptable there, but, coincidentally, probably smacked of 'pop' although it was not deliberate. By 1964, when I got out of school, I was completely preoccupied with my struggle to make a place for myself in the decidedly macho environment in southern California, which involved – among other things – trying to fuse my naturally biomorphic, female-centred imagery (which my male painting teachers despised) with the abstract art language that was dominant, as exemplified by Billy Al Bengston and the 'Ferus Boys'.

Henri Cueco Pop art was generally used as a generic expression to identify recent art from abroad, with artists such as Roy Lichtenstein, Warhol, Claes Oldenburg and David Hockney. When used to speak of French artists it would be rather 'European pop' – a broad term identifying contemporary figurative art. We remember discussions about pop with Pierre Gaudibert, Curator at the Museum of Modern Art in Paris, founder of ARC [Animation/Research/Confrontation – a research and exhibition area dedicated to contemporary artistic creation] in the same museum. 'Pop' was identified/translated as 'popular', meaning something 'aimed at a large audience', but with iconography derived from newspaper and consumer society images. Pop art was then considered with interest for the 'return' of 'figurative concerns' when, at that time, at least in France, abstraction was the dominant recognised contemporary art in the art market and in galleries. Nevertheless, there was some doubt about its 'message' and/or distance from consumer society and advertising stereotypes found in some works from the USA and UK.

Antonio Dias I never used the term pop art in reference to my work, because I found no point of contact with the style as it was understood then, for me so typically American. In 1963, when I started making works such as those included in this exhibition, the term was not well known in Brazil; it only started circulating after Rauschenberg's triumph at the 1964 Venice Biennale. Only later did I begin to see a few reproductions of Jasper Johns's, Rauschenberg's and Warhol's works in magazines. By 1964, my work was more strongly associated with the terms new figuration or narrative figuration [derived from the French nouvelle figuration and figuration narrative].

Romanita Disconzi Not in 1969, and also we didn't have an alternative term. In 1970 I sent my silkscreen prints to São Paulo Pré-Biennial, and got an award, which included an invitation to participate in the 1971 Biennial. It was in this Biennial that I became aware of pop art.

Gérard Fromanger No. New figuration and/or *figuration narrative*.

Ángela García Pop arrived in Spain from the Anglo-Saxon world in the 1960s. Initially the term wasn't popular. It was mainly associated with the avant-garde of the time; later on it gained currency among the general audience. During Franco's dictatorship, pop offered us a subversive language against the regime. On the one hand it represented a change in aesthetic, and on the other hand it offered an opportunity to [visually] translate the social and political reality of the country, through a plastic language with great communicative potential.

Beatriz González In the early 1960s pop was an unknown term. Unlike *neo-figuración* (new figuration) and *interiorismo* (interiorism), pop was part of a discourse happening abroad. Really pop art was absent from the medium in which I specialised: painting. Pop could be fashionable, a classification or an exercise but it wasn't the appropriate label for the work I was doing, or a vision informing my way of painting.

Towards the end of the 1960s, there was a big debate around the term pop. Initially Marta Traba established that (in Colombia) the conditions for pop's existence didn't exist, mainly because we didn't have a consumer society on the scale of other nations. Without a doubt, later on in her critical articles she established the notion of local pop, which referred to artists like Carlos Rojas and Judith Márquez. Once we entered the 1970s, the term gained currency in the artistic language.

Jozef Jankovič The term pop art has been generally used by artists and curators in Slovakia since the early 1960s. It was not used by the official media and, if so, it was given negative connotations.

Vitaly Komar [Komar and Melamid] In 1972 I began working in co-authorship with Alexander Melamid. We coined the term Sots-art. 'Sots' is an abbreviation of 'Socialism', just as 'pop' is abbreviated from 'popular'. Sots-art reflects the images of Soviet agit-pop that surrounded all of us from childhood … Since the USSR was a conceptual state, Sots-art can be understood as 'conceptual pop'. Unlike Western

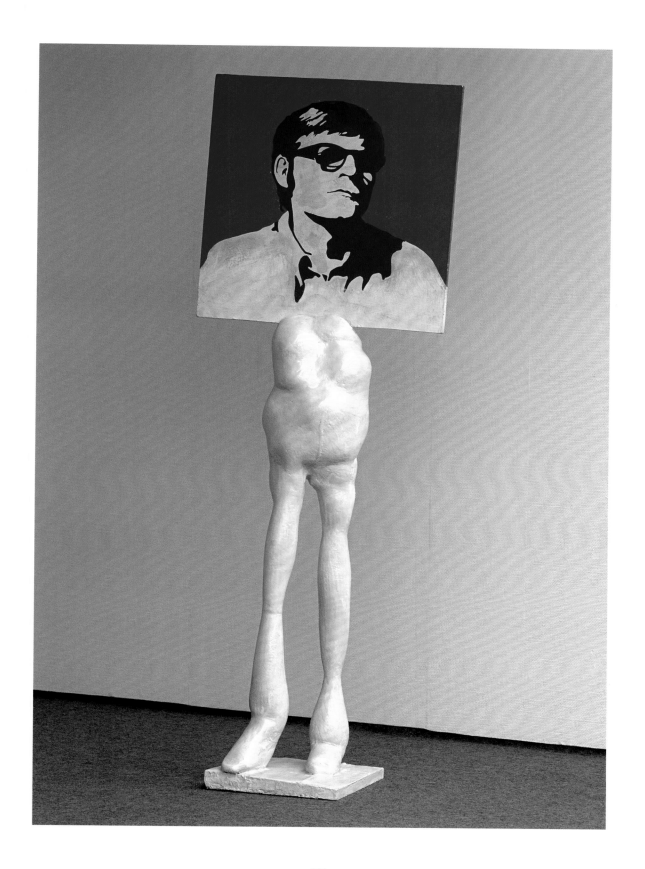

111
Jozef Jankovič
Private Manifestation 1968
Wood, plaster, fabric and
polyester
241 × 90 × 50

129

pop art, which responded to the overproduction of advertising and commercial consumption, Sots-art instead was a comment on the pervasion of Soviet ideology and its propaganda. Of course, advertising and propaganda have a lot of structural similarities. Having lived half a lifetime in Moscow and half a lifetime in New York, I can refer to mass culture in the Soviet Union as the 'advertising of ideology', while in the West it is the 'propaganda of consumerism'. Sots-art was not a part of the Western 'new figuration' of the 1960s and other features of postmodernism were initiated in many of our works of Sots-art.

Nicola L I didn't use the term pop art in relation to my work in the 1960s – for me it was a great new movement only coming from England and America … As a student at the École nationale supérieure des beaux-arts de Paris, and later as a young artist, in the 1960s I felt kind of asphyxiated by the old School of Paris. Especially after my encounter with Alberto Greco, who had just returned from New York City where he had met Marcel Duchamp, when he asked me, 'How can you paint in the 1960s?'.

Anna Maria Maiolino We, Brazilian artists, did not use the term pop art, we talked about new figuration. Even so, our work was parallel to international pop art and we shared in common the same interests of retrieving the figure and developing an artistic perspective with mass culture and without separating high art from popular art.

Marta Minujín We called it 'thing' (*chose* in French). We were creating things that weren't sculptures, we wanted to break with the established easel painting. Our goal was

112
Dušan Otašević
Towards Communism on Lenin's Course 1967
Painted wood
Each 95×95

113
(Opposite)
Joan Rabascall
Atomic Kiss 1968
Acrylic paint on canvas
162×97

to attract the public, to do popular art, then it turned into pop art.

Dušan Otašević I did not declare myself a pop artist, although my works from that period do feature some elements of American pop art. I felt closer to European new figuration because of its more complex choice of topics. I sometimes used to call my artistic products 'OTAŠEVIĆ PROCESSED GOODS.'

Ulrike Ottinger I used both expressions: pop and nouvelle figuration. Of course I was aware of Ileana Sonnabend's exhibition in Paris, but I also felt close to the figuration narrative movement, to which some of my surrealist friends belonged together with the leading critic and theorist Gérard Gassiot-Talabot. I was interested in the narrative of images, and I studied baroque art exploring different dramatic strategies for my paintings.

Joe Overstreet I always thought of pop art as undermining abstraction. Therefore, I had not thought of my painting as pop, but rather as a defined image of an African-American woman who had been marked and subjugated. I don't remember, in general, that the term 'pop art' had much currency among African-American artists at that time.

Bernard Rancillac Artists do not choose the terminologies to define their work. They adopt, if needed, the ones that they are offered. I, with a few friends, created a movement (an exhibition in 1964 titled *Mythologies quotidiennes*) and then Mr Gassiot-Talabot coined the term *figuration narrative*.

Martha Rosler Yes, the term 'pop art' was used by myself and people in my milieu (who

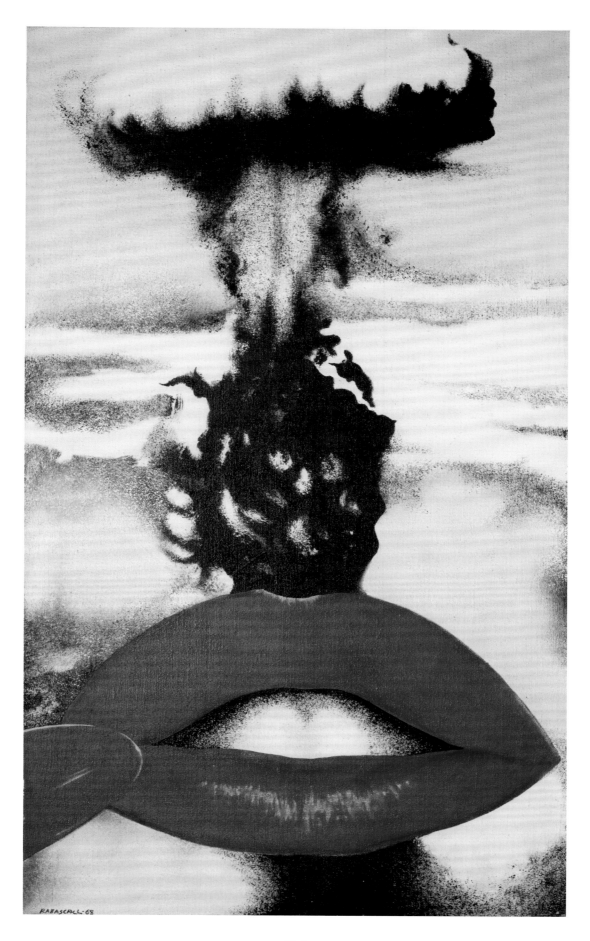

131

got there before me!) by the mid-1960s. But it was not necessarily applied by us, to ourselves. The prevailing model of pop in the USA in the early 1960s had not quite settled on Warhol. He was considered a some-what mystifying hybrid figure and performer, an arrival from fashion illustration, different from those who like James Rosenquist and Lichtenstein had high-art ca-chet – as did the earlier though rowdier Rauschenberg (and, although a bit of a stretch, Willem de Kooning). But initially the painters most attended to were closer to Tom Wesselmann and early 1970s. In Soviet Russia figurative art was revived much earlier, after the death of the Russian avant-garde in the late 1920s and early 1930s – a time that can be called 'post-avant-garde'. This was a time of unique eclecticism, during the transition from avant-gardism to socialist realism. The Russian post-avant-garde was a kind of proto-postmod-ernism, preceding the appearance of postmodernism in the West. From the outset, 'conceptual eclecticism' and (his *Great American Nude* paintings), Oldenburg or Robert Indiana: decorative, smooth, satirical, not too gritty. I drew inspiration from 'cooler' figures, in the Duchampian mode, from outlier influences like the San Franciscan Jess (Collins) and the European surrealist Max Ernst, from some Bauhaus photogra-phy, and the ever-fascinating Eadweard Muybridge.

Dorothée Selz Yes, I was aware of the term pop art since the early 1960s; it was used by my artist friends around me. Later around 1969 I discovered nouveau réalisme and met writer/curator Pierre Restany. In 1965 in Paris, British pop art and North American pop art were not much exhibited; I only knew of Alexandre Iolas gallery, which opened in 1964. The American Centre had an excellent programme showing American, French and international experi-mental avant-garde artists such as Festival Fluxus, John Giorno, John Cage, Marc'O's theatre, Bernard Heidsieck, action poetry or visual poetry, Living Theatre, Philip Glass …

Keiichi Tanaami I think the term pop art was a very common term and anybody interested in art knew about it. Around the same time, in Japan there was an art movement called 'anti-art' (*hangeijutsu*) and artists who deviated from traditional art criteria were creat-ing turmoil in the world. In comparison, pop art was easy to understand and it was associated with a modern, urban image – it was popular.

Claudio Tozzi I would prefer to call it 'nouvelle figura-tion' as, at the time, it referred to Latin-American problems and especially to Brazil, a country that was undergoing political restraints due to the military dictatorship that governed. The 'nouvelle figuration' or 'new objectivity' used a language that was similar to the one used by both the mass media and the messages conveyed by the urban background. We transformed their meanings and suggested images that questioned the social conditions we were going through. We responded to the changes that happened in the arts and especially to the changes that occurred in society and to the new line of thought of the young people. The artworks reached beyond the borders of the fine arts and were exhibited in alternative venues such as public spaces, theatres and trade union headquarters rather than museums and art galleries. We were interested in communicating directly with the public and were eager to follow their responses to them.

Manolo Valdés [Equipo Crónica] We used 'pop' but questioned it. We took the images (language) but knew it had to be different from the United States. We felt that American pop lacked the political con-tent. Lichtenstein, Warhol could be useful, but we had ahead of us quite a distinct challenge, as we faced a political situation very different from that encoun-tered by US artists. Thus to us, pop was a means to engage in a political battle, but also a way out and against the domineering artistic tendencies associated with Informel.

We relied heavily on historical painting, which we converted into pop. For us the Museo del Prado represented the utmost expression of popular culture. Its contents became our main source of inspiration and through our pop language we transformed legendary paintings belonging to the Spanish tradition – Goya, Velázquez – into prints for wide distribution. Turning high culture into mass culture proved to be a strong aesthetic exercise. Multiplication and wide diffusion were important elements for us, and thus we turned to printmaking.

Tadanori Yokoo In the 1960s, I think there were four or five (very few) painters in Japan creating figurative works of art. However, they worked rather individu-ally and I don't think there was a general term for this. Critics only reacted to Japanese figurative art that was influenced by American pop art, which had just emerged. Therefore, apparently there was some resistance among artists against the term pop art. This is surely due to the fact that the moment their works were called 'pop art', they had to think of themselves as imitating American pop art.

Japan at the time was directly influenced by the consumer culture of American society; therefore I don't think it would be wrong to say that it was just very natural to use mass-produced icons and symbols as painting motifs. However, I don't know how individ-ual artists labelled the works of art that they created under these circumstances. Artists probably didn't know how to define them either and perhaps with a quiet voice they called them 'pop-art-like'. However, in the 1960s there was a critic, I think either Nakahara Yūsuke or Hariu Ichirō, who organised an exhibition with works by four artists, including myself, and the exhibition was titled *Sightseeing* (*Kankō*). I think he understood pop art as one form of urban landscape.

Jana Želibská In official art the term 'pop art' was not used, but a certain group of artists working outside

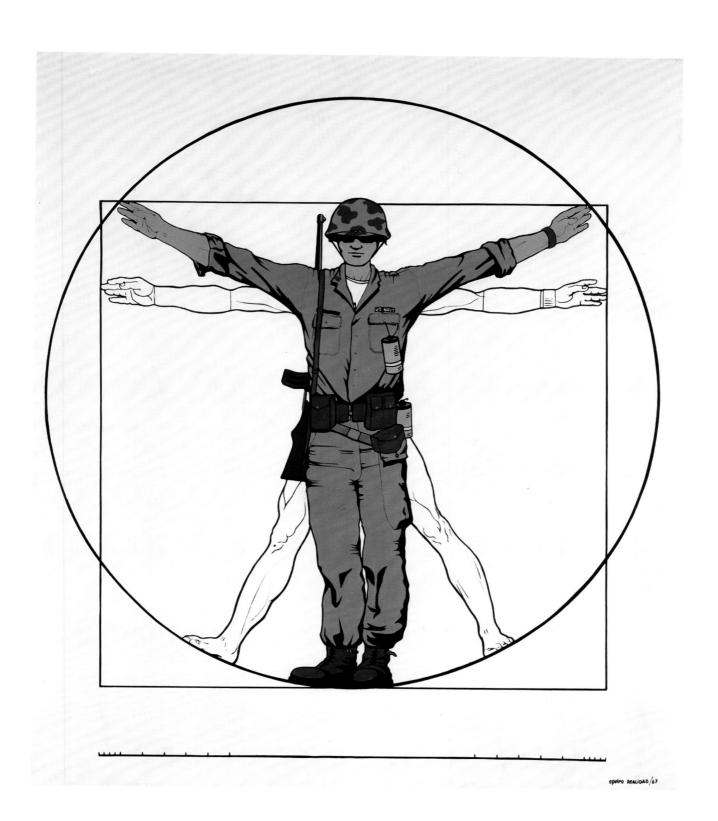

114
Equipo Realidad
Divine Proportion 1967
Acrylic paint on board
131.5×114

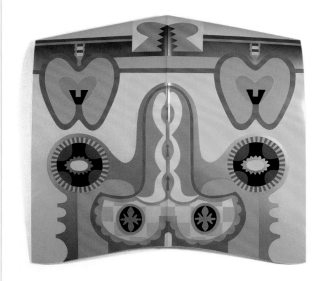

the official circles were familiar with it; for me personally the expression 'pop art' was important and inspiring.

DID YOUR WORK ENGAGE WITH CURRENT EVENTS IN THE 1960S AND EARLY 1970S?

Renate Bertlmann At the start of the 1970s I got engaged in Women's Lib movements. I worked with women's groups on implementing cultural-political demands and on creative projects. The engagement with female creativity, the analyses of patriarchal mechanisms of repression, and all the personal experiences connected with this during this time greatly influenced my artistic practice; they marked both form and content.

Delia Cancela Yes, I was interested in the conditions of women, and in everything that was happening in Europe. For instance, the English cinema and the French Nouvelle Vague, particularly Jean-Luc Godard, European pop music and fashion.

Rafael Canogar My work was responding directly to abstract expressionism – or informalism – that had dominated the art scene up to that point. My work was included in different exhibitions abroad, which attempted to move beyond these movements and open new avenues, including: *Kunst und Politik*, organised by the Badischer Kunstverein in Karlsruhe in 1970; *Menschenbilder*, organised by the Kunsthalle Darmstadt in 1968; and many others focusing on the theme of 'reality'.

Joan Cardells (Equipo Realidad) Yes, our work was closely tied to current international events, more than national or local ones, because of censorship. We were cautious because censorship was watching us: we had a problem with a serigraphy of Che Guevara. But the critical stance was always above the local or the general.

Henri Cueco Indeed yes. Bearing in mind the recent memory of the Second World War, and the Cold War period, most young artists were involved in some political movement – Maoist, Trotskyite or some sort of anarchist group or the French Communist party – even if they criticised, as insiders, some of the positions of that system or party. For art creation, the collective phase of judgement of aesthetic and formalism in the *Salon de la Jeune peinture* was practically an annual event where discourses were elaborated and debates about art and political engagement held, including, specifically, the artist's role and status in/toward society. For example in the *Salle rouge pour le Vietnam* (The Red Room for Vietnam) 'the just war of the Vietnamese people' was the theme of the Salon in 1968, and all works presented had to be related to this. Due to the political events in May, the 'red room' was finally presented in early 1969. The following Salon in 1969 was named *Police and Culture*, denouncing and ironically commenting on the moral and ideological behaviour of the 'Nouvelle Société', an expression coined by the French Prime minister, Jacques Chaban-Delmas.

Antonio Dias When I started this kind of work in 1963, I was nineteen years old. A quick look at my early works reveals my preoccupation with issues such as personal and urban violence, explicit sex, censorship, the police state and nuclear war, in short all the topics that I experienced on a daily basis while living in Brazil. I went to live in Paris in 1966, and references to the war in Vietnam began to appear in some of my paintings, while images related to the dictatorship in Brazil were disappearing. In mid-1968 I stopped making works that used that kind of figuration and I moved to Milan, Italy.

Ángela García Without a doubt. In those years early feminist texts were beginning to reach Spain; they slowly and timidly made their way into the country. As Spanish women we suffered from double repression: the politics imposed by the dictatorship and the inequality towards women. The political climate under the dictatorship had a strong National-Catholic drive, which subtly repressed intimate and moral behaviours, ultimately stressing differences between the sexes. In the most conservative classes, this repressive morality was upheld by the figure of the paterfamilias, whose logic saw women going from father to husband. In my work I reflected on the education imposed on Spanish women, encompassing everything from schooling to the strict sentimental culture they had to adapt to. Attending university proved very important for me, as it allowed me to reflect independently as well as exchange ideas. Women without access to culture didn't have this opportunity.

Beatriz González The idea of taking images from everyday reality runs through my whole career. More than current events I was interested in what Félix Fénéon termed *faits-divers*. Starting with *The Suicides of the Sisga* (nos. 78, 79, 80) and then with the furniture pieces, I appropriated press images. These included: gossip columns, accounts of trips by royalty and advertisements

115
(Top)
Judy Chicago
Bigamy Hood
1965/2011
Sprayed automotive lacquer on car hood
109 × 109 × 10.9

116
(Bottom)
Judy Chicago
Birth Hood
1965/2011
Sprayed automotive lacquer on car hood
109 × 109 × 10.9

that I found in local newspapers (I still do it). I was particularly interested in the relationship between text and image (the captions) and minor printing defects.

As well as images extracted from the press, I also worked on icons from the time, ranging from Simón Bolívar and Queen Isabella of Spain, to the Pope and pocket depictions of saints. Above all I was focusing on a provincial everyday reality, universal symbols that underwent a process of transformation through their re-localisation in the Third World. For instance an odalisque by Jean-Auguste-Dominique Ingres could illustrate a book dealing with exotic sexual practices.

I encountered these images in bookshops in the city centre (Bogotá), discoloured or badly printed and above all decontextualised. At times, without actively searching, I came across images of this sort on common objects, for example, packages that my sister sent me from London, on chocolate wrappings etc. These to a certain extent also belonged to the everyday realm I had an interest in.

Sanja Iveković As a woman and as an artist I was formed by the contentious spirit of 1968. I was following the student demonstrations in Yugoslavia but at the Zagreb Fine Art Academy where I was studying I wasn't generally able to produce works that engaged with the movement. Only on one occasion, for an etching project, did I use a photograph of a well-known female politician who was the president of the Croatian Communist Party. It was my comment on the current political event called the 'Croatian Spring'. It wasn't well received by my professors.

Natalia LL I carried *Consumer Art* (no.24) at a demonstration against Ann Bryant in New York in 1977. I documented that.

Anna Maria Maiolino The military dictatorship took power in Brazil in April 1964 and lasted until 1980. During those years cultural activities for many people meant resisting the political status quo through artistic production and tricking the censorship as far as possible. Therefore, some of my works from the 1960s and 1970s have an obvious political content. This work goes beyond the political pamphlet because it is born from a real need, and driven by an ethical need for conduct in the face of torture and repression by the agencies of the dictatorship. When besieged, the artist invents ways in which to evade censorship

135

117
Joe Overstreet
The New Jemima 1964, 1970
Acrylic paint on fabric over
plywood construction
260 × 154.3 × 43.8

136

118
Romanita Disconzi
Interpretation Totem 1969
Duco paint on plywood
Each 40×40×40

119
(Top)
Parviz Tanavoli
*Poet Squeezing
Lemon* 1974
Screenprint on paper
69.8 × 49.1

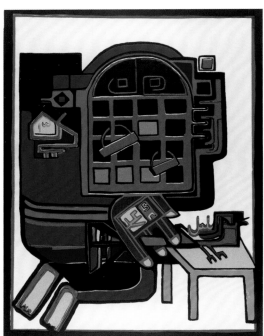

120
(Bottom)
Parviz Tanavoli
*Poet and
Nightingale* 1974
Screenprint on paper
76 × 60

and find new paths for art. He becomes a demiurge and through his works exorcises the enemy: the enemy of human rights, of the right to freedom.

Toshio Matsumoto Thinking about the core of art in the 1960s–70s, it is important to remember its historical background and the fact that there was an overwhelming paradigm change of viewpoints, feelings and values. Naturally, pop art also participated in creating this turning point and I think it opened up new horizons. The relationship between pop art and my works from that time can be seen in different forms, for example in the multilayered appropriations of posters, commercials and popular songs in *For the Damaged Right Eye* 1968; in the manga speech bubble scene and the fragmented mixture of slapstick-comical elements and quotations in *Funeral Parade of Roses* 1969; the introduction of Japanese pop art and its diverse intermixture in *Space Projection Ako, The Expo '70 Textile Pavilion* 1970, that I conceived as the director general of the pavilion; or in the interaction of Duchamp and techno pop in *Metastasis* 1971.

Marta Minujín Yes, *La Menesunda* (no.96) was related to the events in Buenos Aires. It was an abstraction of them.

Marcello Nitsche Yes, I participated in events such as: the 9th and 10th São Paulo Biennials in 1967 and 1969 respectively; the exhibition of the labour trade union of São Paulo; the group exhibition entitled *New Objectivity*, at the Modern Art Museum of Rio de Janeiro in 1967; and the *National Expo of Brasilia* in 1967, where my work was destroyed by the military.

Dušan Otašević Some of my work from that period came into being as a result of my opposition to the ruling socialist ideology in Yugoslavia, or as a reaction to world events such as the senseless war in Vietnam.

Ulrike Ottinger Yes, in the way that I questioned the current social and political events that were becoming more and more ideological, especially the Marxist-Leninist and Maoist groups being very radical, whereas the Trotskyites were more differentiated. My interests in ethnology (Claude Lévi-Strauss, Michel Leiris, Victor Segalen), the Nouveau Roman and the Nouvelle Vague were important sources of inspiration. Structuralism helped me to find visual solutions for the multiple political, social and aesthetic layers I was trying to include in my paintings.

Joe Overstreet I was born in Conehatta, a

138

very rural place, not far from Philadelphia, Mississippi, where three young civil rights workers were murdered in 1964. I have been aware of inequalities in civil rights for most of my adult life. So, absolutely, in the 1960s I was involved in the civil rights struggle so that black people could receive equal opportunities. I demonstrated. I showed paintings in civil rights exhibitions. I worked at the Black Arts Repertory Theater in Harlem. Before that I worked in San Francisco and Oakland as part of the Beat Movement, with Bob Kaufman, Eric 'Big Daddy' Nord and Allen Ginsberg.

Joan Rabascall Yes, since my inspiration was the mass media of the time.

Bernard Rancillac Of course. On 1 January 1966, I decided to devote the entire year to current events. I realised that political events had an impact on me (the Vietnam War, Palestinians, Mao Tse-tung etc.).

Reimo Reinikainen The sketches for the US flag (nos. 29, 30, 31, 32) of course arose from the war that the USA was waging in Vietnam. I was appalled at how the richest country on the planet was trying to ravage one of the world's poorest countries. I was conflicted because I, like other Finnish pop artists, admired American pop art. At the same time, I was angered by the war the bigwigs in the US were waging against Vietnam, so I wanted to express my opposition to it. These four paintings were my protest against the war, but they were interpreted politically. Then again, war is very much a political event.

Colin Self I've created pop in *my* image. It's a vital part of my human character, identity and life experiences.

In those days of the early 1960s there was liberation in the air, colossal leaps and liberation in all arts. 'Conditions' like queen ants were going to fly. One felt it. War Babies young enough to miss National Service and *use* those valuable years. Bright sparks from the working classes (so called) getting a meritocratic chance. Art schools with *space* for inner dreams to get fulfilled. And grants. We repaid ours back to our *society* in better ways than now. Not academics ridden or full of jargon, bull or bankers' loans and debt. These milestones around the necks.

At the Slade School of Fine Art actually, my awful, prejudiced tutors Walter Thomas Monnington, Andrew Forge and others (apart from Frank Auerbach, Michael

121
(Top)
Parviz Tanavoli
Disciples of Sheikh San'an 1975
Wool
206×155

122
(Bottom)
Parviz Tanavoli
Disciples of Sheikh San'an 1974
Screenprint on paper
100×69.8

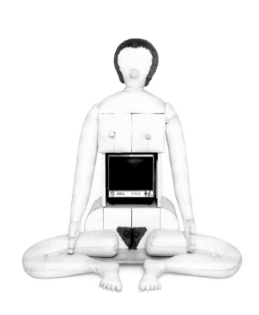

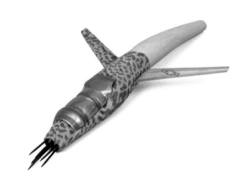

Andrews and Jeffrey Camp) were discouraging staff, and put my works into the Slade's 'worst three students' category … (and told me I would fail). Odd, because Tate Britain and Pallant House Gallery Chichester now own some of those very works …

Leaving the Slade and living in Crouch End, London, in the early 1960s was some kind of liberation from those lousy lecturers. (RCA kicked my friend Allen Jones out and tried to fail Hockney, also my friend).

I was gifted in art – but in working-class culture, this was only acceptable when one was a child. Then you had to 'grow up and get a proper job.' (And not easy either for some of my ex-public-school friends either).

The social *prejudice* against *art* was *shocking*. Modern art came on TV once a year – for people to *laugh at*. At the cinema, Movietone News showed a film of Yves Klein rolling nude women in paint and then they squirmed about on canvas placed on the floor. The ignorant audiences fell about laughing, which was the whole point of showing it.

Dorothée Selz Yes my work was linked to the socio-cultural context of the years from 1960 to 1975. Society was changing as well as behaviours and I felt the necessity to develop new attitudes in my work:

new pictorial subjects linked to
    current socio-political issues;
new modes of action outside galleries
    (performances in the streets to
    de-sacralise art);
new approaches to the public (with
    its active participation);
use of new materials (industrial or
    unusual ones such as the edible);
attempts to destroy a few taboos
    (after our dadaist predecessors).

French society was then fully metamorphosing. I experienced events in Paris in May 1968 with conscience, seriousness and euphoria: students' and workers' protests, feminist movements, sexual liberation, a whole population becoming aware. Current events were also the origin of fear or interrogation:

Algerian War of Independence from
    France (1954–62);
Francisco Franco's dictatorship in
    Spain;
the USA and Vietnam War;
dictatorships in Latin America;

140

Black Power in the USA;
the Cold War and the USA/Soviet Union's
nuclear race.

But the news was also marked by a certain utopia
and poetry, with the Beat generation, the hippie
movement, the new literature and the music boom,
with Woodstock in 1969 and the Isle of Wight festival,
which I went to.

In France, the economic boom enabled women
to be financially independent. There was little unem-
ployment and everyday life didn't cost much. The
changes in traditions and the socio-cultural changes
enabled women to play other roles in society. I was
a feminist and I still am, in the sense of rights to fight
for, for the new social role of women, and for the
changes in intimacy in parallel with the changes in
society. This also implied new sexual/erotic relationships, but of course with males' complicity, in so far
as a new woman also implies a new man, right?!

Teresinha Soares Yes. My work was profoundly
related to the socio-political events of the time, and
it vehemently opposed the Vietnam War, American
imperialism, sexual repression, the oppression
of women, the deaths and torture of political
prisoners in Brazilian prisons and the lack of
freedom of expression in authoritarian regimes.

Ushio Shinohara When creating works, I always intend
to ride the flow of the world and fight at the front. Of
course I also joined the flow at that time.

HOW DID YOU CHOOSE THE SUBJECT MATTER FOR YOUR WORK INCLUDED IN THE WORLD GOES POP?

Joan Cardells [Equipo Realidad] It was an idea we came
across while skimming through art historical images:
the work by Leonardo Da Vinci was a well-respected
image that we altered with a contemporary image of
a North American marine [*Divine Proportion* 1967
(no.114)]. It was an ironical take on the universal repression at the hands of Western powers, the supposed
perfection and kindness of Western repressive powers.
To this end, and more [Jorge] Ballester than myself,
we inherited Josep Renau Berenguer's ironical mechanisms, which were more anecdotal than pictorial.

Judy Chicago These paintings horrified my painting
instructors: 'wombs and breasts' they exclaimed, as
if those body part references were the manifestation
of something hideous. As a result, I eventually
destroyed them even though after graduate school

– when I attended automobile body school to learn to spray paint – I had transferred the images to car hoods (or bonnets). Many years later, in preparation for the Getty Center initiative, *Pacific Standard Time* (2011) I looked through my early work and discovered three unfinished hoods – *Flight Hood, Bigamy Hood, Birth Hood* (nos. 56, 115, 116) – and decided to complete them. Fortunately, I had slides of the original paintings and did colour studies based on those. When they were completed, I realised that there was nothing wrong with my early imagery; in fact, the hoods prefigured a good deal of my later work. Moreover, I was glad I brought those images back; otherwise, they might have languished in my slide files forever as testaments to the power of the male-dominated art world to silence the female voice.

Henri Cueco *Large Protest* (no.6) and *The Red Men, bas-relief* (no.106), the latter being the eponymous work of the series, were part of a 'cycle' presented in ARC in the Museum of Modern Art in Paris in May 1970. Preliminary drawings and sketches were made in 1968 and 1969. Paintings and plywood painted figures were realised from the end of 1968 and into 1969. The topics and imagery derived from the idea of some revolutionary utopia, moral and sexual freedom and fantasy, the concern for working people (*La Grève/The Strike*) and their relationships with the intellectual world. These red men and women flying like rain over the city were protesting and the titles (*Demonstration 1* and *2, La Meute (The Pack), La Grève (The Strike)* are sufficiently explicit when the images are not necessarily so. Of course the figures of screaming women or suffering children in the foreground of some works refer to war bombing (Biafran War, Vietnam War), but also to war in the colonial remains of the empires ... In another painting, Sigmund Freud, Karl Marx and Mao Tse-tung appear ironically in the same bed, which at first glance could be seen as a monument honouring their revolutionary roles but could alternatively be understood as an insult, implying their free sexuality, or that they are in the same tomb, a monument made with paving stones removed from Paris streets in 1968.

Romanita Disconzi [*Interpretation Totem* 1969 (no.118)] I was working with silkscreen printing and developing some sort of individual style, using an iconography taken from urban traffic signs, commercial ads in magazines and newspapers, objects from daily life and Christian iconography (the heart, flowers, palm of the hand). I worked with a kind of language with images, and as we were, by then, having a very politically disturbed time in Brazil, some images are symbolically related to specific local features, like the Brazilian map or the money note. The fist and the gun also appeared, inspired by the strong feelings of tension that were in the air. Although I don't consider my work as politically engaged, I do believe that it may be considered as means by which to reflect on that particular historical moment.

Sanja Iveković The Yugoslavian socialist government practised a Communist ideology combined with consumerist elements. The subject of this early video, *Sweet Violence* (no.23), is a good example of this. I wanted to deal with the manipulative power of the media, which is a subject that I am still interested in working with. The video consists of the commercials that were part of the economic propaganda programme broadcast on Zagreb television. By placing vertical strips of black tape over the television screen I wanted to create a visual reference to the passive viewer's captivity at the hands of the system. In this way I could symbolically disconnect viewers from the 'sweet violence', violence committed in a tender, endearing and efficient way, and thus even more damaging in its effects.

Jozef Jankovič At the time when loyalty to socialism was permanently manifested in the portraits of the icons of socialism (Karl Marx, Vladimir Lenin, Joseph Stalin, Klement Gottwald), I felt the need to counterbalance it with the manifestation of myself [*Private Manifestation* 1968 (no.111)].

Vitaly Komar [Komar and Melamid] The *Post Art* series [*Post Art No 1 (Warhol), Post Art No 2 (Lichtenstein), Post Art No 3 (Indiana) 1973,* nos. 16, 17, 18] is an apocalyptic vision of the future. The viewer can see famous works by Andy Warhol, Roy Lichtenstein, Robert Indiana and other pop artists as they might be after a nuclear war or a political or natural disaster. They would come to be as the ancient frescoes of Pompeii have survived to us, after the eruption of Vesuvius. This project also included *Pictures from the Future*: drawings and landscapes of the ruins of modern architecture, such as the Guggenheim Museum and MoMA in New York. The inspiration for the project came from the fact that in Russia historical antiquities, icons and paintings of old masters were considered to be of higher value than modern art. To this day I love unrenovated, darkened pictures or the dilapidated sculptures of ancient Greece and the ruins of ancient Rome, which I sometimes saw in the works of Giovanni Battista Piranesi and Hubert Robert. In the Soviet museums the restorers were scared of washing off, together with the darkened layers of the old lacquer, the final layer, the layer of the author's glaze, which is often jammed between two layers of lacquer. To me, brought up with such darkened pictures, it seemed that the golden darkness of these old paintings was a thrilling and mysterious symbol of time. The grime of the past separated us from 'the death of the author'. So, for me, seeing contemporary pop art through the patina of time means seeing our own time from the future, along with its tragic history and aesthetic values. To this day, when I see Dutch still lifes of the seventeenth century, with simple pots, herring with beer, clay tobacco pipes, playing cards and the like, the usual subjects of bygone daily life, it seems to me that this is the older sibling of pop art.

126
Ulrike Ottinger
God of War 1967–8
Triptych. Acrylic paint on wood
190 × 260 × 60 (open)

Alexander Melamid [Komar and Melamid]
I believed that these works [*Post Art No 1 (Warhol), Post Art No 2 (Lichtenstein), Post Art No 3 (Indiana)* 1973, nos. 16, 17, 18] represented a revolution that would destroy the works of the revolutionists.

Marcello Nitsche In the work entitled *I Want You* (no.33) the visual language was based on the American propaganda poster of the time bearing the words 'I want you for the US army'.

The work entitled *Kill Fly* (no.46) refers to dictatorship; it was my camouflaged way of speaking against the military regime.

Martha Rosler I wanted to use images of women from mass magazines, virtually all of which were engaged in shameless stereotyping. I felt that the emergent pop painters also repeated those tropes but always denied any depth of social critique beyond an ironic wink. I wanted my work to be seen as what we much later came to refer to as a deconstruction of the image. This group of works (which total more than thirty) I retroactively called *Body Beautiful, or Beauty Knows No Pain* (nos. 59, 60, 61, 62, 63, 125).

Dorothée Selz From 1960 to 1975 the woman was depicted in popular imagery (calendars) or sophisticated imagery (*Playboy* magazine or Allen Jones's works) as a seducer, femme fatale or pseudo prostitute. Or, on the other hand, as a housewife or mother of a family. These two clichés were the most common: mother or femme fatale. I thought that women were in an ambiguous position, between the secret desire to resemble the 'sexy female models' and the rejection of these models. It is in this spirit that I conceived this series where I staged myself as a model, by highlighting with humour the ambivalence of the female image in sexy pictures. By posing as a model – to imitate or to reject? – I was myself becoming *the* model of this tricky topic. What kind of woman shall I become? Which woman would I like to resemble? Which woman am I? I didn't want to 'portray myself' but I couldn't see anyone else but myself illustrating my intention. In fact, I would say that by presenting the model and myself, the subject is double, it is a complex duo: the model and its imitation, the model and its ironical imitation, the anonymous model and myself. The edible-like frame is a deliberately absurd background, with pop patisserie colours: from 1967 I was very interested in the edible as subject, object and material from the

127
(Top)
Dorothée Selz
Relative Mimetism – Woman with Boots and Lamp 1973
Gelatin silver print and coloured mortar on wood
Dyptich, each 30 × 36

128
(Middle)
Dorothée Selz
Relative Mimetism – Panther Woman 1973
Gelatin silver print and coloured mortar on wood
Dyptich, each 30 × 36

129
(Bottom)
Dorothée Selz
Relative Mimetism – 'The Vargas Girl' Woman after Vargas 1973
Gelatin silver print and coloured mortar on wood
Dyptich, each 30 × 36

everyday life. *Relative Mimetism* (nos. 127, 128, 129) with its fake edible appearance was asking the question: how do you make fun of the stereotyped women?

Keiichi Tanaami There was a famous Japanese confectionery company that used an angel as its brand icon. The public was invited to copy and depict this angel, and a number of angels that had been drawn by children with crayons were published in a newspaper. These dimly drawn angels that I saw in the midst of tough war times had a really shocking impact on my soul as a child. The memory of these times did not go away but stayed for a long time and inspired me to create animation works [such as *Crayon Angel* 1975 (no.89)].

Parviz Tanavoli Generally speaking, my main subject matter in the works in *The World Goes Pop* are lovers: perhaps the most favourite theme for Persians. Although *The Poet and the Beloved of the King* 1966 (no.34) was made eight years before the screenprints, (nos. 119, 120, 122) they all share the same stories. The imagery of the lovers mostly appears in Persian miniatures. I deliberately wanted to shake up the Iranians and get them out of their millennia-old shells. In order to do so, I picked up ordinary material and commercial paint to break down the soft lines of the Persian miniatures and those pretty faces. My lovers in new mediums with geometric lines are completely the opposite of the Persian refined taste.

WHERE DID YOU GET YOUR IMAGERY FROM? WHAT IF ANY SOURCES DID YOU USE?

Thomas Bayrle I used magazines and any kind of printed matter I could find. I worked in a small advertising company: Bayrle & Kellermann / the makers of display (from 1969 to 1972).

Renate Bertlmann I developed a particular interest in the commodities acquired from sex shops because they mirror so obviously sexual desires, anxieties and aggression. I have bought many different objects from sex shops and they became again and again readymade parts of my artistic practice.

130
Erró
American Interior No 5 1968
Glycerophtalic paint
on blended fabric
130×162×2.5

131
Erró
American Interior No 9 1968
Glycerophtalic paint
on blended fabric
130×162×2.5

147

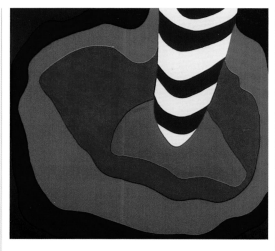

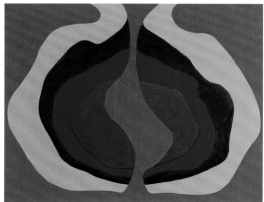

132
(Top)
Mari Chordà
Coitus Pop 1968
Enamel paint
on wood
50 × 60

133
(Bottom)
Mari Chordà
*The Great
Vagina* 1966
Enamel paint and
oil paint on wood
82.1 × 99.7

134
(Opposite)
Renate Bertlmann
Exhibitionism 1973
Wood, tempera,
graphite,
Styrofoam and
acrylic paint
Each 70.8 × 50 × 10

Also, I am always looking out for curious objects and found in an art supply store white Styrofoam eggs, which to me were suggestive of testicles. Thus the working title for this, originally five-part, series was *Hodenbewegung* [Testicle Movement, a pun on 'Frauenbewegung' meaning Women's Lib]. At first I didn't care much for this title but a couple of years later my existence as a female artist allowed for a very fitting title indeed. In 1975 Valie Export organised the first women's exhibition in the Viennese Galerie Nächst St Stephan, entitled *Magna Feminismus: Art and Creativity*. The erstwhile artistic director of the gallery, Oswald Oberhuber, rejected my series *Hodenbewegung*, which had been selected by Export, and wanted to cancel the show, arguing that he felt *'exhibitioniert'* (exposed, put on display). Thus, finally, I found a fitting title for my series of objects, namely *Exhibitionism* (no.134). Another work selected by Export was the object-collage with the title *Le Charme indiscret de la bourgeoisie*, which showed hairy female genitalia. This work did appeal to Oberhuber and thus found its way into the exhibition.

Cornel Brudaşcu I used solarised photographs from my own collection that portrayed friends and colleagues. Also, I was using images from magazines of that period. Sometimes I would have access to magazines form the West, for example the German magazine *Popcorn*, which I borrowed from a friend that had a subscription. A work inspired by an image I saw in *Popcorn* is *Guitarist* (no.12).

Teresa Burga The imagery was drawn from materials found in local markets selling textiles and other products.

Rafael Canogar I became aware that the configuration of a new iconography, as a testament to collective struggle, had to be introduced through a new language, less hermetic than informal abstraction. Realism gave me the possibility to channel my different aesthetic searches, besides giving me a moral support for my socio-political anxieties. This didn't entail going back to figuration; it meant creating a new reality. My need for truthfulness drew me to the use of authentic clothes in which to dress my characters, frozen and hardened with glass fibre and polyester. At times they resembled empty carcasses, without a head, dehumanised, as a way to underline their objective condition: like archaeological

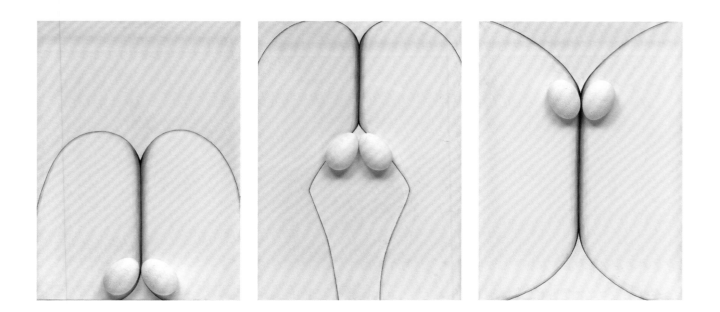

metaphors, the remains of a new Pergamon temple.

Mari Chordà The images and themes that interested me were closely linked to my intimate and emotional life, and to the life of the people I was most close to. Above all, my body was my model. In the case of *The Great Vagina* 1966 (no.133), as in the series of works called *Vaginas* from 1964, I capture my vision of my body, that goes from inside to outside and that re-creates itself in the pleasure of exploring the intimate. In the case of the paintings called *Pregnant Self-portraits* 1966–7 I was my own model. Through the images that I created I was able to understand the gestation of a creature. In painting seven moments of my pregnancy I reflected on the impact this had on my body. *Coitus Pop* 1968 (no.132) represents a great bi-colour phallus, in a vertical position, spreading its semen all around, with arrogance.

Henri Cueco Most of the images were taken from newspapers, news magazines and some photography books, and were impregnated with my reading of anthropology books such as *Tristes Tropiques* by Claude Lévi-Strauss, those by Marxist theoreticians, such as Antonio Gramsci, Louis Althusser and Herbert Marcuse, or those by philosophers, such as Jean-François Lyotard, Gilles Deleuze and Raymond Roussel.

Erró I collect images from all over. In my big loft near the Chelsea Hotel in New York, on the right side were the magazines, on the left newspapers bought by the kilo (it was forbidden to rip pages out). The images for the *American Interiors* series – *American*

135
Beatriz González
The Last Table 1970
Enamel on metal plate mounted within metal furniture
105 × 205 × 75

Interior No 1, American Interior No 5, American Interior No 9 (nos. 100, 130, 131) – were found in Cuba during our trip in 1967. The American paint factory was closed following the coming to power of Fidel Castro. I had to ask permission to get the catalogues with images of various coloured interiors. I found the images of the Viet-Kong soldiers in an underground shop in New York. Walt Disney's 'Tears for Two' I found in a bookshop in Fulton Street along with Pablo Picasso's images [*Big Tears for Two* 1963 (no.102)].

Beatriz González *The Suicide of the Sisga* (nos. 78, 79, 80) was inspired by a story that appeared in the press about a couple of young farmers in love: the man, guided by mystical insanity, convinced his girlfriend to commit suicide in order to preserve the purity of their love. Before jumping from the dam of the Sisga on the outskirts of Bogotá, the couple commissioned a professional photographer to take their portrait. The picture was then sent on to their families and when the news broke it was widely reprinted in black and white in local newspapers. As I already mentioned, the quality, or 'the bad quality' of the image, awoke my interest in this. I was attracted by the plain quality of the printed image, the simplification of the facial features, almost deformed by the discrepancy.

The Last Table (nos. 135, 136) is one of the first furniture pieces I ever made. These qualify as a sort of *objet trouvé*, upon which I intervened. Between 1969 and 1970 I came up with the idea for the furniture works. In front of the building where I

136
Beatriz González
The Last Table 1970
Enamel on metal
plate mounted
within metal
furniture
105 × 205 × 75
(Detail)

lived, there was a parking lot called Libertador, which had a Simón Bolívar painting reproduced on a hoarding. The hoardings of Bogotá were made in metal, rustic, not very big, very different from contemporary ones. One day I dared to approach a man who fabricated hoardings in a garage, and asked him to prepare me metal supports onto which I painted my paintings. A little later, I accompanied my husband, an architect, to buy construction materials in a neighbourhood called Los Mártires, identified by an obelisk celebrating the heroes of independence. There I found a metal bed, imitating wood. This piece of furniture was called 'radio bed', because embedded in its structure was a dedicated space for a radio; also, sectioned off by a sheet of corrugated glass, there was space for a lamp. We bought it with no specific purpose. At home, I was completing a painting on a metal sheet, the *Señor de Monserrate*, to be hung on a wall. When I began to ask myself 'what should we do with the bed?', it dawned on me that I should lie the painting on its back and fit it in the bed structure, and destiny made it fit precisely. The painting measured 120 wide, and the bed was also 120 wide. This moment still seems magical to me.

I didn't paint the furniture; I simply purchased it and assembled it with a painting that matched the feel of the object. Later on I discovered the factory that produced the furniture and it was able to customise the designs for me. I was very interested in factory painters' ability to mimic wood and marble (on metal), the 'falsification of materials': wood wasn't wood; marble wasn't marble; the power of simulation.

The subject matter didn't develop in response to the reproduction of a real artwork, for instance *The Last Table*; it drew instead on popular prints branded Molinari, and printed in Cali, that were sold in stores selling religious objects. The printer Molinari decided to intervene in the work of Leonardo and included the painter in the scene pretending he was one of Christ's disciples. *The Last Supper* was especially popular in Colombia because in every household this image was placed above the main entrance door as a good-luck charm against thieves. In a way the image acquired its own life and many spin-offs were produced.

Vitaly Komar [Komar and Melamid]

The samples used for the *Post Art* project were not originals but reproductions. In Russia in those days it wasn't possible to see the famous original pop art works so I hadn't seen them. The black and white reproductions from Soviet booklets criticising the 'soulless West' were badly printed, like grey ghosts. But for *Post Art* we used brightly coloured pictures from the famous book by Lucy Lippard, *Pop Art* (1966), which was a priceless gift from an American student friend. I'll let you into a professional secret. (Maybe it will come in handy for a young artist.) Firstly, with the help of a projector, we increased the reproduction to the size of the original. Then we made a colour copy and let it dry out. Then we covered it in a dark lacquer and, without allowing it to dry completely, we burnt it with the flame of a gas burner. And finally we let it dry out with a second layer of cracked matt lacquer. After the exhibition in Izmailovsky Park, 'a friend of a friend' carried many Sots-art paintings to New York. There in 1976 they were shown in an exhibition of Komar and Melamid at the Ronald Feldman gallery. We were not allowed out of Russia for our own

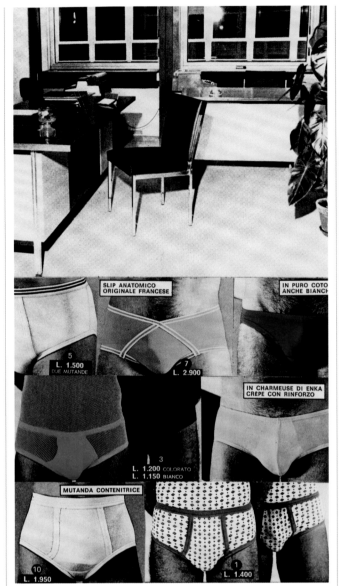

exhibition. The exhibition was unusually successful. Ronald sent us a bunch of reviews from newspapers and magazines. In his words, when Andy Warhol saw *Post Art* [*Post Art No 1 (Warhol)* 1973, no.16] and the future of his soup can, the face of this great artist turned as green as his beloved dollar bill. Only in 1978 was I able to get to New York and see the original pop art. It didn't differ much from the reproductions in Lippard's book.

Nicola L *Little TV Woman: 'I Am the Last Woman Object'* (no.123) was probably inspired by the new feminist movement, in which the woman declares:

> I am the last woman object,
> you can touch my mouth,
> my breasts,
> my stomach,
> but I repeat myself it's the last time.

Iris Clert, the grand and divine art dealer of the 1960s originally from Greece, showed this piece in the vitrine of the famous jeweller Alfred Van Cleef.

Ana Maria Maiolino The imagery works with the objectification of the modern man, specifically with the issue of females in their everyday life and their relationship with society. In several works I approach an ostensibly socially disqualified theme: the feminine. On the other hand, the everyday life oppressed by military repression gave rise to my works with a greater political and social tone, such as *The Hero (O Herói)*, *Glu Glu Glu* (no.36), both from 1966 and *KEHM* from 1967. The written work was also part of my output from that period. The word is a sign that comes to enhance the discourse of the work and leaves no doubt about that which is being represented and indicated in the narrative, like a handbook for children. That same word would also serve as the title for the work.

Toshio Matsumoto There were three motivations for creating *Mona Lisa* 1973 (no.82). Firstly, Leonardo Da Vinci's *Mona Lisa* came from the Louvre to Japan. As an ironic reaction against the extremely exaggerated response to this, I wanted to create a delusionary image of this super-famous person, referencing Andy Warhol's portraits of famous people. Secondly, around that time, the electronic image synthesiser Scanimate from America had been introduced to Japan. Researching how to use it, I found out that with this device it had become easier to combine pictures, photographs, films, CG or television images – images that differ technically – on one screen. Therefore, concrete images for works as well as ideas for their compositions came to my mind continuously. Thirdly, I received a message from Nam Jun Paik and there were more and more artists that worked with the new medium of video. In 1974, the Museum of Modern Art in New York organised an international exhibition and conference entitled *Open Circuits: The*

Future of Television, which was devoted to the medium of video; they invited me to come to America and asked me to create a new work.

Marta Minujín I used all kinds of media sources: electronics, media, neon. I chose the influence of technology in modern life. I also used everyday objects, such as make-up, smells, etc.

Marcello Nitsche In general I sought to use visual elements of everyday life, practising a language that the Brazilian people already knew. Based on this language, I inserted a criticism about the system.

Dušan Otašević My newly acquired knowledge of the existence of pop art as a new artistic expression coincided with my affinity for 'folk art': handmade signs that hang over craft shops, 'cooking poetry' (hand-embroidered motifs and rhymes popular in Central Europe, used as decoration in the kitchen) or fairground treats such as 'gingerbread hearts'. I would sometimes incorporate such a mixture of amateur products and kitsch into my work.

Ulrike Ottinger My inspirations came from very different sources like flipper automats, advertisements, newspapers, cybernetic models and political events. I experimented with photographic *mises en scènes* with my friends and with self-portraits as means to create a sort of fierce theatricality dissecting religious, political, economic or scientific structures.

Joe Overstreet I read in a magazine that Nancy Green, who was born in slavery in Kentucky, cooked around a million pancakes at the 1893 Chicago World's Exposition in order to save a pancake flour company. She made me think of my grandmother, my mother, and I thought she must have been very tired. And I knew Jemima was tired of that role. The painting – *The New Jemima* (no.117) – has a double meaning. So my painting reveals the New Jemima who chose a machine gun as her stove, for her kitchen equipment.

Joan Rabascall *Atomic Kiss* (no.113) reflects the year 1968. It was the year of student protests from Berkeley to Berlin, via Paris. The refusal of Vietnam War, the threat of a possible world war …

Teresinha Soares I consider the body as the axis of my poetics. I reinvented myself by re-discovering my own body as new woman, and in all my artworks, drawings, prints and performances, the leitmotiv is the body. My practice, considered avant-gardist at

137
(Opposite)
Eulàlia Grau
Office (Ethnography)
1973
Photographic emulsion and aniline on canvas
163.5×102.5

138
Eulàlia Grau
Nixon (Ethnography) 1973
Photographic emulsion on canvas
112.5×57

154

the time, continues to be contemporary because it focuses on all the issues that are still of concern today: the taboos of sex, male-female relationships, encounters and dis-encounters, women demanding respect within contemporary society, still fighting for rights and freedom.

Manolo Valdés [Equipo Crónica] Our imagery was borrowed from high culture, it belonged to the art historical cannon promoted by certain museums. They were all images that we had grown up with and respected. We were fascinated by these iconic paintings that appeared everywhere in picture books, photographs and drawings. Ultimately we decided to revisit them ironically.

Tadanori Yokoo In *KISS KISS KISS* (no.87), I assembled a large number of kiss scenes from American comic magazines, copied them and then, always beginning with the part that depicts the lips, I gradually ripped them. At the end, all the pictures were torn and not even one was left. The dada critic and artist Hans Richter saw the work and commented on it very positively, writing about it in a book entitled *Dada: Art and Anti-Art*. Following this, he planned to show it in New York but as I didn't have the financial means to create a copy of the film, I could not take this great opportunity. If the film can be shown in London this time, this would make me happy and I would be really honoured.

WERE YOU AWARE OF POP ART IN OTHER PARTS OF THE WORLD?

Thomas Bayrle Besides the pop art of England and USA, Japanese manga art fascinated me strongly … having visited Japan often since 1978, the way they produced manga images – in order to flow into comics or film – fascinated me (the entire industry of it).

Delia Cancela In 1965 American pop art arrived at the Di Tella Institute. The exhibition *New America Cinema* introduced Andy Warhol and Paul Morrissey movies. Other exhibitions featured paintings from American pop artists. But it was not until the 1970s that I discovered English pop.

Joan Cardells [Equipo Realidad] Yes, through

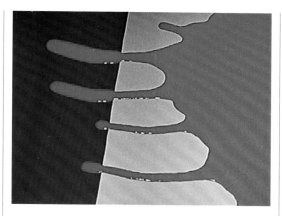

139
(Opposite)
Gérard Fromanger
Album The Red
1968–70
21 Serigraphies
Each 60×90

140
Gérard Fromanger
Film-tract n°: 1968
1968
16mm film, digitalised, colour silent
2 min 49 sec

the magazine *L'Europeo* I became familiar with the work of Robert Rauschenberg, and during the first trip I took to Paris, at the end of 1966, I had the chance to visit the group exhibition, *La Jeune Peinture*, which included Italian and French painters. In our case, in Valencia, and through Tomás Llorens and Julio Aguilera, we tried to adapt pop to a critical figuration, which became known as 'chronic of reality'.

Judy Chicago I only knew what little work was exhibited on the West coast in the 1960s and I don't remember being interested in it.

Mari Chordà Yes, when I lived in Paris. I was informed, mainly about the USA, through the exhibitions and some magazines. I knew the work of Jasper Johns, Andy Warhol, Roy Lichtenstein. The work that most interested me was (Lichtenstein's), although I didn't like the macho inflection of some of his *vignette*. I was excited by Niki de Saint Phalle's *Nanas*. I read it as a glorification of the female body. I also knew the work of Equipo Crónica, a Valencian collective very active and well known in Spain at the end of the 1960s for its collaboration in semi-clandestine activities connected with Estampa Popular.

Antonio Dias In Brazil, a group of artists including Claudio Tozzi, Geraldo de Barros, Nelson Leirner and Rubens Gerchman used a type of figuration that approximated a pop language. When I was living in Paris, I met artists such as Peter Klasen, Jacques Monory and Bernard Rancillac who also used a pop language, albeit with narrative features. In Italy I met the artists Mario Schifano, Sergio Lombardo and Renato Mambor among others.

Erró I arrived in New York in December 1963. My good friend Öyvind Fahlström took me to the studios of all the pop artists who have become close friends since then. Arriving in New York was a kick in the ass. After that I spent several months every winter in New York until 1968.

Ángela García Yes, but I had no knowledge of feminist painters, or the representation of women by other women. For me it was a great surprise, when after some time I became aware of American movements by women artists who were working along the same line of enquiry as mine. I was thrilled by this discovery!

Beatriz González During the 1960s I wasn't aware of it. In the art history classes taught by Marta Traba the furthest we got was abstract expressionism. In 1961 we went with her on a trip to New York. There we visited MoMA and we saw mostly abstract expressionist works, with Jackson Pollock above all. Pop was mentioned at the time but with little enthusiasm. Thinking about it perhaps I knew pop, but I didn't like it. I remember seeing in the Latin American edition of *Life* magazine a critique of Claes Oldenburg's kitchens, but this didn't catch my attention.

Again, in 1966 in Amsterdam I visited the Stedelijk Museum where I came across Robert Indiana's numbers and some works by Tom Wesselmann but they were unrelated and extraneous to my painting. I considered them very distant from what I was doing in painting.

Jozef Jankovič In those days we produced unofficial art that existed on the margins of society. A deeper understanding of this phenomenon requires a greater awareness of the situation. Everything, including the cultural institutions, was controlled by the state, both ideologically and economically. Private galleries, publishing houses and art agencies did not exist. Since there was no art market, commercial art did not influence our work.

Toshio Matsumoto I knew a little bit about what was going on in America and the UK from art journals. However, the first time that real works of pop art came to Japan was in 1974 when the Daimaru Department Store in Tokyo organised an Andy Warhol retrospective solo show.

Joan Rabascall Only in Western parts of the world. American pop through magazines and catalogues. British pop directly through trips to London. Some feeble signals sometimes came from Eastern Europe.

Bernard Rancillac I have been seduced and influenced by the works of Peter Saul, which I discovered from the early 1960s when he lived in Europe. I visited the exhibition of British painters at the Whitechapel Gallery (Derek Boshier, Peter Blake, Patrick Caulfield). They were also, by the way, all exhibited at the Musée d'Art Moderne de la Ville de Paris. Then Mrs Sonnabend opened her gallery on Quai de Seine. We were almost the only ones at her openings. She rapidly made us understand that she was here to 'launch' American pop artists in Europe. This is called landing in military terms: a successful operation. I bought a serigraphy (original and signed) of Andy Warhol's *Marilyn*.

Martha Rosler I knew about British pop by mid-decade: Richard Hamilton was a well-respected figure, and Allen Jones a despised one; but French nouveau réalisme was known to have preceded these trends before Lawrence Alloway disseminated the term 'pop art'. I may have known by then of some Latin American pop. There were a number of women, mostly painters but some sculptors, in New York who were clearly making work that was pop, including Marisol, who was always referred to as Latin American. I don't think I had more than a superficial knowledge of the contents or intentions of pop abroad, however.

Dorothée Selz I had little information about pop art in the UK and USA. I knew the works of Equipo Crónica in Spain, I met Brazilian Antonio Dias in Paris, Lourdes Castro and René Bértholo in Portugal, and Erró and the nouveaux réalistes. But I didn't know anything about pop art in the rest of the world. Information was only circulated by word of mouth, which was more efficient than the press.

Keiichi Tanaami In Tokyo close to Ginza there was a bookshop, Iena, which specialised in Western books.

It was a valuable source of information for me and I went there regularly. I have forgotten the name of the magazine but I remember that I was fascinated by a small photograph that I saw in an American art magazine. This was my first encounter with pop art. I think it was probably a work by Roy Lichtenstein. There was information about works from America and England but I didn't really know anything about works from other countries.

Claudio Tozzi Through publications, books, magazines, conferences and debates that took place in the History department of the Faculdade de Arquitetura e Urbanismo da Universidade de São Paulo (College of Architecture and Urbanism of the University of São Paulo) I acquired a wide range of knowledge of the new figuration and pop art in different countries. At the São Paulo Biennial there was a pop art exhibition room, which showed works by almost all of the American artists of the time. Some Latin American institutions carried out research and organised exhibitions of the new figuration artworks.

WAS COMMERCIAL ART AN INFLUENCE ON YOUR WORK OR THE WAY IN WHICH IT WAS MADE?

Thomas Bayrle Sure – as I mentioned. Working for three years – via advertising companies – I learned a lot about the background to pop art.

Delia Cancela Magazines (all of kinds) were part of my inspiration. My father was working in the press distribution and so all the magazines were available at my house.

Antonio Dias No. Although to make paintings in that period I preferred pigments that were used commercially, such as vinyl, alkyd or acrylic for walls.

Romanita Disconzi Yes, very much, especially commercial advertising imagery and the crude way the images were presented, with pure flat colours and very delimited edges.

Ángela García My work was influenced by the iconography of female mass media, so in this sense I can say yes, through the subversion of the image that became the protagonist of a history very distinct from that of pink glamour.

Sanja Iveković In the 1970s I was working as a graphic designer at a large publishing house in Zagreb. Later I started a collaboration with a number of Croatian non-government women's organisations designing their press material and creating the promotional videos for the television. The knowledge I gained

as a graphic designer definitely influenced the way I deal with my artworks.

Sergio Lombardo Advertisements of commercial products gave me the aesthetic key with which I tried to paint politicians as mass produced products.

Toshio Matsumoto I have never particularly admired commercial art; however, I sometimes get fresh inspiration from its intuitive sense to visualise directly the trends and feelings of an era.

Marta Minujín No. I can only think of the invention of Bazooka bubble gum as one of the greatest inventions. Its colour seemed to me the most pop possible!

Dušan Otašević Commercial art that could be seen at the beginning of the formation of consumer society in our country (Yugoslavia) appealed to me because of its naïve immediacy and freedom from any knowledge about art.

Martha Rosler I felt allergic to commercial art, and most of my work was in one way or another pitched against it. Much of the post-AbEx [post-abstract expressionist] work of the late 1950s and the 1960s was made in the face of the impending tide of commercialism: for example, Allan Kaprow and the birth of 'happenings'. (Fluxus had a different sort of European-derived concern, I felt.)

Dorothée Selz Yes, I was very interested in the industrialisation of the image, through advertising, packaging, press/fashion/food photographs, record covers, film posters, shop windows, large industrial food displays, new architectural techniques, forms, colours, textures: everything in the urban everyday environment was inspiring. For a living I was working for the daily newspaper *France-Soir*, retouching press photographs, and for various fashion magazines.

Ushio Shinohara Commercial art does not allow artists to be too self-satisfied. It is therefore attractive to lonely artists who are working by themselves in their studio.

Parviz Tanavoli The commercial work of the Iranian bazaars, yes (i.e. neon lights, banners, signs and all their kitsch mixtures/blends).

Claudio Tozzi My work in the 1960s moved away from traditional easel painting. I worked on a horizontal surface and used as a support industrially produced agglomerated plates. The ink I used was the same as that commonly used to make traffic signs and urban advertisements. I started to work with Liquitex, an acrylic resin widely used by pop artists, which had characteristics similar to those used in publicity. Some processes such as silkscreen paved the way to the appropriation of photographic images and their coupling to the painting. The traditional processes of printing using typography and offset allowed the creation of photolithography with different graphical particles that were then incorporated into the work.

Tadanori Yokoo Commercial art was my job in order to survive; however, I have never really been influenced by other commercial art. The influence of Japanese *ukiyo-e* woodblock prints, illustrations in old Japanese

141
Eulàlia Grau
Panic (Ethnography) 1973
Photographic emulsion, aniline
and acrylic paint on canvas
98.5×120

142
Eulàlia Grau
Chicks and Cops (Ethnography) 1973
Photographic emulsion, aniline
and acrylic paint on canvas
170.5×120.5

159

De izquierda a derecha: Juan Céspedes Martín, Antonio Ray Cobo y Fernando Vega Ureta, identificados por la Policía como integrantes de la banda de atracadores y que se encuentran en ignorado paradero, aunque se siguen de cerca los pas

143
(Top)
Eulàlia Grau
*Miss and Gangsters
(Ethnography)* 1973
Photographic
emulsion and acrylic
paint on canvas
108.5×115.8

144
Eulàlia Grau
*Rich and Famous
(Ethnography)* 1972
Photographic
emulsion and acrylic
paint on canvas
120.5×124.5

novel books and American as well as European contemporary art was a lot stronger.

WAS THERE A FEELING AT THE TIME THAT YOU WERE DOING SOMETHING IMPORTANT AND NEW, MAKING A CHANGE...?

Renate Bertlmann I have always thought of my artistic practice as serious, but important … ? In retrospect it was obviously very important for myself to discover the creative potential of aggression within me. Not only men resented this but women, too. My radical and uncompromising artistic work embarrassed and appeared strange to both sexes. Perhaps it was novel for me to focus from the very start on investigating and developing a new image of the male by the female and did not restrict myself to developing a new image of the female by the female.

Mari Chordà Yes, on a personal level, as a Catalan woman I had to make difficult decisions. I was born in a village, in Amposta, a few years after the end of the Spanish Civil War, and my life was different from what was expected of a woman at that time. I chose to study Fine Arts at the University of Barcelona. I wanted to be an artist and I moved to live and paint in Paris. They wanted me to marry but I believed in 'free love' and I started making a type of art that people did not understand … All of this was very different from the life that was expected of me and that they forced upon the majority of Catalan and Spanish women. This explains how the changes we made to our personal lives, as women, had repercussions and reflected the changes in all social spheres. We belived in the personal as political, as we used to say at that time.

Once I arrived in Paris, I met men and women who lived and related to each other in very different ways. For a short time I collaborated with a cell of the Spanish Communist party based in the Latin Quarter in Paris. I helped them with the organisation of cultural and solidarity activities in support of the working class, especially those with a Spanish connection. By participating in very present, lively events, I was experiencing a moment of great cultural and political effervescence.

Because of my pregnancy, the political party gradually distanced itself from me. I began to be discriminated against, because of my condition! This situation made me question the hierarchies and the domineering machismo of that group tied to Stalinist Communism.

Henri Cueco Difficult to say, but this idea of diffusing to a large audience paintings and posters (lithographies) and being able to show these works in good conditions in public venues, produced a proximity that changed the relationship between the artist and his public, especially at a period marked by the expanding 'power of the mass media' as it was called at that time. My production of lithographies, distributed through a system of public subscription at a low price, was directly aimed at having a relationship with an extensive audience. For example, a folio of ten images was sold for the equivalent of nowadays €15, or €1 to €1.5 each. These prints produced in large series (around 1,000) were sold as posters at the time of these exhibitions in art or cultural centres or theatres, but also in some supermarkets, such as Prisunic.

Antonio Dias Of course the objective of these works was to present something new. Above all for my own interest. I was young and I aimed to produce works that were completely different from anything that I knew. The conscious and the unconscious mixed. For me it was almost a catharsis. But this made it all very difficult; the paintings were considered aggressive and nothing ever sold.

Romanita Disconzi I think so, I knew then, and now, that in that time this kind of work was quite new in Brazil and the neighbouring countries.

Eulàlia Grau It was a time of great turmoil in Catalonia, we were all aching for change and were under the illusion that we would achieve it.

Jozef Jankovič In the first half of the 1960s, unofficial works were presented in the artists' studios and private apartments. This situation lasted until 1966 when state censorship was abolished. In the second half of the 1960s, when the political situation became more liberal, we were gradually allowed to exhibit in state galleries. During the normalisation period in the 1970s, the majority of nonconformist artists were excluded from the Union of Slovak Visual Artists, which had a total monopoly on the presentation of artists in galleries, in the media and in public. The audience had a limited access to unofficial art. As a result there was little response to this art.

Vitaly Komar [Komar and Melamid] I didn't consider Sots-art to be a commodity, but rather a very important means of 'self-cleansing' from the hypnosis of Soviet propaganda and, primarily, a cleansing from oneself. Sots-art does not try to impose its medicine on everyone. Anton Chekhov, who was not only a writer but also a doctor, wrote of 'squeezing the slave out of oneself, drop by drop'. In the totalitarian society it was important to remember that 'squeezing the slave' meant squeezing it from oneself, not squeezing it from others.

Sergio Lombardo It was clear that my work changed the traditional style and perception of painted human images – no more as a realistic imitation of reality, but a new reality itself – a new artificial reality.

Anna Maria Maiolino When you're young you have the advantage of an enthusiasm for building your own alphabet, your own language. This flourishes into a wonderful adventure of creation, full of previously unknown flavours. It is a constant and gradual discovery of ourselves and of what we are capable. Living in Rio de Janeiro, at such a stimulating and effervescent time in Brazilian life, with art tracing new paths over Brazilian roots and a large portion of society proposing major social changes to build a new future, I certainly felt like I was part of this process and consequently was building something new.

Toshio Matsumoto I think it was right that while echoing the big changes of the 1960s and 1970s, I always tried to fight against psychosomatic rigidity. This mindset has basically not changed to the present day.

Marta Minujín Of course. I thought I was the most avant-garde artist in the world.

Isabel Oliver I was firmly convinced of how important it was to do this kind of work, but I was also well aware that as a woman I would encounter additional obstacles.

Dušan Otašević At the beginning of my artistic activity I felt close to Filippo Tommaso Marinetti's idea of burning down the museum. I tried to move away from the language of painting, acquired at the Academy of Fine Arts in Belgrade, through my choice of topics and mode of execution. I used trivial everyday life moments such as lighting a match or licking ice cream. Instead of classical painting materials I used industrial paints, spray-painted onto aluminium or wooden boards.

Joan Rabascall No, what was I important, I believe, was to get away from abstract art, which was very present in galleries, and do something that was corresponding to the time in which we were living. Move forward and look ahead, not at the rear-view mirror.

Dorothée Selz No, I wasn't conscious of that but I thought I was in the spirit of the times, and that the subject was important. French society in the 1960s was very conservative and living another way of life required a lot of energy. What was important for me was what was experienced, and more than making a change it was I who was changing. I didn't have enough distance to look back at my work and judge it. I thought artists had a role to play in society and should express themselves as much as possible. But I didn't have a career plan and I didn't even think of taking photographs of the work I was producing. This is why there is very little documentation on my works from 1967 to 1975.

Teresinha Soares Yes. I felt that my generation and I were participating in the changing attitudes of men and women in the eyes of the world; we were seeking changes in behaviour, changes in politics, changes in art, changes in the environment and, ultimately, a new libertarian way of being in the world.

Ushio Shinohara During the opening of the Tokyo Olympics in 1964, the whole of Japan was very excited. All of us young artists were feeling a sense of fulfilment while creating works.

Parviz Tanavoli All I knew was that I was going in the wrong direction and I had chosen the wrong path, but I enjoyed it.

Jana Želibská Of course, especially in Slovakia this represented a substantial change in the way art was perceived.

WAS THERE AN AUDIENCE FOR THE WORK AT THE TIME AND, IF SO, WHAT WAS THE REACTION TO IT?

Thomas Bayrle The audience was only in areas of advertising – hardly in the field of art.

Renate Bertlmann Valie Export had discovered two-year-old collages in my studio and she took to them in a big way. But she could not show them in her *Magna Feminismus* exhibition due to the incident described above. Because of that incident I lost any desire to offer these collages to anyone else. I sensed they were too forward, too provocative. Thus I stopped showing them to anybody or suggesting them for exhibitions, since my dogged interest in the male, phallic structure not only lead to repeated irritation and rejection by males but equally by feminist artists and critics. The latter two accused me of being fixated on the phallus, of being obscene and lacking engagement with femininity.

Rafael Canogar In 1965, when I exhibited my first works in Madrid – where I live – there were strong attacks, and curiously, if I'm not mistaken, they attacked me for having turned to and being influenced by 'pop

145
Keiichi Tanaami
Commercial War 1971
Animation film
4 min 30 sec

art'. But a few months later I exhibited these works at the Venice Biennale and they had a huge effect.

Gérard Fromanger Yes, this work – *Album The Red* (no.139) – was immediately internationally acclaimed and was awarded the Tokyo Biennial Print Prize as well as Kyoto Biennial's (before Andy Warhol, Robert Rauschenberg and Jasper Johns!). With it I also earned Jean-Luc Godard's friendship and collaboration.

Beatriz González People couldn't understand why I had abandoned my refined early paintings. With *The Suicides of Sisga* (nos. 78, 79, 80) I changed, and shifted on the one hand, my interest from images inspired by Johannes Vermeer and Diego Velázquez to Antonio Molinari's images, and on the other hand, I turned to bright colours and flat figures. This was considered a stark departure and was immediately rejected. Afterwards, when I exhibited my furniture pieces in the São Paulo Biennial in 1971, they didn't encounter much appreciation among specialist and general audiences. At the time abstraction still prevailed. Nevertheless, in the catalogue Marta Traba described it as marginal art. It was the first time that the term marginality was used in relation to Latin American art. With the furniture pieces I had attached, without realising it, a counter proposal to international art.

Eulàlia Grau The majority of the audience were intellectuals and young people, students that were ready for a cultural change, but on the other side we were fiercely criticised by the reactionaries and left wing people with fascist inclinations!

Sergio Lombardo We were considered as an insane group of subversive agitators, especially by the artists of Realismo Socialista, like Renato Guttuso and his followers: they were the establishment. When I was seventeen I was expelled from a conference and as accused of being 'bourgeois'. My paintings were shown as examples of how not to paint.

Marta Minujín It was a giant success for the public. Audiences of all kinds came to participate and to live the work. People that never consumed art had this first experience. *La Menesunda* (no.96) was installed in the Di Tella Institute, an intellectual centre. In spite of this, there was a queue each day eight blocks long.

Ulrike Ottinger There was a split between the audiences. My work was shocking for the followers of the École de Paris but was received enthusiastically by the people of the Biennale international de l'Éstampe in Paris.

Joe Overstreet In 1964 I made a large painting (260×154.3) of Jemima: *The New Jemima* (no.117). Larry Rivers saw it around 1970, and he said that if I made it larger, he would include it in the *Some American History* exhibition at Rice University. So I made a kind of wooden armature so that the painting would resemble something like a pancake box. I enlarged it especially for this art project, which was part of the effort in 1971 to desegregate Rice University. Rice had a codicil that blacks could never attend that institution.

Bernard Rancillac My first exhibition described as pop at Mathias Fels gallery in 1965 (I think) only caused me to receive sarcasm and insults.

Reimo Reinikainen The sketches for the US flag were displayed in Helsinki in 1966, at the first exhibition of my own. The displayed works were mostly circle and line paintings. Some works featured collage materials. As a generalisation, you could say that the critics failed to understand the art and were dismissive. It is rare for an artist to know how the audiences reacted.

Ushio Shinohara The Japan of that time did not have any art dealers. We as artists organised group exhibitions to present our works and only related people from the art world were excited about them. There were no collectors either.

Teresinha Soares Yes, record audiences attended all exhibitions of my works. Perhaps it was due to a curiosity for the new, for the playfulness and eroticism of the works; or, who knows, for my privileged social position, or for being a married woman, mother to five children. We made happenings, performances and the public engaged with our proposals. We were featured in some of the country's major newspapers. 'La fin du siècle est arrivée à Belo Horizonte' was one of the great headlines in the *O Estado de Minas* newspaper in the state of Minas Gerais. The avant-garde critics supported us, but the general public outside (the art scene), the traditional families of Minas Gerais, the military and the representatives of the Catholic Church, reacted against our boldness.

Keiichi Tanaami Regarding animation works, there were only very few visitors and few places where we showed these films. At the time, animation films by Disney and such were well known but there were hardly any opportunities to see experimental animation films and there were not many people making them either.

Around 1964, an animation festival started in Tokyo and it became possible to see works from overseas. Around the same time the dramatist Terayama Shūji opened the Tenjō Sajiki theatre and approached me as I had been looking for a place to show my work. It would be in the middle of the night or early in the morning when there were no

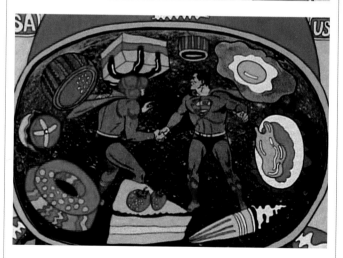

146
Cornel Brudaşcu
Composition 1970
Oil paint on canvas
118× 165

147
Cornel Brudaşcu
Youth on the Building Yard 1972
Oil paint on canvas
149.5 × 157

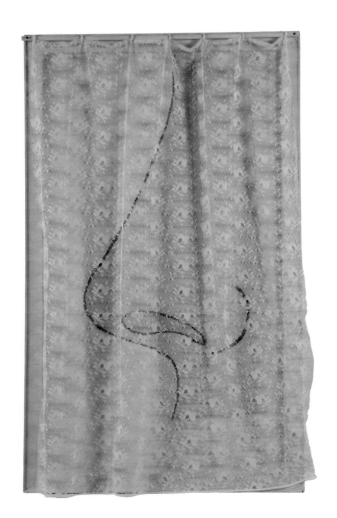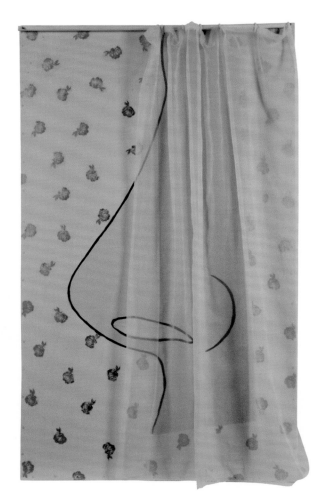

148
Jana Želibská
Nose I – II 1967
Diptych. Plywood
and mixed media
Each 120 × 70

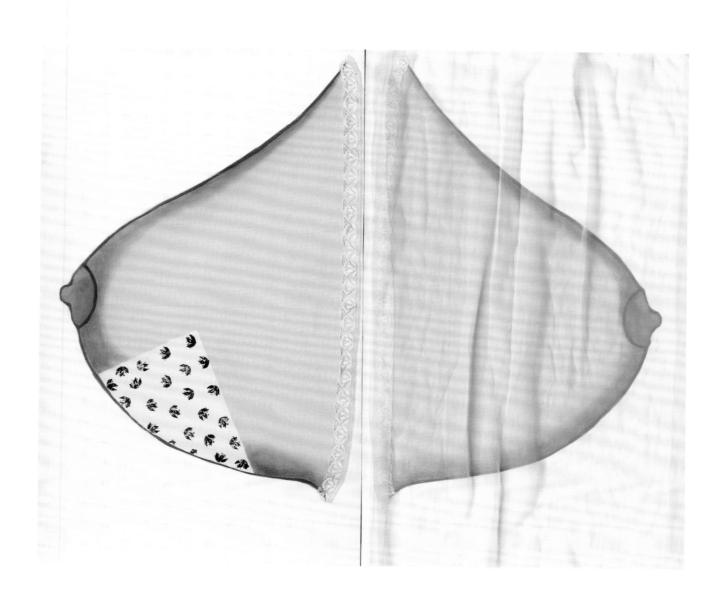

149
Jana Želibská
Breasts 1967
Diptych. Plywood
and mixed media
Each 120 × 70

public theatre performances but nevertheless I was thankful for his proposal. However, there were also days when it was really empty and only two or three people came. There was also a situation when some people came who expected a normal film and then said 'Give me my money back' – that was a real shock.

Claudio Tozzi The public interested in the fine arts was very restricted at the time. In order to enlarge it we used alternative venues to divulge our work. Silkscreen was widely used to reproduce the images without attributing numbers to the series as is used today and thus keep them far from commercial purposes. We produced images of popular idols on paper, fabrics, T-shirts and other items that transgressed the traditional ones. We organised an exhibition entitled *Flags* in a public square, which drew a large number of people. Another exhibition focused on stamps with images that were chosen by the audience. Spectators stamped the chosen image on paper and took them home. These were actions that aimed to make people connect and get more used to artworks.

Tadanori Yokoo In Japan at the time it was not possible yet for young artists to have a solo exhibition in an art museum; however, there were art exhibitions in the exhibition spaces of department stores instead. In 1970, 70,000 visitors came to my solo exhibition at the Matsuya Ginza department store within just six days, which was a record. Ninety per cent of the visitors were young people in their twenties and they were queuing on the stairs from the first to the seventh floor. When Mishima Yukio saw this, he also wanted to have a solo exhibition and in the same year he had a solo show in a different department store. Two or three months later, he rushed into the self-defence forces, failed to inspire a coup d'état and committed suicide (*seppuku*).

LOOKING BACK AT THESE WORKS, WHAT DO YOU THINK ABOUT THEM NOW?

Renate Bertlmann Pornographic jokes have always been a male domain, made at the exclusive expense of women. I consider my series of objects an accomplished example of an obscene female joke. This joke has hit home; it targets the deadly serious, male sexual arrogance. My works could be created only because I was obviously able, despite my anxieties, to discuss sexuality and sexual repression simultaneously through desire and ironic distance.

Cornel Brudaşcu Looking back, I'm glad that I was part of that moment. It was the correct time for

experiments, important for my artistic endeavour. Looking at these works now, I have a feeling of satisfaction that they are the result of my own research regarding representation and that these were not made using other techniques, like the projector or transfer techniques such as monoprint.

Teresa Burga I'm still interested in this period as it represents a special time in all the arts, fashion, music, dance, theatre and movies.

Pop iconography still influences contemporary pictorial forms, in the same way that musical tunes do. It is also important to bear in mind that many of the artists who are making conceptual art, are also turning to pop art, to present their imagery.

Judy Chicago I'm very glad I decided to bring new life to that early work. It taught me that one should always trust one's own impulses as an artist, even in the face of rejection, ridicule or silence.

Antonio Dias I feel that they were the first steps of a staircase that I am still climbing today. To me they seem fun and frank. I do not see them as outdated; they are an experiment I conducted, an experience that gave me a lot of awareness about what I understood artistic practice to be.

Gérard Fromanger It was a great moment of unity between art and life. This emotion is still present. Art can be at the same time knowledgeable and popular. It is only in this perspective (and not historically) that I can consider myself a 'pop artist'.

Beatriz González I'm surprised by myself, for having taken such a valiant position in this moment. Yes, sometimes I see myself like a transgressor that didn't fit in her time.

Jozef Jankovič This is part of my early work and, as it happens, memories of youth are always nice, even though I lived in a terrible period.

Natalia LL I think that their deeper meaning and artistic importance is continually rediscovered anew. Especially by young people, the next generation who have been educated in a different context of reality.

Ana Maria Maiolino Examining my oeuvre from the beginning to now, I think that the works produced with a figurative narrative in the 1960s and those produced after abandoning figuration in the 1970s have remained strong and vivid over time, because they carry certain seminal aspects that remain active to this day in my work, for example: food, digestion, the body, the inside and the outside, the development and appropriation of aspects of the quotidian, life as art, the word as sign, and finally the political. These questions indicate my inner needs, of my soul and my mind. These points, where my imagery, my seemingly non-linear work, returns and, in spiral movements, is fed and born again in cycles.

Marta Minujín I think they were brilliant and totally avant-garde. *La Menesunda* (no.96) was the first work of art where a TV and an undressed couple were presented.

150
Cornel Brudaşcu
Group Portrait 1970
Oil paint on canvas
161×180

151
Sergio Lombardo
John F. Kennedy 1962
Enamel paint on canvas
170×200

152
Sergio Lombardo
Nikita Krusciov 1962
Enamel paint on canvas
190×250

Marcello Nitsche I decided to complement our interview with a conversation that I had with the artist Robert Rauschenberg, when he was in São Paulo for the Biennial in 1967. I had the opportunity to exchange ideas with him about the works exhibited, and he told me that one of the interesting features of his observations was that the works of art were not finished as well as those of the Americans, and that they were more consistent with our reality!

Isabel Oliver I think they reflect the role assigned to women in society at that time and that the paintings perform a role of denunciation in the struggle for equal rights. With time I understand them as achievements.

Joe Overstreet In my painting, I think it is also easy for people to understand the rage, political consciousness, even the irony of the subject. 'Mammy' was one of the favourite stereotypes created by whites to control African Americans. Black folks were disgusted with these old, tired and exasperating ideas. In the new world of intergalactic space travel, New Jemima decided to take a stand. So my painting reveals the New Jemima who chose a machine gun as her stove, for her kitchen equipment. She is shooting rapid-fire pancakes.

Joan Rabascall I think they correspond to a past moment when the youngest protagonists appropriated the large field of the possible. Laboratory came before market. Today it is the contrary: art is dependent on the globalised market society of spectacle.

Reimo Reinikainen Next year marks the fiftieth anniversary of my first exhibition. I am originally from Helsinki, but I now live in a sparsely populated forest region in central Finland, which I moved to from a small town in southern Finland. I live in the middle of nowhere and have to travel long distances to get anywhere. What could I say about the art I made when I was young?

Martha Rosler I hardly know how to talk about my own work with any distance. *Woman with Vacuum, or Vacuuming Pop Art* (no.63) is one of the earliest of this 'series'; it announces the theme I would pursue for quite a few years. It is a retrograde image of a happy housewife with a snaky appliance, which implicitly compares the bright colours of pop art – embodied by images of women and romance – with the professional, almost claustrophobic decor. The rest are much later and take on the theme 'the (female) body in pieces', dismembered for delectation in high-end, soft-core pornographic magazines, encoded into wallpaper (painting is flat!) on the one hand and kitchen appliance adverts on the other. I should think that the reading of 'woman = good mother = food' is apparent in the kitchen set; you might say its theme is 'consumption'. I am surprised at the consumability of the latter set today, as I see them as flatly, obviously, inarguably symbolic.

Dorothée Selz Today, I think that the concept and realisation of these works are good, but I notice that their subject is still current, and that I could produce more works of this series today. In 1970 I thought that pin-up's imagery would disappear, how naïve I was! The male body also rapidly became a pin-up in every visual media.

Keiichi Tanaami Today, I still create works that deal with my experience of war as a child. This moment of fear that a whole city can disappear just within a moment is a memory that has been recorded deep in my mind; it does not go away. Bomb blasts that burn the skin; weirdly shining orange flares; enormous bright red columns of flames; machine gun fire from combat planes; the smell of scorching corpses lying on the streets. This extreme reality attacked the young me. The fact that it almost feels like yesterday, although it is far away in the past, shows that to me it really was a big incident. In *Crayon Angel* (no.89), real bombing moments from contemporary news films that I had seen in the cinemas as well as from newspapers and magazines telling of military war situations are overlapping, perhaps like in a collage. This film was the starting point for the works that I have been creating until today.

153
Nicola L
Red Coat 1969
Vinyl
Eleven slits and
eleven hooded jackets
Dimensions variable

ARTIST BIOGRAPHIES

Elsa Coustou, Lina Džuverović, Sofia Gotti

EVELYNE AXELL

b.1935 Evelyne Devaux, in Namur, Belgium.
d. 1972, in Zwijnaerde.

One of the first female European artists to fully embrace pop art from the mid-1960s, Evelyne Axell engaged, throughout her short career as an artist, with a proto-feminist depiction of the emancipation of woman's sexuality. An acclaimed theatre and film actress, Axell turned to painting in 1964, taking lessons with family friend René Magritte. Her husband, film director Jean Antoine, had just produced a documentary on American pop artists and, while filming another one, introduced Axell to British pop artists Patrick Caulfield, Pauline Boty, Peter Blake, Allen Jones and Joe Tilson. Fascinated by their work, Axell immediately drew on pop's visual vocabulary. In 1967, discovering plastic materials, she developed her signature technique, adapting her painting to the possibilities offered by the new material. Cutting female silhouettes into translucent plastic sheets and enamel painting, she created provocative works infused with desire and eroticism. From her early works until her premature death, Axell has depicted the female body and glorified female sexuality and fantasies.

Tackling the deep changes occurring within an increasingly disputed, gendered, social order, Axell's early works *Licensed in Both Ways* 1965 (no.55) and *Valentine* 1966 (no.35) depict the liberation of the female body and the uncovering of a feminist intimacy, within the context of the 1960s space race. *Licensed in Both Ways* builds on the motif of erotic voyeurism with added complexity: the viewer is at the same time being watched and invited to watch through the holes of the helmet, a metaphor for the head in which hidden erotic desires take place. The helmet is also present in *Valentine*, a direct homage to Valentina Tereshkova, the first woman to fly in space, who can be unzipped in this work, referring to the conquest of new territories, including uncensored sexuality. Also addressing social and sexual liberation, *The Pretty Month of May* 1970 (no.58) is considered Axell's most political work. Framed by a self-portrait and a portrait of her friend, critic Pierre Restany, founder of nouveau réalisme, the revolutionary crowd of women in this triptych refers to the protest movements from May 1968. – EC

JOAV BAREL

b. 1933 in Tel Aviv, Israel. d. 1977, in Tel Aviv.

Joav BarEl was a Tel Aviv-based multidisciplinary artist, art critic, writer and lecturer. He studied psychology and philosophy at Tel Aviv University and subsequently clinical psychology, graduating in 1969. In parallel with his artistic practice, he remained active as an art critic and lecturer, profoundly impacting future generations of Israeli artists.

In 1965, alongside follow artists Raffi Lavie, Ran Sheckori and several others, BarEl formed the group '10+', a gathering of rebellious young artists looking to 'shake up' what they deemed to be a stagnant art scene dominated by lyrical abstraction. Their guiding principle was the idea of 'doing things differently' aiming to transcend the artists' individual styles through collaboration and non-conventional exhibitions.

Joav BarEl's artistic practice was eclectic, encompassing pop art paintings, expressionistic stone and plaster reliefs, ink drawings, installations as well as works on paper inspired by Franz Kafka's stories. Strongly influenced by American pop art, between 1967 and 1970 BarEl produced acrylic paintings, collages and photographic transfer works using magazine advertisements as his source. In his paintings BarEl used industrial spray paint and primary colours, often playing with the visual effects of complementary glowing colours. His painting *Kennedy Assassination* 1968 (no.10) was first shown at the *Political* exhibition organised by '10+' in Tel Aviv and received critical responses due to its overtly political nature. The work consists of a schematic depiction of a male profile, painted in blocks of phosphorescent orange and green, the face framed by a target. An arrow diagrammatically tracing the path of the bullet that killed John F. Kennedy is shown across the neck. Aside from references to Jasper Johns's target paintings and Andy Warhol's *16 Jackies* series, the work also uses the well-known diagram associated with the 'magic bullet theory' that developed around Kennedy's assassination. – LD

THOMAS BAYRLE

b.1937 in Berlin, Germany.
Lives and works in Frankfurt am Main.

Thomas Bayrle's pioneering work is characterised by
an obsessive preoccupation with repetition and grid
structures, conceiving and representing the world around
him as a multitude of social threads. Bayrle began his
career as a designer and, after an apprenticeship within
a textile factory, he became fascinated by mechanisation
and its repetitive patterns and rhythms. From this
experience, Bayrle's work retained the motif of the
human figure in the machine age and the structure of
the grid. Influenced by pop art, and notably Sigmar Polke
in Germany, the Frankfurt School, the economic postwar boom, and most importantly the large American
presence in Frankfurt, Bayrle abandoned painting in 1967
to produce serigraphic works reflecting on mass society.
Like fellow Frankfurt artist and friend Peter Roehr, Bayrle
adopted serial repetition as a means to critically engage
with mass consumerism. Placing objects and motives
from the daily life and mass advertising into serial
patterns, Bayrle's work reflects on the individual within
socio-political, industrial, and technological entities.

With his wallpaper *The Laughing Cow* 1967 (see
endpapers/inside cover of this book), Bayrle multiplied
in the weaves of the fabric the cheese brand's logo of the
laughing cow, mimicking the mechanical mass-production
process of the product. The re-appropriation of the logo,
endlessly repeated, also questions the status of the artist
and the artwork, through the principle of seriality, which
was developed by pop artists in opposition to the claims
to individuality of informel painting and abstract
expressionism. – EC

RENATE BERTLMANN

b. 1943 in Vienna, Austria, where she lives and works.

Since the early 1970s Renate Bertlmann, feminist avant-garde artist, has explored issues around the representation of sexuality and eroticism within a social context. Despite its closeness to the nascent women's art movement in the 1970s, revolting against a male-dominated world and developing new aesthetics to represent the female body, Bertlmann's work distinguished itself by its inclusion of the masculine point of view. Working with collages, drawings, photographs, photo-films, performances and objects, her work has always played, not without humour, on the ambivalence of the feminine and masculine relationship in terms of sexuality and desire, challenging the stereotyped, preconceived roles assigned by society. Deepening society's preconceptions, from 1975 she developed a series of works using latex teats and inflated condoms, associating the phallic with the feminine and addressing issues of contraception and motherhood. Including pornography in her work from the 1980s onwards, Bertlmann has pursued throughout her career an interrogation on gender relations.

This is particularly visible in her series of works *Exhibitionism* 1973 (no. 134), in which curved abstract forms and soft pale pink colours evoke the contours of a feminine body, while the two egg-shaped protruding objects directly allude to male genitals. What look at first sight like abstract lines refers in fact to male and female corporeality, furtively displaying a pair of legs and a backside that support two testicles. As the title suggests, the viewer is presented with an act of exhibitionism. In her constant work on the interrelationship between the masculine and the feminine, Bertlmann manages to render the interchangeability of sexes and of sexual desires by deceiving conventions. – EC

CORNEL BRUDAŞCU

b.1937 in Tusa, Romania. Lives and works in Cluj-Napoca.

Cornel Brudaşcu studied at the Institute of Arts Ion Andreescu in Cluj, graduating in 1962. He is one of the few Romanian artists associated with pop art, and one of the mentors of the group of younger figurative painters known internationally as the Cluj School. In the 1970s he got acquainted with contemporary American art and consequently embarked on a series of portraits, of both his fellow artists from Cluj and of Western pop icons, based on images seen in Western newspapers and magazines. Nicolae Ceauşescu's Romania in the 1970s was the only period of his regime that was open to international exchanges, therefore even though travel abroad was banned, especially to Western countries, information about new experiments in art was disseminated. Counter-culture, music and art influences were experienced both through Western magazines found in reading rooms, or via informal networks of shared information. The German magazine *Popcorn*, for instance provided a point of departure for some of his paintings, as well as his own experiments with solarised photography.

Cornel Brudaşcu's paintings from this period include *Guitarist, Youth on the Building Yard, Composition, Group Portrait* and *Portrait (Ion Munteanu)*, all 1970 (nos. 12, 147, 146, 150, 13). They use pop art's block colour and flat surfaces, but depart from pop's sharp edges in the use of blurred boundaries and lack of definition. His compositions often feature family members and close friends from his artistic milieu as, for example, in the painting *Portrait (Ion Munteanu)* dedicated to the deceased artist and close friend. At the same time, his paintings speak to the political context in which they were made under Communist rule in Romania. The title and narrative theme of *Youth on the Building Yard* (no.147), for example, is characteristic of official *proletcult* art of this period, whose ideological imperative was to form a new culture that would reflect the spirit of the collective and the desire to build a new Communist society. Brudaşcu's striking use of bright colour and his experimental use of photography, however, mark a departure from the ideologically sanctioned art of this period. – LD

BORIS BUĆAN

b.1947 of Ukrainian-Jewish origin in Zagreb, Croatia, where he lives and works.

Boris Bućan is a Croatian artist and graphic designer. He studied at the School of Applied Arts in Zagreb, the Academy of Visual Arts in Ljubljana and the Academy of Plastic Arts in Zagreb, graduating in painting in 1972. Bućan belongs to the New Art Practice generation of artists who took an interest in combining visual art with newly available technologies such as photography, Polaroids, photocopies, film, video and graphic design. Their conceptual practices gravitated toward public space, breaking away from the gallery system, as an act of resistance against institutional infrastructures, which, at the time, were dominated by lyrical abstraction. Bućan first came to prominence in Zagreb in the late 1960s through his public interventions. These consisted, for instance, of painting the pavement of a street in central Zagreb bright blue or placing a brightly coloured image, reminiscent of pop art's flat imagery and strong palette, in the courtyard of a Zagreb gallery. In parallel with painting, he has maintained a prolific career as a graphic designer, producing posters for galleries, theatre, the Croatian Radio and Television, and National Theatre. In 1984 Bućan represented Yugoslavia at the Venice Biennale with a series of theatre posters.

Bućan Art 1972 (no.27 A–T) is a series of fifty paintings featuring appropriated and modified corporate logos. The highly recognisable brand logos, such as Coca Cola, IBM, Swissair, BMW and others, were modified to replace the company name with the word 'art.' Created at the height of Yugoslavia's economic boom and the invasion of consumerism in the country, the work responded to the omnipresence of global brands, media and advertising that suddenly flooded the Yugoslav public space. For Boris Bućan, inserting the word 'art' symbolically placed corporate culture at the service of art. The semantic play in the work comments on the commodification of art while proposing the possibility of art superseding global capitalism. – LD

TERESA BURGA

b.1935 in Iquitos, Peru. Lives and works in Lima.

After completing her studies at the Catholic University of Peru in Lima, Teresa Burga joined the group Arte Nuevo (1966–1968) alongside Luis Arias Vera, Gloria Gómez-Sánchez and Jaime Dávila, among others. Arte Nuevo is one of the most celebrated catalysts for the redefinition of art practices in Peru in the late 1960s. Burga's main concern in this period was to question and redefine accepted notions of femininity in relation to the mass media and domestic labour. Her early environments presented domestic scenes oversaturated by the colours and symbols of pop culture. Her female figures, painted over two-dimensional, bright surfaces – sometimes over furniture – parody portrayals of femininity, while humorously reminding the viewer of children's toys: dysfunctional apparatuses that pre-date her later investigations into diagrammatic representation.

Cubes 1968 (no.99) is a collection of plywood blocks painted with graphic signs and partial depictions of female bodies. The modular objects reflect on the idea of the 'system' as intended by Jorge Glusberg, luminary and director of the Centre of Art and Communication (CAyC) in Buenos Aires. Understood as an organism formed of singular entities that relate to one another dynamically, yet only within a given structure, Teresa Burga's cubes originate a semiotic game where meaning is never univocal. By suggesting a multiplicity of arrangements, Burga's dynamic visual narrative experiments with the deconstruction of information and understanding. The palette and iconography reference the pop culture motifs of her larger environments. Like many works produced in this period, *Cubes* was made in collaboration with third parties. Burga sought to explore notions of mechanisation and division of labour so as to eliminate traces of feminine subjectivity and artistic gesture. – SG

DELIA CANCELA

b. 1940 in Buenos Aires, Argentina. Lives and works between Buenos Aires and Paris, France.

Delia Cancela studied at the Escuela Superior de Bellas Artes in Buenos Aires. From 1962, Cancela exhibited widely including at the prestigious Ver y Estimar award at the Museo Nacional de Bellas Artes and in exhibitions such as *New Art of Argentina* (1964), which travelled to Buenos Aires, Rio de Janeiro and Minneapolis. Her early canvases incorporated images drawn from popular culture – for example, photographs of Elvis Presley – placing her work at the core of the pop art scene in Buenos Aires. In 1965 Cancela started working in close collaboration with her partner Pablo Mesejean, until 1980. The duo sought to counter the traditionalism that pervaded most of cultural institutions in Buenos Aires, crossing the boundaries between theatre, fine art and fashion. In 1966 at the celebrated Torcuato Di Tella Institute (ITDT), Cancela and Mesejean exhibited a manifesto known as *Nosotros Amamos* (We Love) in which they proclaimed their love of popular culture and the acceptation of gender identity.

At the 1964 yearly national award at the ITDT, Delia Cancela presented the work *Broken Heart* 1964 (no.91), which exaggerates the cliché of heartbreak that is conventionally associated with feminine sentimentality. The work is composed of two disparate elements: a flat and homogenous red heart painted onto canvas, and its broken fragments hanging from silk ribbons beneath it. The effort to break away from the two-dimensional canvas acts as a metaphor for the need to renegotiate a space for sentimentality within contemporary society. *Broken Heart* seeks the spectator's participation to enliven its torn, wounded flesh. Cancela's gesture is both destructive and creative, anticipating the necessity for viewer participation, which would become a *sine qua non* among the Argentine avant-garde. – SG

RAFAEL CANOGAR

b. 1935 in Toledo, Spain. Lives and works in Madrid.

After the Spanish Civil War and a period of transition, Rafael Canogar and his family took up residence in Madrid in 1944. He began his training with painter Daniel Vázquez Díaz, with whom he mastered a figurative language inspired by the work of Georges Braque, Pablo Picasso and Joan Miró. In 1954 Canogar began to experiment with abstraction and informalism, motivated by Michel Tapié's call for a collective art phenomenon. His canvases, increasingly monochromatic, sought to achieve a balance between form and matter, between formal and informal painting. Within this trajectory he formed the group El Paso (1957–60) alongside Luis Feito, Manolo Millares, Manuel Rivera, Antonio Saura among others, which ushered in a key phase in the modernisation of the Spanish avant-garde. Following a trip to the USA in the early 1960s, and a peak in his international recognition in 1964, Canogar abandoned informalism, which had become assimilated by Francisco Franco's regime as 'official' art.

The Punishment 1969 (no. 107) typifies a key aspect of Rafael Canogar's practice from the 1960s. Owning the vocabulary of narrative figuration, which had begun to spread among the Spanish avant-garde of the time, his work invoked the aesthetics of commercial culture and of the mass media. Yet, in contrast with his contemporaries (including Equipo Crónica and Equipo Realidad), his subjects did not exist within an iconographic superstructure, but were deeply rooted in social realities. Using wood and polyester reinforced fibreglass, Canogar escaped the boundaries of the canvas adding three-dimensionality, volume and flesh to his figures. *The Punishment* represents a man being beaten by a policeman, which would not have been an unfamiliar scene in the late 1960s. The disturbing vignette, which physically invades the viewer's domain, was interpreted as a wakeup call to engage with the social unrest that defined those turbulent years in Francoist Spain. – SG

181

JUDY CHICAGO

b.1939 in Chicago, United States of America.
Lives and works in New Mexico.

Judy Chicago is an artist, author, feminist and educator whose career spans five decades. Chicago studied at the University of California, Los Angeles, graduating with a Master's Degree in painting and sculpture in 1964. In 1970 she launched the first feminist art programme at the California State University, Fresno. At the same time Chicago dropped her birth name in favour of her birthplace, as a gesture of breaking away from the patriarchal tradition of a woman taking their father's or husband's name. Chicago works across media, often using traditional crafts such as needlework and china-painting. She has sometimes enlisted the participation of hundreds of people to create monumental works which are realised collaboratively over a number of years. The unifying goal of her work is to make a place for female-centred imagery and to overcome the erasure of women's achievements in art and society. Chicago's most influential work, and a milestone in twentieth-century art, is the iconic installation *The Dinner Party* (1974–9), today a permanent exhibition housed at the Elizabeth A. Sackler Center for Feminist Art at the Brooklyn Museum.

Bigamy Hood, Birth Hood and *Flight Hood* 1965/2011 (nos. 115, 116, 56) are painted car hoods sprayed with acrylic automotive lacquer. The brightly coloured patterns are created by redeploying the techniques that Judy Chicago learned at an auto-body school in Los Angeles, which she attended as a student – the only woman in a class of 250 men. The work appropriates the car hood, a symbol of machismo, to address the challenges that she encountered both in the art world and the custom car shop in LA. The pattern and colouring evoke both male and female forms, in her effort to both 'feminise' a traditional icon of masculinity and establish a gender balance in the work, which reflects her long-standing goals as an artist. – LD

MARI CHORDÀ

b. 1942 in Amposta, Spain.
Lives and works in Barcelona.

Mari Chordà was one of the most eclectic personalities
of the Spanish feminist movement, actively participating
as an artist, poet, editor, screenwriter and co-founder of
the legendary feminist bar/library/publishing house laSal,
created in Barcelona in 1976. During her studies at the
Escola Superior de Bellas Artes in Barcelona, Chordà
began to experiment with pictorial representations of
female sexuality. Despite having received a Catholic
traditionalist education she sought to explore and expand
tabooed conceptions of femininity by unveiling the body,
treating it as a landscape and generating new references
to signify femininity.
   Mari Chordà's *The Great Vagina* 1966 (no. 133),
represents the culmination of an artistic process that
investigated the visual representation of femininity from
a physiological perspective. From 1964 she began to
explore ways to counter the inherent voyeurism of many
North American pop art works that represented women
in the unrealistic, idealised fashion allowed by mass
culture. In the 1960s Chordà began painting female
genitalia in what she defined as a 'non-figurative'
language: an aesthetic in between abstraction and
close-up photography. Chordà's investigation is further
developed in *Coitus Pop* 1968 (no. 132), a work which
depicts the sexual act with the same 'non-figurative'
approach. By sacrificing the alibi of a commercial
aesthetic, yet maintaining its bright and appealing palette,
the depiction of a vagina and a phallus in *Coitus Pop*
addresses the explicit eroticism at the base of
consumption – one intrinsically connected to sexuality
and desire (also evident in the title). By treating the
body as a landscape, Chordà strips it of any subjectivity
or sentimentality, once again forcefully problematising
the issues behind the stereotypical representation of
women. – SG

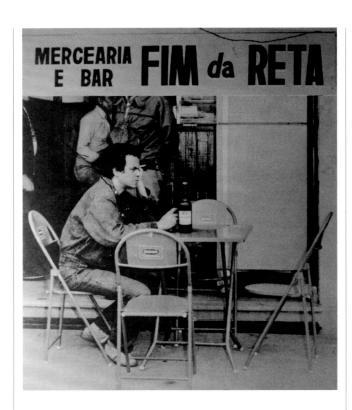

RAYMUNDO COLARES

b. 1944 in Grão Mogol, Minas Gerais, Brazil.
d. 1986 in Montes Claros, Minas Gerais.

In 1964 Raymundo Colares moved from Grão Mogol to Salvador de Bahia with a scholarship to study engineering, but he soon gave up his studies to pursue art, inspired by the works of Piet Mondrian and Paul Klee. He settled in Rio de Janeiro in 1965 where he worked as a jewellery designer at H. Stern. The following year he was admitted into the Escola de Belas Artes where he met Antonio Dias, Antonio Manuel, Wanda Pimentel and Hélio Oiticica, among others, and associated with the Brazilian new figuration. In 1967 he abandoned his studies once again to join artist Ivan Serpa's independent studio at the Museo de Arte Moderna. In this period Colares's painting reached a phase of maturation where he developed an aesthetic that would define his practice for over a decade. He participated in the landmark exhibition *Nova Objetividade Brasileira*, marking his alignment with the objectives of the Brazilian avant-garde.

Raymundo Colares produced the *Untitled* (no.44) aluminium foldable panel in 1969. Exhibited in his first solo show in Rio de Janeiro, the panel captures the artist's ambivalent relationship with the urban landscape, a persistent theme throughout his practice. Both fascinated and disturbed by their prominence, his work depicts the geometric designs commonly found on the sides of buses, the quintessential symbols of urban dynamism and motion. Through the use of crisp edges, familiar commercial enamel colouring, numbers and a rational division of space, Colares's panel unfolds a visual narrative on multiple spatial planes, imposing order on the confusion of the city. In contrast with his early works on canvas, the rhythm asserted by the three-dimensional panel acquires a corporeal aspect. The viewer's body is traversed by the vertigo of the city's frenetic pace. Strengthening a connection with motors, movement and urban life, the aluminium panel combined the aesthetics of Brazilian concretism and pop art with the mechanical dynamism of futurism. – SG

EQUIPO CRÓNICA

Rafael Solbes, b. 1940 in Valencia, Spain.
d. 1981 in Valencia.
Manuel Valdes, b. 1942 in Valencia.
Lives and works between Madrid and New York City,
United States of America.
Juan Antonio Toledo, b 1940 in Valencia.
d. 1995 in Valencia.

Equipo Crónica was founded in 1965 in Valencia by artists Rafael Solbes, Manuel Valdés and Juan Antonio Toledo. Toledo left the group shortly after their first exhibition. Emerging under the umbrella of Estampa Popular (popular print) and the influence of critics Vincente Aguilera Cerni and Tomàs Llorens, Equipo Crónica was in firm opposition to the abstract and informal tendencies championed by Francisco Franco's administration. Solbes and Valdès signed a manifesto in 1965 establishing the group's objectives to adopt a widely intelligible style that would reference everyday life. Among the most celebrated series that critiqued Spanish academicism are *Guernica '69* 1969, in reference to Pablo Picasso's iconic work, and *Police and Culture* 1971, reproducing contemporary art imagery combined with representation of the police, a symbol of oppression. Alongside other artists such as Eduardo Arroyo and Equipo Realidad, Equipo Crónica is associated with the artists who contested Franco's regime, questioning its official culture as repressive.

Concentration or Quantity becomes Quality 1966 (no. 39) belongs to an early series of works by Equipo Crónica, which manipulated photographs from the daily press. The black and white images of a developing crowd are presented on nine canvases in sequence in grey tones, denoting the threat posed by collective gatherings to Franco's regime. *Socialist Realism and Pop Art in the Battlefield* 1969 (no. 1) reflects a further phase in Equipo Crónica's oeuvre that questioned Spanish identity as the sterile product of a long gone 'Golden Era'. The bright acrylic painting borrows the iconography of comics, showing the painter El Greco with a speech bubble containing imagery as disparate as Andy Warhol's Campbell's soup cans and revolutionary workers in Maoist China. Oscillating between the iconography of socialist realism and North American pop art, the work encapsulates the global debate over figuration during the Cold War. – SG

185

HENRI CUECO

b.1929 in Uzerche, France. Lives in Paris.

A painter associated with the *figuration narrative* group of artists in France in the 1960s, Henri Cueco has been concerned, since the beginning of his career, with the socio-political role of the artist and the construction of images. Copying nature from a young age, Cueco started re-appropriating photographs from magazines and books from 1964, giving painting a political function. Questioning bourgeois postwar society and his desire for social rupture his work is also marked by his affiliation to various collaborative practices. A member of the French Communist Party from 1956 to 1976, his militancy is seen in his prominent role in the annual group exhibition *Salon de la Jeune Peinture*, organised to generate collective discussion around painting and creation processes. He also developed his work at this time with the Atelier Populaire in May 1968 in Paris, and through the collective work of the Coopérative des Malassis, which he co-founded in 1970.

Exhibited with his series *The Red Men* at Musée d'art moderne de Paris in 1970, *Large Protest* 1969 (no.6) and *The Red Men, bas-relief* 1969 (no.106) are part of a body of works that reflects Henri Cueco's concerns and affiliation with figuration narrative artists, who distinguished themselves from American pop artists by deliberately focusing on political themes. This series of red men evokes the political context of the May 1968 protests, the Vietnam War and the Western fear of communism in the context of the Cold War. Around a female figure, an allegory of revolution, several silhouettes spring out of the painting in *The Red Men, bas-relief*. Fragmented in *Large Protest*, these cut-out figures drawn in comic-strip style float suspended above the floor, creating a dreamy atmosphere. Having worked with a theatre company, Cueco uses theatre lighting in this installation, accentuating the dramatic effect of the floating figures' projected shadows. Taken from images found in magazines, newspapers and books, these figures were inspired by Cueco's interest in Marxist theories and his reading of Claude Lévi-Strauss's anthropological writing, as well as by Raymond Roussel's fantastical universe. – EC

ANTONIO DIAS

b.1944 in Campina Grande, Paraiba, Brazil. Lives and works between Rio de Janeiro and Milan, Italy.

In 1957, when Antonio Dias moved to Rio de Janeiro with his family, he began working as a draughtsman and graphic designer, cultivating art as an autodidact in his spare time. In the early 1960s, Dias began frequenting the studio of Oswaldo Goeldi, the celebrated modernist printmaker, at the Escola Nacional de Belas Artes. Although Dias was grouped with the Brazilian new figuration, his practice is interwoven with the legacy of the concretist movement and the revolutionary impetus of tropicalia. While his early sculptural works contained an abstract geometric vocabulary, Dias's training drew him to paper and canvas. In 1965 he won the painting award from the Paris Youth Biennale where he lived between 1967 and 1968. After May 1968, he was denied having his French papers extended and decided to go to Italy, where he settled in Milan.

Antonio Dias's works from the mid-1960s are distinguished by visceral red, black and white imagery, symbolic of the blood and the dirt of the urban underbelly, accentuated by the early stages of the military dictatorship in Brazil. The corporeal presence of the paintings is achieved by the addition of three-dimensional elements. *Accident at the Game* 1964 (no.45) incorporates a protruding red phallus in the midst of stylised skulls and bones, evoking a destructive, yet deeply satirical sexuality. *Note on the Unforeseen Death* 1965 (no.5) presents a parody of the political situation juxtaposing comical images of asphyxiating nuclear clouds, toxic gases and soldiers with a realistic bloodstain held in the soft shrine at its centre. By borrowing elements from the structure of comics and the iconography of graffiti, Dias sabotaged commercial culture's semiotic structure forcing viewers to confront the traumas of their environment. – SG

ROMANITA DISCONZI

b. 1940 in Santiago, Rio Grande do Sul, Brazil.
Lives and works in Porto Alegre.

In the late 1960s Romanita Disconzi studied painting, drawing and printing in Porto Alegre with artists Ado Malagoli, Luiz Solari and Julio Plaza. In 1970, for her second solo show in Brazil at the North American Cultural Institute in Porto Alegre, Disconzi exhibited a series of silkscreens representing graphic symbols, emblematic of the first phase of her practice. In the 1970s Disconzi began to teach at the Instituto das Artes Plasticas in Porto Alegre and continued to exhibit internationally in Poland, Puerto Rico, at the second British International Print Biennial in Yorkshire and at the X–XI São Paulo Biennial.

In *Interpretation Totem* 1969 (no.118), Romanita Disconzi uses arrows, guns, no-entry signs, hearts and telephones as building blocks of a semiotic system of her own assembly. The work consists of cubes, cylinders and various polygons that resemble children's toys on an enlarged scale, stacked in an unspecified order. The work invites viewers to 'figure it out themselves' and to establish a unique structure creating arbitrary associations and new meanings. By materialising an investigation revolved around semiotics, *Interpretation Totem* encourages the viewer to renegotiate the boundaries of a society increasingly defined by the images and norms established by the mass media. Disconzi appropriated graphic symbols in the pursuit of exchanging their immediate meaning with a reality of her own construction, while enabling the viewer/participant to do the same. *Interpretation Totem* is the first of a series of experiments that sought to decode, dismember and restructure semiotic systems. – SG

WESLEY DUKE LEE

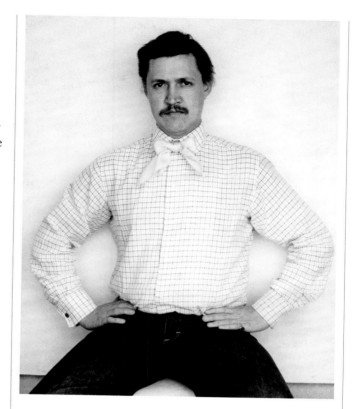

b. 1931 in São Paulo, Brazil. d. 2010, São Paulo.

Grandson of American missionaries and Brazilian merchants of Portuguese descent, Wesley Duke Lee grew up in São Paulo. His training began at the Museo de Arte de São Paulo Assis Chateaubriand (MASP) and in 1951 he enrolled at the Parsons School of Design to study graphic arts. In New York, Lee met Marcel Duchamp, Robert Rauschenberg, Jasper Johns and John Cage, who significantly informed his practice. In 1960 he formed the *realismo magico* (magic realism) movement in São Paulo, which initiated a return to figurative painting. In 1963 Lee organised one of the first happenings to take place in Brazil titled *The Great Spectacle of the Arts* in the landmark Bar João Sebastião, a Bossa Nova meeting place for cultural activists. In 1966, alongside Nelson Leirner, Geraldo De Barros and others, he founded the Grupo REX and REX Gallery (1966–7). REX sought to propose an alternative to the existing market system and offered a programme of free exhibitions, as well as a bimonthly bulletin.

    Trapeze or a Confession 1966 (no. 15) is a key work in Wesley Duke's Lee's oeuvre and was first exhibited at the 33rd Venice Biennale. Inspired by Kurt Schwitters's *Merzhaus*, *Trapeze or a Confession* is an immersive cubic environment constructed of acrylic and wooden panels that represent aspects of human intimacy. The title *Trapeze or a Confession* reflects two layers of the work's meaning. 'Trapeze' refers to an Italian song entitled *Acrobats* that inspired the male and female archetypal silhouettes suspended above ground and connected by transparent ropes on the green and yellow acrylic sheets. 'Confession' refers to the effect the work has on the viewer. Placed between the two figures, the spectator is cross-examined. The intimate space dissipates inhibitions, leaving the viewer with no choice but to confess his/her secrets. In its original version the work incorporated a sound machine that produced a monotonous and consistent noise that further isolated the viewer's perception. – SG

189

ERRÓ

b. 1932 Gudmundur Gudmundsson, in Olafsvik, Iceland.
Lives and works in Paris, France.

Erró was one of the radical artists of the late 1950s to
early 1960s on the Paris art scene to commit to a newly
figurative painting, critical of its socio-political context.
After he left Reykjavik to study in Oslo and Florence,
Erró settled in Paris in 1958, taking part from 1961 in
new figuration exhibitions alongside Gérard Fromanger,
Jacques Monory, Bernard Rancillac, Valerio Adami and
Peter Klasen, among others, and seeing his works exhibited in the seminal *Mythologies Quotidiennes* exhibition
in 1964. Seeking a de-mythologisation of everyday life
in consumer society, Erró and his fellow artists manifested the power structures that constituted these myths
by drawing awareness to the procedures behind image-
making, and thus the manipulative power behind them.
His visual vocabulary drew on popular imagery found
in everyday life, political events and history of art,
increasingly integrating comic-strip's language into his
work. During several trips to New York between 1966
and 1971, Erró met American pop artists Roy Lichtenstein, Robert Rauschenberg and Jim Dine, among others.

The *American Interiors* series of 1968 (nos. 100, 130,
131) shows the reversal of American military intervention
by staging the invasion of peaceful and idealised
American bourgeois home interiors by armed Viet-Cong
and Maoist troops. These two opposite images, as found
in the press, are juxtaposed to provoke critical awareness
of media-constructed clichés as well as of reality. This
series of political fiction denounces the American
hysteria during the Vietnam War and Cold War. The
collage technique enables Erró to reveal the way socio-
political clichés are constructed and conveyed, as well
as creating new narratives. Frequently re-appropriating
art historical images, he paid tribute to old masters at
the same time as he was affirming a new figurative and
political art. With *Big Tears for Two* 1963 (no. 102),
Erró revisits Pablo Picasso's *Weeping Woman* 1937,
in a comic-strip style, which extends to the work a
tragicomic effect. – EC

ÖYVIND FAHLSTRÖM

b. 1928 in São Paulo, Brazil.
d. 1976 in Stockholm, Sweden.

A poet and painter whose work was shaped by his affinity
with concrete music and poetry, Öyvind Fahlström
borrowed pop imagery and vocabulary, particularly comic
strips' language, in a radically critical way. Transposing
the anxiety and precariousness characterising the context
of the Cold War era, he created what he called 'variable
paintings' and 'painting games'. An acute observer of the
global political events and financial processes around
him, Fahlström illustrated through interactive works the
manipulation of information and data, and the ratios of
power controlling the world in its globality. His thorough
analysis of the international economic and political
context of the mid-1960s to the mid-1970s is directly
reflected in his work, through the metaphor of the game
and the presence of interchangeable elements in many
of his works. By requiring the active participation of the
viewer, the performativity and theatricality of his works
offer a plurality of readings. Possessing strong political
content, Fahlström's work was conceived as poetic
visual associations of signs.

In 1965, Öyvind Fahlström was invited along with
eight artists, among whom were John Cage, Steve Paxton,
Yvonne Rainer and Robert Rauschenberg, to create
a work for a series of performance, theatre, music and
dance events, *9 Evenings: Theatre and Engineering*. For
his evening, Fahlström made the piece *Kisses Sweeter
Than Wine*, for which the film *Mao-Hope March* (no. 40)
was produced. This fake street demonstration was staged
in the streets of New York, with seven people carrying
murals of portraits of American actor Bob Hope and
one portrait of Chairman of the Communist Party of
China Mao Tse-tung. These murals were used in
Fahlström's performance *Kisses Sweeter Than Wine*,
along with the projected film. The film of the fake
demonstration includes commentaries of passers-by
answering the question 'are you happy?', offering a
multiplicity of views on the socio-political context of
the mid-1960s, and an ironic and sharp criticism of the
political and entertainment industries. – EC

RUTH FRANCKEN

b. 1924 Ruth Steinreich, in Prague, Czechoslovakia.
d. 2006 in Paris, France.

Born in Prague and exiled in Vienna during the interwar years, Ruth Francken took painting classes with Arthur Segal in Oxford, and lived in New York from 1940 to 1950, receiving American nationality, before settling in Paris in 1952. Francken's career was marked by her uprooted life and early frustration with the medium of painting. In Paris, her work was associated with art informel, but her dissatisfaction with abstract expressionism's model and her own paintings led her to abandon the medium in 1964. While in Berlin on a grant, she started experimenting with sculpture, soon turning toward the ordinary language of industrial objects, privileging metal and creating works at the border between painting and sculpture. Her work from 1967 to the early 1970s is marked by an obsession with technology, as developed in her series of photo-metallic reliefs and collages. The incorporation of industrial objects in her practice associated her with pop artists, despite her desire to escape any categorisation, her prime interest in industrial language lying in its conflictual relationship to art.

Breaking the boundaries between sculpture and functional object, *Man Chair* 1971 (no.81) was directly plaster cast on a male model. The industrial plastic object thus retains a bodily texture, which questions the relationship between artworks and manufactured products. The hybridity of this anthropomorphic, faceless chair turns the idealised male body into a mass-produced, functional object. It also blurs the boundaries between model and artwork, both being amalgamated in this work. – EC

GÉRARD FROMANGER

b. 1939 in Pontchartrain, France.
Lives and works in Paris, France and Siena, Italy

One of the pioneers of the return to figuration in the
late 1950s and early 1960s in France, Gérard Fromanger
became a leading figure of *figuration narrative*. Friend
of sculptor César, with whom he shared a studio, and
of Alberto Giacometti, Fromanger joined the figuration
narrative artists at the Salon de mai in 1964 and 1965 and
soon became involved in the Salon de la Jeune Peinture.
Depicting urban environments and anonymous passers-
by, his painting technique was close to photography.
As a founding member of the Atelier Populaire at the
École des Beaux-Arts in Paris, he also produced various
collective and political serigraphy works during the May
1968 events.

One of the works that Gérard Fromanger submitted
to his peers at Atelier Populaire was the first serigraphy
of his *Album The Red* 1968–70, (no.139) depicting the
French flag with the red stripe dripping across the rest of
the lower portion of the flag suggesting the loss of blood.
Although the work was rejected, he created a series of
twenty other serigraphs to accompany this first work.
Developing the thematic of the flag, Fromanger realised
nine other serigraphs of capitalist and communist
nations' flags, the red elements of which are dripping,
along with serigraphs of scenes of urban protests in
which the figures are transformed in red silhouettes.
From these anonymous urban scenes, he reused the red
silhouettes throughout his future work. When presented
for the first time to the public, this series of silkscreens
was quickly hailed as a milestone for the political and
subversive stance it embodied. The filmmaker Jean-Luc
Godard, drawn to this series of works, asked Fromanger
to create with him what became their *ciné-tracts*, a series
of short films based on *Album The Red* such as his
Film-tract n° : 1968 (no.140). From 1970, widely
acclaimed globally, *Album The Red* established not
only Fromanger's artistic career, but also reinforced the
divergence between the figuration narrative artists, whose
approach to art was distinctively politicised, and the
American pop artists' approach. – EC

ÁNGELA GARCÍA

b.1944 in Valencia, Spain, where she lives and works.

Ángela García's practice developed alongside that of neo-figurative groups such as Equipo Crónica and Equipo Realidad, whose quest to democratise art and establish a Spanish identity led them to draw images from Spain's heritage in dialogue with the contemporary mass media. García, conversely, sought to question the identity of the Spanish woman. One of her main sources was the magazine *Triunfo* (1946–82), which addressed issues such as sexual liberation, the role of women and marriage, and also provided Equipo Crónica and Realidad with key iconographic references. While Francisco Franco's death ushered in a discursive expansion of gender issues, García examines in her work the 'crafts' normally associated with femininity, never elevated to the status of fine art. Throughout the decade she exhibited periodically in Spain, especially at Val I 30 Gallery in Valencia, yet her work has been largely undervalued as a woman within the neo-figurative movement.

Confronting women's struggle for autonomy in Francoist Spain, Ángela García's paintings from the early 1970s are characterised by a deconstruction of the female iconicity championed by the mass media. Following a phase of experimentation with the collage and silkscreen of found images, her *Self-Distraction*, *Divertimento* and *Breathing Out* (nos. 108, 109, 110) all from 1973, use acrylic paint on wooden panels to depict truncated and abstracted female bodies. García's 'market flesh' rendition of nudes challenged accepted canons associated with beauty, traditionalism and propriety, advocating the sexual liberation of women. By abandoning the aesthetics of the commercial media and presenting unadulterated and eroticised images of women, these works demystify the stereotypes that associated femininity with fairy tales, soap operas, popular magazines and beauty pageants, which were considered the only acceptable public arenas for women. While many of her contemporaries directly appropriated images found in the press, García championed fragmentation and discontinuity as critical tools to renegotiate representations of femininity. – SG

BEATRIZ GONZÁLEZ

b.1938 in Bucaramanga, Colombia.
Lives and works in Bogotá.

Considered one of the founders of Colombian art today,
Beatriz González occupies a unique and distinctive
position in South American art history. Growing up in the
1940s and 1950s, her work developed during a period of
social and political upheaval known as La Violencia (the
violence), which largely influenced her understanding of
Colombian society. Following her studies in architecture
and fine arts, González soon stood out from her
contemporaries as one of the first painters in Colombia
to draw inspiration from the mass media, inserting a
dialogue between popular narratives and formal painting.
She attracted the attention of critic Marta Traba who
addressed her oeuvre widely in her writing. González's
early works demonstrate a pronounced critique of the
diluted academicism present in Bogota. In particular the
artist resisted the shared predilection for European art,
a synonym for mastery and good taste that circulated
through cheap black and white reproductions.

Beatriz González's iconic work *The Suicides of Sisga
I, II, III* 1965 (nos. 78, 79, 80) appropriated a photograph
left behind by two lovers who had drowned themselves
in the Sisga dam – a sinister incident, reproduced in
national newspapers. The couple, motivated by deep
religious beliefs, had decided to end their lives together,
to liberate her from sin and preserve both from evil.
González, fascinated and moved by the story, borrowed
the image to denounce its rootedness in the violent facet
of Colombian identity, while critiquing its misuse by the
media. In the early 1970s her reflection on consumption
and materiality led her to incorporate mass-produced
items within her paintings, once more using the
'impoverished' language of Colombian mass culture.
In *The Last Table* 1970 (no.135), the first work of an
extended series, González incorporated a reinterpretation
of Leonardo da Vinci's *Last Supper* into an average
mass-produced faux wood table. The latter circulated
widely as a cheap reproduction, a symbol of Colombia's
Eurocentric gaze. – SG

EULÀLIA GRAU

b. 1946 in Terrassa, Spain.
Lives and works in Barcelona.

Eulàlia Grau was a pioneer artist in the development of feminist art in Spain. In her photomontages she criticised the ideological and repressive forces of capitalist society. After studying fine art and cinema, and having worked in Milan for a design studio, Grau conceived her first series of works, *Ethnographies*, in 1973. Using the technique of photomontage, extracting images from the press and recomposing the conflicting fragments, she created a political commentary on the reality that surrounded her. Grau's work denounces the contradictions of Francisco Franco's regime and the capitalist mass-consumption society. Revealing the manipulative processes behind press advertisements, she tackled the deepest issues of a male-dominated and repressive society, advocating a rebalance of powers, notably through women's liberation from their subordinated role as promoted by the mass media.

The title of Eulàlia Grau's *Ethnographies* 1972–3 (nos. 73, 137, 138, 141, 142, 143, 144) series suggests the description of a human group's habits, traditions and way of life, and she analysed the multiple facets of Spanish society under Franco's repressive dictatorship. The juxtaposition of sharp contrasted images captures a condensed portrayal of excesses, clichés and contradictions of society in the early 1970s as presented and trivialised by the mass media. Grau's analysis covered all aspects of society: the alienation of women in the confined domestic sphere and in the institution of marriage, women's sexuality and abortion, the male-dominated political sphere, the advertisement diktat that imposes idealised bodies, the futility and artificiality of ephemeral fame, sports and beauty celebrities, the horrors of commercial and political wars, and the outrageous discrepancies between social classes. As feminist and critical commentaries, Grau's *Ethnographies* appropriate the language of mass-media society in order to reveal its failures and, more generally, the failures of society as a whole. – EC

SANJA IVEKOVIĆ

b. 1949 in Zagreb, Croatia, where she lives and works.

Sanja Iveković studied at the Zagreb Academy of Fine
Arts, graduating in 1971 from the department of graphics.
Coming of age during the 1968 student protests,
which swept across Yugoslav cities, Iveković belongs
to the New Art Practice (NAP), a generation of artists
whose conceptual practices gravitated toward the
use of public space, breaking away from institutional
infrastructures. As an act of resistance against lyrical
abstraction, these artists combined visual art with newly
available technologies such as photography, Polaroids,
photocopies, film, video and graphic design. In 1978
Iveković co-founded the Podroom Gallery with fellow
artist Dalibor Martinis, which became a hub for her
generation of artists. Iveković was the first artist in
Yugoslavia to actively engage with gender difference,
tackling the commodification of women's roles with
the onset of consumerism in the country. She began
experimenting with pop art techniques while she was
still a student. Using television advertisements, tabloid
magazines and current affairs as her sources, Iveković
juxtaposed these with images of her own life, addressing
the discrepancy between public and private discourses,
and pointing to the hypocrisy of the public declarations
of gender equality in socialist Yugoslavia.

Sweet Violence 1974 (no.23) uses the footage of the
daily economic propaganda programme (EPP) – a cluster
of advertisements broadcast daily on Yugoslav television.
The work highlights the idiosyncrasy of the Yugoslav
situation: a single party socialist state, built on the legacy
of the anti-fascist partisan struggle and principles of
solidarity, egalitarianism and self-management,
simultaneously immersed in what has been termed
'utopian consumerism'. In the work, Iveković visually
disconnects the viewer from the persuasive messages
of product advertising by inserting black vertical bars
in front of the image, enabling a critical distance from
the 'sweet violence' of media culture. – LD

JOZEF JANKOVIČ

b. 1937 in Bratislava, Slovakia, where he lives and works.

Since the early 1960s, Jozef Jankovič's work has been marked by his attempt to claim the place of the individual within a repressive political regime. After studying at the School of Applied Arts in Bratislava, where socialist realism was imposed, he graduated from the Academy of Fine Arts in Bratislava in 1962. To bypass official control on visual art activities, Jankovič participated until 1964 in the private exhibitions organised by the Confrontations movement, an informal association of visual artists. His early sculptures and reliefs integrated found objects similar to those seen in the works of artists in the nouveau réalisme movement. Oscillating between figurative and abstract forms, Jankovič's works of the 1960s include characteristic motifs of fragmented, deformed and atrophied body parts. Another recurrent motif is the imprisonment of his faceless human forms in metallic structures or under coloured polyester layers on canvas, in nets or in a fragile state of balance. While also creating memorial monuments for public display, Jankovič saw his work barred from all public exhibitions by the government during the Normalisation regime (1969–89), leading him to find alternative strategies of production. These included architectural designs, jewellery and computer graphics.

Private Manifestation 1968 (no.111) was made as an attack directed towards official demonstrations, at which the public was encouraged to hold portraits of Vladimir Lenin, Karl Marx or Joseph Stalin. Combining sculpture and painting, as in many of his works from the 1960s, in *Private Manifestation* Jozef Jankovič rebels against the regime not only by replacing the socialist icons with a self-portrait, but also by depicting himself with a radically anti-socialist realism treatment, inspired by pop art. Speaking for the masses of individuals, *Private Manifestation* criticised a regime of censorship and the cult of personality. – EC

KIKI KOGELNIK

b.1935, Graz, Austria. d.1997, Vienna.

Turning away from European abstraction and the Viennese avant-garde art scene, Kiki Kogelnik moved to Santa Monica in 1961 and relocated to New York in 1962, where she met American pop artists Roy Lichtenstein, Andy Warhol, Tom Wesselmann, Robert Rauschenberg and Claes Oldenburg, among others. Influenced by their works, she became increasingly fascinated by new technologies and newly available materials. With a humorous and feminist take on a male-dominated art scene, she explored the human body and the construction of the self within the booming technological environment of postwar consumer society. Experimenting with found objects, assemblage, plastic and vinyl, while also spraying and printing on paper, Kogelnik developed a new visual language, increasingly characterised by weightlessness and the flattening of the human figures. This can be seen in her signature *Hanging* works and cut-out silhouettes of her friends, developed from the early 1960s.

This series of cut-out *Hangings* originated in her early works on paper – on which Kiki Kogelnik traced the life-size contours of her friends, among them Lichtenstein and Oldenburg – before she started using vinyl. Parts of this body of works – *Fallout* c.1964 (no.57), *Hanging* 1970 (no.54) and *Friends* 1971 (no.41) – display dismembered, brightly coloured forms. Alluding to the technological developments of the space race and the presence of humans in space, they question the dehumanisation and faceless social skin of the individual self within a mass-consumerist society marked by violent political conflicts. With humour, she also points to international conflicts of the early 1960s in her work *Bombs in Love* 1962 (no.14), a sculpture of two found bomb casings, which she painted with bright colours, referencing the 'Love & Peace' generation, and reinterpreting the symbolic of Eros and Thanatos. – EC

KOMAR AND MELAMID

Vitaly Komar
b.1943 in Moscow, Russia (former USSR); lives and
works in New York, United States of America.
Alexander Melamid
b.1945 in Moscow, Russia (former USSR); lives and
works in New York

Vitaly Komar and Alexander Melamid are Moscow-born artists who emigrated to Israel in 1977 and then to New York in 1978. The two artists first collaborated on a joint exhibition entitled *Retrospectivism in Moscow* in 1967, and from 1972 started signing all their works with both names, regardless of whether they were made collaboratively. They continued to collaborate until the early 2000s, referring to their work as 'not just an artist, but a movement'. Komar and Melamid are the founders of Sots-art (socialist art), a critical, nonconformist, conceptual form of pop art, based on the appropriation and subversion of socialist realist iconography and street propaganda, creating humorous, often grotesque, posters, paintings and banners. Both artists took part in the notorious 'Bulldozer Exhibition' held in a vacant plot in Moscow's Belyayevo in 1974, which showcased nonconformist art by Moscow avant-garde artists that was swiftly destroyed by the authorities with bulldozers and water cannons.

Post Art 1973–4 is a series of six paintings depicting canonical pop art works by Andy Warhol, Roy Lichtenstein, Jasper Johns, Robert Indiana, Tom Wesselmann and Peter Phillips, portrayed as if they had undergone severe physical damage by war, fire or earthquake. The aesthetic of the works is reminiscent of the decay of frescoes, bringing into question the artistic value of canonical artworks over time. *Post Art No 1 (Warhol)* (no.16) is a discoloured, frayed fragment of Andy Warhol Campbell's soup can, while *Post Art No 2 (Lichtenstein)* (no.17) and *Post Art No 3 (Indiana)* (no.18) apply the same treatment to one of Lichtenstein's comic strips and Robert Indiana's circular motifs respectively, rendering the works barely legible, but nevertheless recognisable. – LD

NICOLA L

b. French in Mazagah, Morocco. Lives and works in New York City, United States of America.

Since the mid-1960s, French-born artist Nicola L has interrogated the integration of the human body within the space of the artwork, developing conceptual works, functional objects, installations, performances and films. After studying painting at the École nationale supérieure des Beaux-Arts in Paris, she regularly met art critic Pierre Restany and artists from the *nouveau réalisme* group, as well as other artists such as Marta Minujin and Erró. Her encounter with Argentinean artist Alberto Greco in 1964 had a decisive impact on her work: giving up painting, she developed her *Pénétrables*, a series of canvases in which the viewers could introduce parts of their body and get into the skin of the painting. Behind their playfulness, these works were conceived as a political statement addressing, beyond the boundaries of painting, the individual's social skin. In 1967, Nicola L made *Cylinder for 3* with the English rock group Soft Machine for a performance at the Paris biennale. Ellen Stuart, director of La Mama Theatre in New York, invited her to continue the performance there. In New York, Nicola encountered Robert Filiou, Emmett Williams and Carolee Schneemann and fully embraced all aspects of the city's turmoil, adopting pop's bright colours and use of plastics. From 1967, she transposed her research on the human body to furniture objects, creating her first functional works.

Woman Sofa 1968 (no.101) and *Little TV Woman: 'I Am the Last Woman Object'* 1969 (no.123) exemplify Nicola L's attempt to overcome the limits of traditional sculpture by creating functional objects. Exploring the female body as an instrument and object, the anthropomorphic sofa and cabinet playfully reflect on the construction of female identity and her role within the domestic space. Influenced by the socio-political context of the late 1960s upheavals, *Red Coat* 1969 (no.153) was designed for a concert by Brazilian musicians Gilberto Gil and Caetano Veloso, which took place at the Isle of Wight Festival in 1969. Created for various improvised performances in public spaces, the *Red Coat* is exemplary of Nicola L's experimentation with the manner in which the body interacts with the artwork and the self is exposed to the other. Designed to be embodied, the *Red Coat* invites the desire to share a collective skin. – EC

UWE LAUSEN

b. 1941 in Stuttgart, Germany. d. 1970 in Beilstein.

In only nine years of art production, autodidact Uwe Lausen created a provocative and stylistically hybrid body of paintings that translate the tensions and contradictions inherent in postwar Germany. From 1960, in reaction to the middle-class milieu where he grew up and the socio-political context of West Germany, Lausen developed a personal vocabulary. His exploration of the human figure is haunted by the cohabitation of younger and older generations, the latter held responsible for Third Reich politics. His paintings conflate many influences, from Francis Bacon to British pop artists Peter Blake and Allen Jones. Close to the SPUR group of artists based in Munich, Lausen lived in Hans-Peter Zimmer's studio and met the revolutionary Situationist International group in Paris in 1961, taking part in their activities until his eviction in 1965. In an effort to reflect on and extract from the socio-cultural and political establishment of his time, Lausen created a singular pictorial language marked by his resolutely rebellious character and experimentation with drugs.

Uwe Lausen's painting *Geometer* 1965 (no. 104) is emblematic of his pictorial experimentation and re-appropriation of various stylistic influences. A complex work, *Geometer* is composed of two parts, seemingly of the same scene, from which unfold multiple readings. The headless and colourless suit, depicted in a comic-strip style, contrasts with the painterly female nude, whose pose evokes Gustave Courbet's *The Origin of the World*. This painting within the painting suggests the elaboration of a meta-discourse on the medium of painting. The pop archetype in the foreground both looks back and turns its back on the figurative and painterly, as well as the angular lines hinting at geometric abstraction in the background. Acknowledging artistic styles from the past, Lausen places the viewer in the same position as his metaphorical pop character: future artistic trends are also looking at this painting, which belongs simultaneously to the past. Recalling his beheaded *Geometer*, Lausen's *Pilot* 1966 (no. 38) depicts an anonymous war pilot, and applies the painterly and comic-strip technique characteristic of his paintings into sculpture, a medium he hardly ever used. – EC

NATALIA LACH-LACHOWICZ (NATALIA LL)

b. 1937 in Żywiec, Poland.
Lives and works in Wrocław.

Natalia Lach-Lachowicz, or Natalia LL, is a pioneer of feminist art in Poland. LL's photographs, drawings, moving image works and installations have from the outset addressed the female subject in a patriarchal, increasingly consumerist society, and as a result she was soon noticed by Western feminist critics, including Lucy Lippard, providing her with international exhibition opportunities from the mid-1970s onwards. LL studied at the PWSSP (today the Academy of Fine Arts) in Wrocław, graduating in 1963. In 1970, she co-founded PERMAFO (short for permanent formalisation) Gallery in Wrocław, with fellow artists Zbigniew Dłubak, Andrzej Lachowicz and Antoni Dzieduszycki, which was set up as a home for artists' experiments in photography.

Using photography to depict small, everyday actions such as eating, sleeping, copulation, resting and speaking, LL introduced the notion of 'permanent registration' seeing art as 'a process that generates successive phases of reality', rather than a sphere divorced from the everyday. As one of the most prominent conceptual artists in Poland, she was critical of conceptualism's cold, rational detachment from physical sensuality and the everyday, which led her to incorporate popular culture and the possibilities of mechanical registration and distribution into her work.

Following the *Permanent Registration* body of work (1970–2), Natalia LL embarked on a series of film and photographic works entitled *Consumer Art* 1972–5 – a critique of the commodification of women's bodies in pornography. The sixteen-minute silent film *Consumer Art* 1972, 1974, 1975 (no.24) features young, attractive female models provocatively eating a variety of suggestively shaped foods, emulating the style of pornographic films. The women gaze at the camera seductively as they perform the erotically charged 'play' with bananas, sausages, ice cream and other food filled with sexual innuendo. Unlike pornography, in *Consumer Art* the models are given agency, their actions teetering between seduction and humour, as they gaze back, reversing the dynamics from objects of male gaze and consumption, to being active protagonists in control of the situation. – LD

203

SERGIO LOMBARDO

b. 1939, Rome, Italy, where he lives and works.

At a very young age, Sergio Lombardo abandoned his studies in law and psychology to pursue his passion for art. His first body of work, produced between 1958 and 1961, was a series of paintings made of paper squares pasted on canvas in the shape of a grid, coated with layers of monochrome enamel. Lombardo opposed the notion of the artist-as-genius, and sought to produce works that were non-artistic, drained of any subjective mark. From 1961 he grew closer to the Scuola di Piazza del Popolo (Piazza del Popolo School, also known as the Pop artists of Rome), composed of Mario Schifano, Cesare Tacchi and Renato Mambor among others, participating in some of the most important group exhibitions at the Galleria Tartaruga. As he developed a greater aperture towards the world of the mass media, he began to work on the series *Gesti Tipici* (*Typical Gestures* 1961–3), which portrayed, first in black in white, then also in colour, some of the most relevant and iconic political figures of the time, including Malcolm X, McNamara, Rockefeller, and De Gaulle.

The works *Nikita Krusciov* (no. 152) and *John F. Kennedy* (no. 151), both from 1962, depict the black and white silhouettes of the politicians, leaders of the world's two superpowers during the Cold War. Belonging to the series *Typical Gestures* (first exhibited at the Galleria Tartaruga in 1963), the works immortalise the authoritative postures, and formal clothing of the figures, which retain their unmistakeable (or 'typical') aura. Lombardo's choice to use black and white, and to reduce the images to their bare silhouettes, relates to his understanding of 'industrial aesthetics,' drawn from black and white television, and from the press. Lombardo underlined the non-figurative quality of his works, which were documents, as opposed to representations or portraits; their grand scale, and the deliberately impersonal manner in which they are represented, heightens the sense of grandiosity and iconicity attributed to his subjects, familiar to the viewer's perception because of their omnipresence in the media. – SG

ANNA MARIA MAIOLINO

b.1942 in Scalea, Italy.
Lives and works in São Paulo, Brazil.

Central to Anna Maria Maiolino's practice are notions of subjectivity, belonging and place. Maiolino was born in southern Italy and moved to Venezuela in 1954 with her parents where she began her artistic training. In 1960 she moved to Rio de Janeiro where she joined the independent studio run by printmaker Ivan Serpa at the Museum of Modern Art. Maiolino's work perfected a dialogue with contemporary movements in Brazil at the time, such as new figuration. Given her eclectic background, Maiolino's works reflect a negotiation of identity. In the mid-1960s, she adopted woodcutting, a typically north-eastern Brazilian technique, as her preferred medium. In 1966 she began to experiment with non-traditional media such as upholstery stuffing, strengthening her connection to new figuration. In 1967 Maiolino participated in the landmark exhibition *New Brazilian Objectivity* alongside Helio Oiticica, Rubens Gerchman, Raymundo Colares, Antonio Dias and others, cementing her place in the Brazilian art scene.

Anna Maria Maiolino's iconic work *Glu Glu Glu* 1966 (no.36) presents an open-mouthed, red-lipped dismembered female figure, with its digestive apparatus in view. This work reflects her concern about the effects of mass culture on the realm of domesticity and the subjectivity of women. The marked division between the upper part of the body, contained within a box, and its organs, strengthens the symbolic disconnection between body and mind. The fragmented figure, with its open, toothy mouth and insides, bears witness to the effects of outmoded consumption on subjectivity, left fragile and exposed. *Glu Glu Glu* retains the hard-edge aesthetic of Maiolino's early experiments with woodcutting, a craft that for the artist encapsulated the multiple facets of Brazilian vernacular culture. The colour and garish quality of the work, made of stuffed upholstery, overrides its grotesque subject matter. Its three-dimensionality provides it with 'flesh' and Eros, pronouncing an increasing sensitivity towards the notion of the body as commodity. – SG

MARISOL

b. 1930 Marisol Escobar, in Paris, France.
Lives and works in New York City,
United States of America.

Marisol Escobar is most commonly referred to as Marisol after she renounced her surname in order to 'stand out from the crowd'. The artist, whose practice revolved around a negotiation of identity, spent her childhood between Paris, Venezuela (her parents' native country) and the USA. In 1949 she enrolled at the École des Beaux-Arts in Paris after which she returned to New York, where she studied with Japanese photographer Yasuo Kunioshi and abstract expressionist Hans Hofmann. Despite her affinity with abstract painting, Marisol increasingly turned to three-dimensional work with terracotta, wood and plaster, inspired by pre-Columbian cultures. In 1958 she had her first solo show, at Leo Castelli's prestigious gallery in New York, receiving great acclaim; in 1961 she also participated in the exhibition *The Art of Assemblage* at MoMA, New York. In this period Marisol had friendships with Andy Warhol and Roy Lichtenstein, and appeared in Warhol's films *Kiss* (1963) and *13 Most Beautiful Girls* (1965).

Marisol's *My Mum and I* 1968 (no.2) belongs to a series of works started in the early 1960s that made way for in-depth re-evaluations of pop art as an all male, Anglo-American phenomenon. Marisol's immersion within the New York pop art scene inspired her to experiment with mediated imagery and unconventional materials. The body of work that emerged – comprised of heterogeneous figure-sculpture-portraits of assembled carved and painted wood – manifested her omnipresent concern for portraiture and representation, combined with a renewed attention to elements from popular culture, photographs and found objects. In *My Mum and I* the two figures, pink boxes, humanised by protruding faces, hands and feet, stand frozen in time. Evoking her mother's passing, when Marisol was only eleven, the work is imbued by a sense of nostalgia. The sculptures are adorned with fragments from Marisol's heritage, exemplified by the typically Latin American cast hat worn by the mother figure. – SG

RAÚL MARTÍNEZ

b. 1927 in Ciego de Avila, Cuba. d. 1995 in La Havana.

Raúl Martínez was the leading Cuban artist after the
revolution of 1959. The son of a sugar mill worker and
a teacher, Martínez moved to Havana in 1940 where
he began his fine art training at the San Alejandro
Academy. Encouraged by abstract artist Sandu Darie,
and after reading *Vision in Motion* by Bauhaus professor
László Moholy-Nagy, Martínez enrolled in the Chicago
Design Institute where his canvases took an abstract
expressionist turn. In 1953, back in Cuba, he joined the
group Los Once with whom he exhibited until 1956.
Establishing his presence within the Havana avant-garde,
Martínez also worked as a freelance graphic artist for
magazines and publishing houses. Between 1960 and
1961 he was appointed artistic director of the cultural
magazine *Lunes de Revolución*, and in the following
years he also participated in the foundation of the Cuban
Film Institute (ICAIC) and the Cuban Book Institute.

The large-scale painting *Listen America* c. 1967
(no. 105) is emblematic of an abrupt stylistic shift in Raúl
Martínez's oeuvre. After deciding to take a break from
painting in 1966, he focused on his work in graphic
design, a medium he considered more socially relevant.
Having observed the visual impact of the murals and
graffiti that appeared across the island to celebrate the
revolution, he returned to painting in 1967, renouncing
abstraction in favour of a more direct aesthetic language.
Together with paintings of revolutionary heroes Che
Guevara and Camilo Cienfuegos, *Listen America* was one
of Martínez's first figurative artworks to seek to capture
the popular revolutionary fervour. While maintaining a
connection with modernist abstraction, evident in the use
of repetition within a grid-like structure, his depiction of
Cuba's leader Fidel Castro in a naïve painterly style
rendered the work intelligible and connected it to local
folk tradition. Immortalised during one of his memorable
speeches, Martínez's Fidel salutes America, transmitting
Cuba's revolutionary message. – SG

TOSHIO MATSUMOTO

b. 1932 in Nagoya, Japan.
Lives and works in Tokyo, Japan.

Film director, video artist and film theoretician, Toshio Matsumoto was a pioneer of Japanese 1960s experimental cinema. Pursuing documentary filmmaking, he produced radical and provocative short and feature films, while at the same time theorising the documentary form in his critical writing. In the late 1950s, he collaborated with the collective Jikken Kobo (Experimental Workshop), soon integrating avant-garde elements into his documentary practice. In his influential essays and experimental films, Matsumoto developed in the 1960s what he coined 'neo-documentarism', an expressive type of documentary rejecting documentary's traditional objective nature for one that would reveal internal mental states and subjectivities. Facing the contradictions of cultural and political systems of postwar Japanese society, Matsumoto appropriated television and journalistic media forms and images to reveal the manipulative forces behind them. From the 1970s, he increasingly experimented with video, using devices that alter images and colours, laying out the very processes of image manipulation.

This approach is illustrated in his short film *Mona Lisa* 1973 (no.82), for which Toshio Matsumoto used an electric image synthesiser, generating psychedelic colour effects. Anticipating the travel to Japan of Leonardo da Vinci's masterpiece in 1974, Matsumoto refers to the multiple reinterpretations and copies of the *Mona Lisa* throughout the history of art, notably those by Marcel Duchamp and Andy Warhol. Directly referencing the mass-reproduced icon but also her mythical mysterious inner life, he projects found images and abstract brightly coloured forms onto the image of the painting. At once the subject before a changing background and receptacle for the background image, the figure of Mona Lisa is the only fixed element against which a succession of constructed images are set. Applying a number of colour effects to the *Mona Lisa*, Matsumoto gradually produces multiple impressions, which seem echoed or provoked by the altering of images in the background. The original painting is transformed into a powerful surrealist and psychedelic vision, tinted by a certain anxiety of loss of control and enhanced by the musical track. Projecting his own fantasy onto the painting, Matsumoto confronts his subjectivity with the animated object, which acquires through this process a seemingly internal, active life. – EC

MARTA MINUJÍN

b.1943 in Buenos Aires, Argentina,
where she lives and works.

After attending the National School of Fine Arts, Marta
Minujín frequented the studio of informal painter Jorge
López Anaya, where she developed her first canvases.
As a very young student, in 1961 Minujín travelled to
Paris where, with the guidance of her mentor Alberto
Greco, she began to develop a participatory vocabulary.
From the mid-1960s Minujín became one of the most
energetic contributors to the pop art scene in Buenos
Aires. In 1964 she won first prize at the yearly national
awards of the Torcuato Di Tella Institute with her seminal
work ¡Revuélquese y Viva! (Roll Around and Live! 1964),
a construction made of hand-painted mattresses that
invited the viewer to release his/her inhibitions and roll
within the object/sculpture. Throughout her practice
Minujín explores the value of participation in
the redefinition of art's purpose.

Mattress 1962 (no.95) is one of Marta Minujin's
earliest experiments with the manipulation of mattresses
into sculptural interactive forms, which took place in
Paris in the early 1960s. The hand-painted colourful
objects emerged from an interest in urban debris and
found objects. Their malleable quality, soon led Minujin
to further investigate their participative potential,
a pursuit, which characterised her oeuvre throughout
the decade. La Menesunda 1965 (no.96) is a project she
conceived in collaboration with Rubèn Santantonín,
Pablo Suárez, Floreal Amor, Rodolfo Prayon, Leopoldo
Maler, David Lamelas and others associated to the
Torcuato Di Tella Institute in Buenos Aires. One of the
most celebrated works of the decade, La Menesunda
consisted of a visual itinerary made of sixteen
environments: these included a room with a couple in
bed, a dental surgery, a walk-in freezer and a beauty salon
housed in a structure in the shape of a woman's head.
La Menesunda sought to transform the passive spectator
into an active participant. Over 30,000 visitors flocked
to see Minujín's curious environment, seeking to
experience the irreverent yet playful spirit that pervaded
the Di Tella Institute. – SG

MARCELLO NITSCHE

b. 1942 in São Paulo, Brazil,
where he lives and works.

Born and bred in São Paulo, Marcello Nitsche began his artistic training at the School of Fine Arts Armando Alvares Penteado. In the mid-1960s he became increasingly drawn to painting, under the growing influence of the neo-figurative movement and the aesthetics of pop art. After the military coup in 1964, Nitsche's works began to reference overtly political themes such as the financial relationship that tied Brazil to the USA and the Vietnam War. Between 1966 and 1967 he frequented the REX Gallery where he met artists Wesley Duke Lee, Nelson Leirner and others. An integral part in REX's operation was spectator participation and the construction of environments, which greatly influenced Nitsche's output. In 1967 he participated in the exhibition at the Museum of Modern Art in Rio de Janeiro, *New Brazilian Objectivity*, and won several painting awards across Brazil, which established his place among the Brazilian avant-garde.

I Want You 1966 (no.33) appropriates the USA's iconic military recruitment advertising campaign's slogan and its unmistakeable pointing finger – also adopted by Roy Lichtenstein earlier in the decade. The addition of a drop of blood made from stuffed painted canvas hijacks the image's traditional meaning. While in the USA the image was unavoidably connected to military recruitment, in Brazil it invoked the cultural and political imperialism that it exerted: by 1966 the USA was highly invested in the Vietnam War, and just two years earlier it had largely subsidised the military coup in Brazil. Similarly, *Kill Fly* 1967 (no.46), a suspended papier-mâché sculpture of a giant hand holding a fly squat, also plays on the notion of command and punishment. First exhibited at the IX São Paulo Biennial, remembered as the Pop Biennial, *Kill Fly* seeks to further involve spectators by placing them at the mercy of a larger entity, ready to punish, squat in hand. – SG

ISABEL OLIVER

b. 1946 in Valencia, Spain,
where she lives and works.

In 1965 Isabel Oliver began her training at the Facultad
de Bellas Artes of Valencia. Between 1970 and 1971 she
began experimenting with figurative painting, which
increasingly defined her visual trajectory. In 1971 Equipo
Crónica, the noted collective founded by Rafael Solbes
and Manuel Valdés in 1965, noticed Oliver's work and
invited her to join them. Under the umbrella of estampa
popular – a group that ushered in a return to figuration
during Francisco Fanco's regime – Equipo Crónica sought
to appropriate the language of the mass media in order
to highlight issues tied to Spanish national identity.
Inspired by Andy Warhol's Factory, Equipo Crónica
produced paintings collectively, in order to eliminate
individual authorship. Before and throughout the period
of collaboration with Crónica, Oliver produced a parallel
body of work about the portrayal of women in Spanish
society. While Crónica questioned what it meant to be
Spanish, Oliver questioned what it meant to be female.

In the series *The Woman* 1970–3 Isabel Oliver
portrays women in domestic or imaginary scenes in order
to critique their role in Spanish society. By using the
impersonal figurative aesthetic of the mass media, Oliver
sought to examine how commercial culture shaped
common perceptions of femininity. *Beauty Products*
(no. 69) and *Surgery* (no. 70) respectively depict a woman
sprinting over a sea of cosmetics and another undergoing
plastic surgery. The disturbing *tableau vivant* question
the paradoxical expectations of women's appearance. *The
Family* (no. 64) and *Happy Reunion* (no. 72) reproduce
domestic scenes in which the notion of appearance is
once again confronted through the lens of social norms
and behaviours. In *Family,* the parents of a family of four,
beneath the outline of the board game Parchís, seem
visibly disinterested despite their nudity. *Happy Reunion,*
presents a group of women conversing in a living room.
The macabre palette and the expressions of the women
in the group, suggest the notion of a façade upheld by
society. Lastly, *It is a Girl* (no. 71), portrays the negative
photograph of a toddler (the artist's mother), posing for
a portrait at the end of the nineteenth century, a symbol
of a secular sedimentation of values associated to
femininity. – SG

DUŠAN OTAŠEVIĆ

b. 1940 in Belgrade, Serbia (former Yugoslavia), where he lives and works.

Dušan Otašević graduated from the Academy of Fine Arts in Belgrade in 1966. In the same year his work was included in the exhibition *New Figuration of the Belgrade Circle* at the Cultural Centre Gallery. While still a student, he turned away from the lyrical abstraction and tonal painting taught at the academy, instead finding his inspiration in Belgrade's everyday life and in the popular culture of the rapidly developing 'utopian consumerism' in the country. Given Yugoslavia's turn to the West, a unique hybrid of Western-style consumerism and socialist self-management – the Yugoslav 'socialism with a human face', emerged. Keen to shed the romantic myth of the artist, Otašević chose to refer to himself as a craftsman rather than a painter or sculptor, using non-art tools and materials such as wood, glue, a chisel and industrial paint. Like many Western pop artists, he addressed consumer culture by appropriating its signs and visual language in his sculptural objects. Sharing much with American pop in his aesthetics and methods, in particular the oversized objects of Claes Oldenburg, Robert Indiana's signs, and Warhol's 'before and after' images, Otašević's turn to the vernacular looked to comic strips and advertisements, traffic signs as well as hand-painted artisan shop signs. His ironic and humorous quotations often depict mundane processes and actions – such as smoking, eating and cutting – often shown in several stages, in comic-book-like frames with white backgrounds.

Frequently referring to the political situation in Yugoslavia, Dušan Otašević's controversial work *Comrade Tito, White Violet, Our Youth Loves You* 1969, named after a patriotic song expressing the people's love of the Yugoslav leader, depicts Tito as a pop icon – an act perceived as dissident given that any unofficial representation of the leader would automatically be read as a critique of the system. *Towards Communism on Lenin's Course* 1967 (no.112), a work made as a result of a student trip to Moscow, similarly reflects on Yugoslavia's 1948 split from the USSR. The triptych shows the socialist red star, part of the Yugoslav flag, an image of Lenin and a traffic sign forbidding a right turn. – LD

ULRIKE OTTINGER

b.1942 in Konstanz, Germany.
Lives and works in Berlin.

Mostly known for her avant-garde, transgressive
filmmaking practice, Ulrike Ottinger lived in Paris from
1962 to 1968, creating paintings influenced by pop art.
Engaging with mass media, Ottinger's *peinture nouvelle*,
developed in Paris, constituted a meta-discourse on the
myths of mass culture by adopting a visual language that
was simultaneously influenced by and critical of pop's
aesthetics. Exhibited at the *Salon de la Jeune Peinture*
alongside works by artists of figuration narrative Gérard
Fromanger, Öyvind Fahlström, Peter Klasen, Peter Saul,
Hervé Télémaque and Eduardo Arroyo, among others, her
paintings engaged with the socio-political context of the
mid-1960s. Her treatment of images, a superimposition
of references from everyday motifs, already suggested
a cinematic, montage-like narrative technique.

Emblematic of Ulrike Ottinger's *peinture nouvelle*
is her triptych *God of War* 1967–8 (no.126), which
re-appropriates the pop aesthetics of the pinball machine
and the traditional artistic genre of religious altar
painting. Infused with images directly referencing the
Vietnam War as well as political tensions in France
leading to the May 1968 events, this work addresses the
sacralisation of everyday life in mass-consumption
societies, as well as the idea of war as a game, in which
players score points by striking various targets. Ottinger's
fragmentary narrative technique is translated into her
sculptural work *Female Mannequin – Legs Under Water*
1966 (no.7), which sequences a female body into three
assembled distinctive parts. Immersed in the
anthropologic writings of Claude Lévi-Strauss, Michel
Leiris and Victor Segalen, as well as influenced by her
visits to the Musée de l'Homme in Paris, Ottinger infused
her work with symbolism found in ethnographic studies.
Drinking from the ornamental heart and from the
female's genitalia, the rats here are closely linked to fertile
energy. In various civilisations and religions, notably
Hinduism, black or white rats represent diverse deities
and symbolic characteristics. – EC

213

JOE OVERSTREET

b.1933 in Conehatta, Mississippi, United States of America. Lives and works in New York City.

Joe Overstreet moved from his native Mississippi to California as a child. He studied at Contra Cost College and the California College of Arts in the 1950s. He was mentored by the sculptor Sargent Johnson, a passionate advocate and supporter of black artists. In 1955 Overstreet moved to Los Angeles and started working for Walt Disney as an animator. The repetition involved in hand-drawn animation soon proved frustrating, and in 1957 Overstreet moved to New York City where he designed department store windows while also studying art. He soon immersed himself in the Harlem artistic scene, working as an art director for Harlem's Black Arts Repertory Theater/School, becoming an advocate for African-American artists' rights. His work at the time was abstract expressionist. With the 1964 Civil Rights Act and Overstreet's engagement with the civil rights movement, his work shifted towards protest painting. Works such as *Strange Fruit* c.1965, based on Billy Holliday's anti-lynching song, and *The New Jemima* 1964 directly address black oppression, challenging stereotypical images of blackness. In 1974 Joe Overstreet founded Kenkeleba House on the Lower East Side, an alternative gallery space dedicated to exhibiting work by African-American, Latino, Asian-American and Native American artists, which he still runs and where his studio is based today.

The New Jemima 1964 (no.117) reimagines the racist stereotypical image of Aunt Jemima – a quintessential black servant who cooks, cleans, and looks after the children and the house, originally inspired by the Mammy character in Southern literature and the 'Minstrel Shows'. The New Jemima in Overstreet's painting is imbued with agency, fuelled by black pride and anger at centuries of oppression. His Jemima is a powerful figure, confidently gazing at the viewer, machine gun in hand, ready to fight for her rights. The 'Made in USA' sign in the painting is a reminder of the need to acknowledge African-Americans as equal citizens. – LD

MARIA PININSKA - BERES

b.1931 in Poznan, Poland. d.1999 in Kraków

Maria Pinińska-Bereś was a Kraków-based artist
whose work encompassed performance, sculpture and
installation. She studied at the School of Art in Katowice
and the Academy of Fine Arts in Kraków, graduating
in sculpture in 1962. Pinińska-Bereś initially made
figurative sculpture but by 1965 her practice shifted
towards abstraction and the use of soft, lightweight
materials as a 'medium close to women's practice'.
From this point on, in her immersive, often dimly-lit
environments, Pinińska-Bereś explored gender difference
in a patriarchal, increasingly consumerist society by
tapping into what she referred to as a 'reservoir of
femininity-related' issues. Her installations featured fleshy,
organic quasi-bodies placed inside display cases. With a
pop art sensibility of appropriating non-art materials for
her immersive installations, the artist claimed domestic
processes by combining papier mâché, sewn or quilted
materials, cushions and sponge trimmed with fabric.
Although Pinińska-Bereś did not wish to be associated
with feminism, following a negative response to her early
'soft' works, she is nevertheless considered as one of the
feminist pioneers in Poland alongside her slightly younger
fellow Polish artists Natalia LL and Ewa Partum.

In 1968 Maria Pinińska-Bereś began a body of
work entitled *Psycho Furniture*, shown at the exhibition
Women's Art at the Galeria ON in Poznan. The series
addressed the objectification of women for the benefit
of male pleasure, featuring sewn pink shapes fashioned
after female body parts, combined into absurd, utilitarian
machines aimed to serve, despite their owners'
dismemberment. One of them, *Love Machine* 1969
(no.76), invites the user to turn a handle on a box, as if
grilling meat. The handle activates a sinister 'machine'
consisting of shapes reminiscent of woman's sexual
organs, a pair of breasts and three legs that turn endlessly
as if they were a propeller. In *Screen* 1973 (no.77) a soft
organic bright pink shape can be seen, as if hiding behind
a white partition with the words 'screen' – 'is good' –
'for everything' scrolled onto it, suggesting the hypocrisy
involved in 'screening off' female subjectivity. – LD

215

JOAN RABASCALL

b.1935 in Barcelona, Spain.
Lives and works in Paris, France.

Since the mid-1960s Joan Rabascall has worked
on unveiling the mechanisms behind image-making,
and in particular the mass media's manipulation of
representation. After he was exiled to Paris from
Francoist Spain in 1962, Rabascall met avant-garde
artists of the Independent Group in London, the
nouveaux réalistes in Paris, theorist Lawrence Alloway
and critic Pierre Restany who exhibited his works in
1966. With other Catalan artists – Jaume Xifra, Antoni
Miralda and his wife Dorothée Selz – he organised a
series of collective dinner performances in 1969 and 1970.
His collage technique interrogates the very essence of
image construction, offering a re-reading of existing
images, subverting their original content and context.
By reframing and associating contrasted images taken
from everyday life, Rabascall turned the communication
tools of mass media against themselves.

Joan Rabascall started using the technique of
photomontage and photographic emulsion on canvas
at the end of the 1960s, working with cut-outs from
magazines, newspapers and advertising posters. *Atomic
Kiss* 1968 (no.113) is emblematic of Rabascall's interest
in reactivating the meaning of an image by means of
associations with conflicted images. Responding to the
bombardment of images by the mass media, *Atomic Kiss*
superimposes an iconic, sensual and Hollywood-inspired
red lipsticked female mouth with an image of an atomic
explosion. An ironic and violent portrayal of the socio-
political context of the upheavals in the late 1960s, this
work depicts the ambiguities of American consumerist
society, which hid behind its glamorous cinema icons
a mass destructive military power. – EC

BERNARD RANCILLAC

b.1931 in Paris, France,
where he lives and works.

As the co-organiser of the seminal exhibition
Mythologies Quotidiennes in 1964 in Paris, considered
to be the founding point of *figuration narrative*,
Bernard Rancillac was at a very early stage engaged
with a critical re-appropriation of pop art's *figurative
language*. Abandoning informal and abstract painting
in 1962, he became a pioneer of French figuration
narrative, working from photographic images in magazines, advertisements, popular imagery and comic
strips and reinterpreting them to highlight their political
implications. Increasingly preoccupied by the socio-
political context in which he was painting, in 1966
Rancillac decided to illustrate all key events of that year.
Developing the process of juxtaposition of images taken
from the press, Rancillac offered critical commentaries
on topical issues, notably the Vietnam War, decoloni-
sation, military dictatorships, poverty in developing
countries and socio-cultural changes in Western societies. He participated in the production of posters at the
Atelier Populaire in May 1968 and pursued his political
paintings throughout the 1970s.

In May 1966, social and celebrity magazine *Paris
Match* published a photograph of an African art collector's
dinner, showing the wealthily dressed guests sat around the
dinner table, in a lavish Parisian interior, posing with
African masks covering their faces. This was concurrent
with the opening of the World Festival of Black Arts,
organised in Dakar by the Republic of Senegal's President,
Leopold Sedar Senghor – a major international event for
the recognition of African arts in Western countries, where
they were becoming luxury items in the 1960s. Re-
appropriating this photograph and its title in *Dinner-Party
of the Head-Hunters* 1966 (no.103), Bernard Rancillac
critiqued this bourgeois scene by incorporating three
moveable sections with the portraits of Frantz Fanon,
Patrice Lumumba and Malcom X, iconic activists in the
anti-colonial independence struggles in Algeria, Congo
and the USA, all of whom had died in the early 1960s.
A direct reference to Fanon's book *Black Skin, White
Masks* (1952), this painting addressed issues around
(de)colonisation. Revealing what is hidden behind mass-
consumer society lies at the heart of *At Last, a Silhouette
Slimmed to the Waist* 1966 (no.28), which juxtaposes two
images top to tail and can be hung either way, in order to
emphasise either the advertisement for female underwear
or the horrors of the Vietnam War. Other societal issues
were addressed by Rancillac in 1966, such as the
controversial debate around the legalisation of the
contraceptive pill and the conquest of new territories
within the private and public realms by women in *Pilules
Capsules Conciliabules* 1966 (no.37). – EC

217

EQUIPO REALIDAD

Joan Cardells
b. 1948 in Valencia, Spain, where he lives and works
Jorge Ballester
b. 1941 in Valencia where he died in 2014.

Equipo Realidad (Group Reality) was formed by Joan Cardells and Jorge Ballester in Valencia in 1966. In alignment with a return to figuration that was rising in Spain, as exemplified by artist group Equipo Crónica and Estampa Popular, Cardells and Ballester founded Equipo Realidad, with the mandate to serve society through art. The two Valencian artists, born in 1941 and 1948 respectively, met at the San Carlos Fine Arts School in 1964, where they both participated in the activities of the Free Students' Union, increasingly resistant to Francisco Franco's government. In the first few years of its operation, Equipo Realidad worked extensively with the Students' Union and for alternative bookshops in Valencia producing decorative panels in acrylic paint. In the late 1960s the group began to address individual themes articulated in four series including *Hogar, dulce hogar* (*Home Sweet Home*), and *Cuadros de Historia* (*History Paintings*).

From the outset Equipo Realidad confronted the themes of war, politics, consumerism, femininity and the role of Art with a capital 'A'. *Divine Proportion* 1967 (no. 114), exhibited during the group's first trip to Italy in 1967, revisits Leonardo da Vinci's iconic Vitruvian Man. By substituting the anatomical study with the depiction of a North American soldier, Equipo Realidad activates a twofold critique. Firstly, an association is established between the Vietnam War and a European cultural icon, warning against the threat of US cultural and economic imperialism – heightened in Spain by the neoliberal policies implemented by Francisco Franco's administration. Secondly, the manipulation of the same icon reflects Equipo Realidad's discontent with the official culture promoted by the regime, still anchored to past achievements. Through the approachable aesthetic of the mass media, Equipo Realidad strove to encourage the viewer to participate in a re-evaluation of Spanish culture, caught between imperialism and academicism. – SG

RAIMO REINIKAINEN

b.1939 in Helsinki, Finland.
Lives and works in Väätäiskylä.

Raimo Reinikainen trained in fine art at the Helsinki
Fine Arts Academy between 1961 and 1966. From the
outset, Reinikainen's fascination with the metaphysical
beauty of both nature and of his urban surroundings
informed his relationship with art. Considered one of the
young avant-garde rebels in the early 1960s, he developed
his practice in opposition to the stale academicism that
pervaded the institutions, which were champions of
non-figurative abstraction. Seeking to approach universal
themes, such as everyday life, death, violence and love,
Reinikainen became fascinated with the anti-elitism and
accessibility of pop art, in particular the work of Robert
Rauschenberg. Among the paintings exhibited at his first
solo show at the E-Kerho Gallery in 1966 were a series of
'Bright Targets', reminiscent of Jasper Johns, and canvases
that incorporated cut-outs from popular magazines and
newspapers in the mode of assemblage.

Raimo Reinikainen's series *Sketch for the U.S. Flag 1,
2, 3, 4* 1966 (nos. 29, 31, 30, 32) is a deeply anti-war pop
art work emblematic of his political orientation in the
mid-1960s. During the Cold War, Finland was one of the
few capitalist economies bordering the Soviet Union,
whose political influence was widely felt, especially
among the younger generations in Helsinki. He became
highly sensitive to the effects of commercial culture, often
imported from the USA, which inspired his early
artworks. In *Sketch for the U.S. Flag 1, 2, 3, 4* Reinikainen
replaced the stars and stripes of the American ensign
with rainbows and crude press photographs of the
Vietnam War. As the series progresses, the stripes become
wider, the collaged images gradually move towards the
centre of the canvas, and the specific reference to the US
flag is attenuated. The juxtaposition of the background,
a possible reference to hippy culture, and the military
images, perhaps suggests the universal concerns raised
by the ignominies of war. – SG

GLAUCO RODRIGUES

b. 1929 in Octavius Castillos, in Bage, Brazil.
d. 2004 in Rio de Janeiro.

Glauco Rodrigues began painting in 1945, as an autodidact. After a brief period of training in Bage with painter José Moraes, Rodrigues received a scholarship to attend the National Fine Arts School in Rio de Janeiro for three months. Between 1951 and 1954 he participated in several engraving collectives in Bage and Porto Alegre, where his aim was to express through drawing and engraving the rural character and traditions of southern Brazil, an objective that defined his practice. In 1958 he settled in Rio de Janeiro where he worked as a graphic designer, an illustrator and later as the director of the popular *Senhor* magazine. Between 1962 and 1965 Rodrigues lived in Rome, a period during which he adopted an abstract vocabulary. After participating at the 1964 Venice Biennale (the so-called 'pop Biennale'), Rodrigues returned to a figurative lexicon under the umbrella of Brazilian new figuration. In Rio de Janeiro, he took part in the exhibition *Opinao '66* at the Museum of Modern Art.

The Song of Solomon – Concha Shell 1967 (from the series *Concha Shell*) (no.43) belongs to a body of work that Glauco Rodrigues developed in the mid-1960s, which humorously dealt with themes related to Brazilian national identity, as a means of questioning the socio-political context that erupted following the military coup of 1964. *The Song of Solomon* appropriates the logo of the Shell Corporation in the depiction of a woman, with her breasts exposed, in a sensual pose – a subtle allusion to Brazil's economic relationship with the USA. By equating Shell's economic presence with a sexualised image, Rodrigues activated a mockery of Brazilian culture, prone to exploitation and associated with pleasure and female sensuality, a recurrent theme throughout his practice. Working with a bright palette, canvas, plastic objects and discarded materials, Rodrigues represented aspects of Brazilian visual culture as portrayed by the mass media, as methods of questioning the tension between Brazilian politics and the exponential growth of consumer culture. – SG

PETER ROEHR

b. 1944 in Lauenburg, Germany.
d. 1968 in Frankfurt am Main.

Despite having only a brief artistic career, spanning from 1962 to 1967, Peter Roehr left behind him a prolific oeuvre of pioneering collages, photo and sound montages and films. Refusing to belong to any artistic movement of the early 1960s or to the then emerging art scene in West Germany, Roehr developed a proto-conceptual practice borrowing from pop art and minimalism. His practice was based on the principle of serial organisation and montage, focusing on the effects produced by unvaried repetition. In order to achieve the impression of sameness, Roehr used industrially manufactured products. For his *Film-Montages* 1965–8 he had access to spots from American television commercials, which he manually mounted to create a series of short films comprising approximately ten identical short sequences. His re-appropriation of advertisements for mass-consumption products was aimed at dissolving the original message.

The twenty-two short films that constitute Peter Roehr's *Film-Montages I–III* 1965 (nos. 160, 161) are repeated sequences taken from television spots. Both the sequences of images and their accompanying soundtracks are repeated about ten times, with the effect of a skipping record. Lights in a car tunnel, views of skyscrapers, cars passing by, a woman flicking her hair, two men wrestling: all of the brief excerpts, when repeated, acquire a self-referential dimension. At first the clip is clearly anchored in a specific context, such as that of an advertisement, but its repetition creates a distancing effect from the original image, which no longer refers to an external reality. The images lose their referential and representational power, each sequence referring to the one before, creating at the same time anticipation in the viewer's mind and an effect of difference among sameness. Similarly, the *Sound Montages I+III* 1966 are repeated sequences of audio clips taken from German and American advertisements. – EC

221

MARTHA ROSLER

b. in Brooklyn, New York, United States of America,
where she lives and works.

Martha Rosler is an eminent artist, theorist and
educator as well as a leading contemporary critical voice
within feminist discourses. Rosler's work encompasses
photography, video, installation, photomontage and
performance. She has also published over fifteen books
of her works and essays exploring the role of
photography and art, public space, transportation, as well
as public housing and homelessness. Rosler studied at
Brooklyn College in New York and subsequently at the
University of California, San Diego, obtaining her MFA
there in 1974. Her widely seen video work *Semiotics of
the Kitchen* 1975, reflecting her longstanding interest in
the position of the female subject within patriarchy, uses
humour in this parody of cooking shows to address
the implications of traditional female roles.

Appropriating elements of pop culture in her work,
such as television and magazine advertising, Rosler
produced a now well-known set of photomontages,
in which she collages magazine photography with
depictions of ideal homes, producing a single
incongruous frame as a way of highlighting the false
disconnection between these two public discourses.
In *House Beautiful: Bringing the War Home*,
c. 1967–72, for instance, a series produced at the peak
of the Vietnam War, Rosler combined images of
Vietnamese civilians and U.S. soldiers with those of
pristine dwellings. Remaining outside the art context,
Rosler distributed photocopies of these works among
the anti-war community and published them in
'underground' periodicals.

In the series *Body Beautiful, or Beauty Knows No
Pain*, made between 1965 and 1972, Rosler deconstructs
representations of women in mass circulation magazines.
In the works in this series – *Cold Meat I*, *Cold Meat II* or
Kitchen II, *Kitchen I*, *or Hot Meat* and *Damp Meat* (nos.
61, 62, 60, 59) – parts of women's torsos are merged with
kitchen appliances, placing the commodified female flesh
within the arena of food preparation and consumption.
Similarly, in *Pop Art, or Wallpaper* (no. 125) parts of a
female body from a *Playboy* magazine centerfold become
a patterned wallpaper and are systematically arranged,
grid-like, on a wood-grain surface. In *Woman with
Vacuum, or Vacuuming Pop Art* (no. 63) Martha Rosler
addresses the marginalisation of women in pop art. The
work features a well-groomed woman vacuuming a
corridor filled with well-known pop art works by male
artists – for instance a work by Tom Wesselmann. The
vacuuming woman is smiling, as if resigned to her
invisibility and subservient role within the dominant
patriarchal discourse. – LD

MARIO SCHIFANO

b.1934 in Homs, Libya. d.1998 in Rome, Italy.

Following the end of the Second World War, Mario Schifano moved with his family from his native Libya to Rome. Showing little interest in school, he soon began restoring ceramics, a trade learned from his archaeologist and restorer father. An autodidact, Schifano soon took up painting, initially producing bold monochrome canvases, with strips of glued wrapping paper and stencils applied to them. His work was critically acclaimed, leading to several exhibitions in Italy and later in the USA, capturing the attention of the internationally renowned art dealer Ileana Sonnabend. In the early 1960s Schifano's interest turned to the urban landscape of Rome and he began using coloured Perspex, corporate logos and layered paper like billboards in an exploration of the street and popular culture. He frequently travelled to the USA, where his works were exhibited alongside those of American pop artists. In the mid-1960s, in parallel with painting, he started directing 16mm films, inspired by Jean-Luc Goddard's principles of improvisation.

In 1968, in response to the global wave of protests, Schifano made a number of political works. Among them are the three *Comrades comrades* 1968 (nos. 4, 158, 159) paintings belonging to the *Comrades* series. Black spray-painted silhouettes of political protestors holding the Communist symbol of hammer and sickle inhabit these works. The same motif, accompanied by a political slogan calling for a fair solution to society's social and political contradictions, is repeated across the series. While the silhouettes are fixed the background varies, shifting from bold block-like colours to decorative patterns. By endlessly repeating the same motif Schifano shows how protest, slogans and politics generally fall prey to serialisation. – LD

COLIN SELF

b. 1941 in Rackheath, Norfolk, United Kingdom.
Lives and works in Norwich.

Colin Self studied at the Norwich Art School and London's Slade School of Fine Art, graduating in 1963. A maverick from the outset, Self rejected conventions of representational drawing, embracing popular culture and eclectically combining everyday materials, drawing, collage, sculpture, printmaking and painting. The visiting lecturers, David Hockney and Peter Blake, recognised Self's potential, encouraging him to pursue his own artistic vocabulary. His early work addressed the socio-political reality of the Cold War and the nuclear threat. He was one of the first artists in Britain to engage with these topics while also commenting on the increasing consumerism, sexual violence and the artifice of the art establishment. His early works depicted glamorous *Vogue* models with nuclear bombers looming above their heads, fallout shelters and nuclear victims. Self's materials combined leopard skin, fur, wood and metal with meticulous drawing and painting.

Colin Self's 1962–3 series of *Nuclear Bombers*, made while he was still a student, equated animal predatory impulses with male aggression and sexual violence *Leopardskin Nuclear Bomber No.2* 1963 (no.124) is a phallic object shaped to resemble bomber planes, made of painted wood and scrap metal, and adorned with fashionable fur as a symbol of the artifice of the consumer society. – LD

DOROTHÉE SELZ

b. 1946 in Paris, France, where she lives and works.

Dorothée Selz's oeuvre is focused on an interrogation of the ephemeral as manifest by her espousal of the edible in her work. Directly influenced by the context and spirit of the late 1960s, May 1968 events, and counter-culture movements, her early work bears the impact of the artistic experimentation of these years. At first working with collages of magazine photography and street posters, she soon decided to turn towards a new popular material, the edible. In 1969, with fellow artists Antoni Miralda, Jaume Xifra and Joan Rabascall, she organised her first ritual performative dinner, which was followed by other similar events in the 1970s. Selz's use of the edible, close to the 'eat art' movement and the work of Daniel Spoerri, revolved around the idea that food offers the public a direct and immediate relation to its environment, the ephemeral artwork being consumed at these events. Her pictorial works, pursued in parallel to her edible works, re-appropriate and bring new life to popular, found imagery, emphasising the fleetingness of these images, often 'consumed' by the eye very briefly and thrown away immediately.

In the wake of feminist movements and pop art, Dorothée Selz's series of *Relative Mimetism* 1973 (nos. 127, 128, 129) appears as a humorous and critical series addressing the image of the 'seductive' woman as conveyed by fashion magazines, calendars or pop art works by Allen Jones. Placing side by side a photograph taken from an advertisement and a picture of Selz mimicking the image, the artist questions the very process of creation – and consequent desire – in consumer society. The conflation of the role of artist and model also highlights the artificiality of the constructed pin-up image. The brightly coloured frames, decorated with icing from piping bags, evoke children's crafts and edible ornaments. At a time when feminist movements were denouncing and rejecting the idealisation and objectification of women's bodies as conveyed by magazines, Selz's re-appropriation of popular imagery stages the ambiguous desire to both reject and resemble those icons. – EC

225

USHIO SHINOHARA

b. 1932 in Tokyo, Japan. Lives and works
in New York City, United States of America.

A founding member of the Neo Dada group, Ushio
Shinohara embraced pop art as early as 1963 with his
Imitation Art series, a critical and provocative take on
the work of American pop artists Jasper Johns and Robert
Rauschenberg. These imitations – rough copies
of works by the American artists – reflected on the notion
of newness and originality in art, as well as on Japanese
modern art's relationship to Western art. Growing up
in Japan during the Second World War, Shinohara
witnessed the rapid Americanisation of his country.
After inventing his famous *Boxing Paintings* in 1960–1,
he gave up gesture-based painting and turned towards
more mechanical means of production using new
industrial materials and airbrush. Revisiting traditional
Japanese art, from 1965 he developed a series of *Oiran*
works imbued with pop's aesthetics. Modernising the
motif of *oiran*, a high-class courtesan traditionally
depicted in woodblock prints from the Edo period
(1603–1868), he adapted it to the context of pop art.
Shinohara settled in New York in 1969 where he
refused to partake in the minimalist and conceptual art
movements, pursuing in the 1970s figurative works such
as his series of cardboard *Motorcycle Sculptures*.

Presented at Ushio Shinohara's debut exhibition
Doll Festival at the commercial Tokyo Gallery in 1965,
the *Oiran* series transformed traditional imagery into
a groundbreaking body of work using fluorescent paint,
plastic and aluminium sheets. His eponymous *Doll
Festival* 1966 (no.83) is emblematic of this series, with
its pop treatment of the traditional subject. Although the
faceless characters have been denied expression, their
positions and attires in the painting introduce a narrative:
the five figures are both actors and spectators of a scene
withheld from the viewer. At the centre of the triptych,
a man wearing a Western outfit is surrounded by four
traditional Japanese figures: on the left a parade leader
and a townswoman, and on the right a young male
prostitute and an oiran. Inspired by the annual festival
organised to pray for young girls' growth and good
development, *Doll Festival* reflects on the prevalence
of symbols embedded in society at the time of
modernisation and Americanisation of Japanese
society. – EC

TERESINHA SOARES

b.1927 in Araxá, Minas Gerais, Brazil.
Lives and works in Belo Horizonte.

Advancing from a career in literature and acting,
Teresinha Soares began her fine arts training at the
Universidad Mineira das Artes in Belo Horizonte in
1965; the following year, she moved to Rio de Janeiro
to study engraving at the independent studios
organised by the Museum of Modern Art. Working with
printmaking, painting and object/sculptures made of
wood (later also complemented by performance), Soares's
works were distinguished by a hard-edge aesthetic,
which connected her to new figuration. Throughout
her practice, she explored the power and limitations
of femininity in a continuous effort against chauvinism
and repression. Because of the delicacy of these themes
during the initial stages of the military dictatorship in
Brazil, Soares's critique emerged through an exaggerated
and humorous language. By 1967 she was celebrated
in the national press as the new artistic revelation from
Minas Gerais and her works were exhibited widely across
the country.

The 1968 *Vietnam* series encapsulates many of
Teresinha Soares's omnipresent motifs revolving around
sexuality and liberation, while also being one of her most
politicised pieces. In this series, composed of three works
in total, she applied wooden sheets and frames re-creating
the geometry of television sets, film reels and screens.
The images that appear in the three-dimensional panels
alternate between sexualised silhouettes and violent
imagery of battle and war. Soares juxtaposes war and
love, the balance between Eros and Thanatos, but
distances them from the viewer through the image of
the television set or the film reel – symbolic of the mass
media's alienating effect. The fierce imagery, disguised
by the title's reference to the Vietnam War, also spoke
out against the violence perpetrated by the dictatorship
in Brazil. *So Many Men Die and I Am Here So Lonely*
(no.50) and *Die Wearing the Legitimate Espadrille*
(no.51) force the viewers to examine the sexual and
violent imagery in dialogue, and to determine their
position within this dichotomy. – SG

227

SHINKICHI TAJIRI

b. 1923 in Los Angeles, United States of America.
d. 2009 in Baarlo, Netherlands.

Shinkichi Tajiri, a child of first-generation immigrants to the USA from Japan, spent his childhood in Los Angeles and San Diego. Following the 1941 attack on the US airfield in Hawaii by the Japanese army, Tajiri's family was sent to the Poston War Relocation Center, an internment camp in Arizona. In a combination of patriotism and his wish to leave the camp, Tajiri soon volunteered for the army and joined the all-Japanese American regiment, which later became the most decorated regiment of its size in American military history. He subsequently attended the Chicago Art Institute from 1946 to 1948, also working for the sculptor Isamu Noguchi in New York. In 1949 he moved to Paris and studied with Ossip Zadkine and Fernand Léger. Primarily a sculptor, Tajiri also made a number of award-winning films, videos, stereo and panoramic photos and works on paper.

Shinkichi Tajiri saw the war as catalyst for his becoming an artist and he regarded his imagery as a way of crystallising his war experiences. The main themes of his work are speed, erotica and violence in an ongoing confrontation with the tragedies of the Second World War and its aftermath. In 1967 and 1968 he made a series of sculptures entitled *Machines* as a form of protest against the violence of the Vietnam War. *Machine No 7* 1967–8 (no.11) is a steel, aluminium, Plexiglas and chromed iron sculpture shaped like a hybrid of a fighter plane and a gun, embodying Tajiri's experiences of the violence of war. – LD

KEIICHI TANAAMI

b. 1936 in Tokyo, Japan, where he lives and works.

Keiichi Tanaami's childhood was marked by the chaos brought about by the Second World War. He was only nine during the Tokyo Air Raid of 1945 and his family relocated from their Tokyo home to Meguro, a suburban residential district, from where he observed over a hundred firebombing attacks on his native city. Images of roaring American airplanes, searchlights, bombs and fleeing masses were deeply lodged in his memory, later becoming his core iconography – a blur of his nightmares and real memories. A talented draughtsman, Tanaami graduated in graphic design from the Musashino Art University in 1960. He quickly forged a successful career in design and advertising, illustrating the Japanese releases of record covers for Jefferson Airplane and The Monkees, among other projects. An encounter with the Japanese neo-dada scene centred around the studio of the artist Ushio Shinohara, as well as Manga-style cartoons, inspired Tanaami's foray into art. His colourful, overpopulated psychedelic collages, animations and drawings frequently juxtapose war imagery with American and Japanese pop culture, communicating the underlying peace message.

Keiichi Tanaami's first trip to New York in the late 1960s introduced him to the work of Andy Warhol, whose interdisciplinary approach constantly shifting between art and advertising echoed Tanaami's own path. He would later visit Warhol's Factory, as the first art director of the Japanese edition of *Playboy* magazine. From 1965 Tanaami began to work with video and animation in collaboration with Yoji Kuri's Experimental Animation School. *Commercial War* 1971 (no. 145) takes the emblems associated with American consumer society – like Coca-Cola – and juxtaposes them with Tanaami's own visual vocabulary. The effect is a comic-strip-like critical take on the advent and impact of American consumer culture on foreign nations. Also commenting on the American invasion of Japan both in military and cultural terms is *Crayon Angel* 1975 (no. 89). Opening with the sound of sirens and dramatic drumming over images of fighter jets and explosions, the fast-paced video goes on to combine black and white photographs of Japanese families and children, often seen through black prison-like bars which evoke Japanese *fusuma* (sliding doors used to partition spaces within a room), with psychedelic characters and superheroes appearing on traditional Japanese patterns. The incongruity of such imagery points to Japan's difficult past, its growing consumerism and the pervasive nature of global pop culture. – LD

PARVIZ TANAVOLI

b.1937 in Tehran, Iran.
Lives and works in Vancouver, Canada and Tehran.

From 1960 on, Parviz Tanavoli became a pioneering figure in contemporary Iranian art, revisiting Persian traditions and modern sculpture. While he was studying art in Tehran in the mid-1950s, the Iranian government's cultural policy was opening to Western practices, at the same time as encouraging the development of national and traditional arts. This led Tanavoli to study sculpture in Milan at the end of the 1950s and teach for two and a half years in Minneapolis in the early 1960s. Returning to Tehran and reflecting on the modernisation of Iranian art, his studio soon transformed into a hub for exhibitions and collective reflection. Gathering artists and poets, his studio, Atelier Kaboud, was the fertile ground for the formation of the Saqqakhaneh School. The most influential avant-garde movement in 1960s Iran, the Saqqakhaneh School developed a visual language drawing on popular culture and its symbols, re-appropriating traditions with a modernist stance.

Parviz Tanavoli's practice, developed throughout the 1960s and 1970s, is characterised by the modern incorporation of traditional techniques, notably everyday handicrafts found in the blacksmiths, foundries and pottery workshops of Tehran, and traditional subjects such as popular love stories as depicted in Persian poetry. Recurrent in his works are motifs taken from religious folk art, especially the saqqakhaneh, a votive fountain protected by metal grills. *The Poet and the Beloved of the King* 1964–6 (no.34) is a striking example of Tanavoli's re-appropriation of the evocative grill element, but extracted from its original significance by applying it to robot-like figures made out of brightly coloured, pop-inspired material. Revisiting poetic traditional love stories, his series of screenprints celebrates idiomatic Persian myths and symbols through a resolutely modernist visual language (nos. 119, 120, 122). Many of his works pay tribute to the legendary love story of Farhad, the only sculptor mentioned in classical Persian poetry, who challenged the Sassanian King Khosrow Parviz, his rival for the hand of the beloved princess Shirin. Tanavoli reinterprets, throughout his works, this poetic legend as well as icons found in Shiite folk art, such as the cage, the lion, the lock and the bird, using geometric forms and new mediums. – EC

JOE TILSON

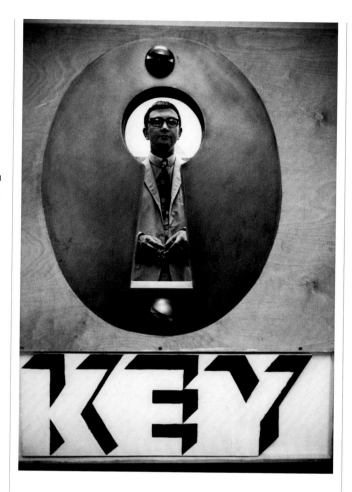

b. 1928 in London, UK.
Lives and works between London and Venice, Italy.

Following initial training and work as a carpenter, and
three years in the Royal Air Force, Joe Tilson enrolled
at St Martin's School of Art and the Royal College of
Art in London, studying alongside Frank Auerbach, Leon
Kossoff and Peter Blake, and graduated in 1955. Winning
the Roma prize, Tilson moved to Rome, where he met
and married artist Joslyn Morton. The two returned to
the UK for Tilson to take up a teaching post at St
Martin's, and later at the Slade School of Art in London.
Using his experience as a carpenter and joiner, in the
late 1950s Tilson produced wooden reliefs in addition to
prints and paintings. His work reflected a preoccupation
with language, puzzle-making and symbols. It also
revealed a desire to disrupt the hierarchy between
the copy and original, which he shared with other
pop artists of his generation.

Joe Tilson's work gradually shifted to reflect his
growing political activism and his critique of
consumerism. In 1969 he embarked on a series entitled
Pages – three-dimensional wooden grids that mimicked
the layout of radical newspapers and magazines of the
period, such as *Black Dwarf* and *International Times*.
The content sections, slotted within the wooden grids,
featured screenprints of articles and images, printed on
soft pillow-like fabric, sewn by Tilson's wife Morton.

Page 7 Snow White and the Black Dwarf 1969
(no. 156) and *Page 9 Black Dwarf* 1969 (no. 157) refer
to the political magazine *Black Dwarf* and the latter
includes extracts from Norman O. Brown's book *Life
Against Death*, an influential publication critical of
Sigmund Freud's theories. *Page 19 He, She & It* 1969–70
(no. 154) and *Page 20 He, She & It* 1969–70 (no. 155)
both represent *International Times*. The latter also
references James Whale's adaptation of Mary Shelley's
Frankenstein, W.B. Yeats's poetry and excerpts from
James Joyce's writing, while *Page 18 Muhammad Speaks*
1969–70 (no. 3) is entirely devoted to the American boxer
Muhammad Ali. – LD

CLAUDIO TOZZI

b.1944 in São Paulo, Brazil, where he lives and works.

Claudio Tozzi joined the University of Sao Paulo's Faculty of Architecture and Urbanism (FAU) in 1964, yet never practiced architecture, working as a graphic artist instead. While at university he met luminary, critic and physicist Mário Schenberg, who quickly identified his work with Brazilian new figuration, a contemporary alternative to the concrete avant-gardes, alongside Wesley Duke Lee, Antonio Dias and Roberto Magalhães, among others. Tozzi's interest in figuration developed from a necessity to popularise art in São Paulo, which offered very few platforms for young artists to exhibit, besides in yearly salons. He responded to the lacuna of official exhibition spaces by appropriating the intelligible language of commercial culture, through the aesthetics of pop art. In his works Tozzi addressed current political issues reported widely in the media including the space race and the Cuban revolution. Among his most iconic works are representations of astronauts and Che Guevara.

Claudio Tozzi's effort to popularise art led him to draw images from the mass media, challenging accepted socio-cultural values as well as satirising the Brazilian information network, which was plagued by censorship during the military dictatorship. In the mid-1960s, crowds and political icons are among Tozzi's recurrent subjects. *Multitude* 1968 (no.42) reflects one of his persistent motifs: the crowd in protest. In 1968 the military regime in Brazil became notoriously more oppressive, to the extent that many artists and intellectuals were forced to flee the country. In São Paulo and Rio de Janeiro, political protests became a daily occurrence, in parallel to the May 1968 student revolts in Paris. Tozzi's depiction of the crowd, through enlarged details juxtaposed with a series of raised fists, accentuates his effort to highlight the power of the individual within the multitude. By adopting pop's accessible language, he proposed to sensitise a wider audience to the mobilising potential of art. – SG

CHRYSSA VARDEA

b.1933 in Athens, Greece, where she died in 2013.

Chryssa Vardea-Mavromichali was a Greek-born American sculptor best known for her monumental assemblages combining neon, bronze, aluminium, plaster, wood, canvas and paint as well as found objects, which prefigured both pop art and minimalism. Vardea studied in Paris and San Francisco, and in 1955 moved to New York, finding inspiration in the spectacle of the advertising neon signs of Times Square. Her interest in communication and the use of letters was first expressed through small baked-clay tablets entitled *Cycladic Books* 1955, followed by tablets and plaques with single letters, or variations on letter forms. Using neon since 1962, Vardea was one of the first artists to transform it from an advertising tool into an art material.

It was the same interest in the written word that inspired Chryssa Vardea's most ambitious, monumental work, *The Gates to Times Square* (also known as 'The Gates'), which was realised between 1964 and 1966. The work is Vardea's homage to her experience of New York, to popular culture, advertising and mass communication. Consisting of two monumental letter As, incorporating fragments of commercial signs, the just under one-metre-square stainless steel, Plexiglas and neon sculpture invites visitors to walk through it, becoming physically immersed in the pale blue neon light with changing intensity and rhythm. *Study for Gates No.4* 1967 (no.162) is one of sixteen sculptures entitled *Studies for Gates*, which the artist produced both before and after the completion of the main work itself. The work takes a fragment of the monumental work, resembling the letter S, repeating it sixteen times, in eight double sets of blue neon lights, which light up in sequence. – LD

233

TADANORI YOKOO

b.1936 in Nishiwaki, Hyogo Prefecture, Japan.
Lives and works in Tokyo.

Tadanori Yokoo is one of Japan's most well-known artists, who began working with painting in 1966. In parallel, Yokoo's early screenprints combined photographs with the influence of traditional Japanese *ukiyo-e* (woodblock prints) and pop art's flat colours and overtly sexual content. Awarded the Grand Prize for Prints at the 6th Paris Youth Biennale in 1969, Yokoo experimented with collage and illustration, re-appropriating found photographs and images, which reflected on the rapid changes and Westernisation of Japan post-war society. His work became influenced by mysticism following his trip to India in the 1970s, resulting in posters with eclectic imagery sharing the aesthetics of the underground psychedelic magazines of the time.

Tadanori Yokoo's animation *KISS KISS KISS* 1964 (no.87) uses the pop art strategy of appropriating comic-book images of kissing couples complete with speech bubbles spelling 'kiss'. The work starts off with the soundtrack of Dean Martin's popular song *Kiss*, changing moments later to the otherworldly sounds of a theremin, suggesting the emergence of a darker side to the kissing couple's bliss. As the animation progresses, the images are manipulated through hand colouring, rhythm, rotation and the effect of ripped paper, speeding up only to once again end with Martin's song. – LD

JANA ŽELIBSKÁ

b. 1941 in Olomouc, Czechoslovakia.
Lives and works in Bratislava, Slovakia.

Jana Želibská studied at the Academy of Fine Art and
Design in Bratislava and graduated in graphics and
book illustration in 1965. In 1968 Želibská received
a scholarship for a residency in Paris, where she
witnessed the 1968 protests. Belonging to a generation
of progressive artists in Czechoslovakia, she was inspired
by nouveau réalisme as well as pop art. Želibská rapidly
moved on from experimenting with lyrical painting
and prints in her early years, to creating immersive
environments, using mixed media and non-art materials.

Jana Želibská created the first of such environments,
entitled *The Possibility of Exposure* 1967, for a solo
exhibition at the Cyprian Majernik Gallery in Bratislava
and comprised paintings, assemblages and freestanding
objects. Viewers could manipulate elements of the
exhibited paintings and assemblages, featuring fragments
of female bodies, divided by sheer curtains. Inspired by
nouveau realisme's use of non-art material, the work
combined mirrors, fabric, neon and plastics. In one of the
paintings shown within the installation, entitled *Breasts*
1967 (no.149), a breast adorned with lace and a
patterned fabric is shown with its mirror image lightly
concealed behind a sheer curtain. The viewer is
encouraged to move the curtain to reveal the painting
in its entirety, emulating intimate moments and engaging
with the tactile qualities of the work.

Similarly, in *Nose I – II* 1967 (no.148), two
diagrammatic images are shown next to each other,
reminiscent of 'before and after' pictures depicting
cosmetic surgery or self-improvement techniques. The
two noses are, however, identical. Other works within
the environment include *Object II* 1967 (no.75) and a
column entitled *Kandarya-Mahadeva* 1969/2010 –12
(no.8), which refers to the eponymous temple in India
and draws in elements of tantric Hinduism and erotic
rituals. Covered in neon-outlined bodies of female
dancers, with mirrors in place of their private parts,
Želibská originally intended this work to be shown
on the street, but was prohibited from doing so as
the work was deemed too explicit. – LD

JERZY RYSZARD 'JURRY' ZIELINSKI

b. 1943 in Kazimierzów, Poland. d. 1980 in Warsaw.

Jerzy Ryszard 'Jurry' Zieliński studied sculpture and painting at the Warsaw Academy of Fine Arts, graduating in 1968 with a diploma in painting. Zieliński was an active opponent of the political administration in Poland. His artistic vocabulary combined pop art influences with those of the Polish Poster School, but above all his subject matter remained rooted in the social reality of the political context of communist Poland. Zieliński's use of flat surfaces and simplified shapes in bright poster-like colours stood in sharp contrast to the academic post-impressionistic painting taught across polish academies at the time. In 1967, while still a student, Zieliński founded the collaborative project Neo-Neo-Neo with fellow artist Jan 'Dobson' Dobkowski. Formed a year prior to a major political crisis in Poland that saw the workers' militia suppress student protests at Warsaw University, Neo-Neo-Neo sought to 'present the world's problems, without excluding the person' as stated in their 1969 manifesto. Neo-Neo-Neo's projects were multidisciplinary including writing and performative displays, such as 'parodies of happenings' consisting of flat chipboard cut-outs that were then filmed and animated.

   In 1970 Zieliński's work *Without Rebellion* 1970 (no. 26) was first exhibited at the *Information – Painting – Action* exhibition at the Gallery of Contemporary Art in Warsaw. A simplified portrait of a face expands into three dimensions through the use of a red satin pillow, standing in for a tongue pierced and secured to the floor with a nail. The eyes are symbolised by two Polish eagles in front of a red sun – a legendary symbol of Poland's foundations, only here shown in black. The 1967/1974 painting *The Smile, or Thirty Years, Ha, Ha, Ha* (no. 25) depicts a mouth, sewn shut with three × symbols. The work subverts the official iconography in a critical take on Polish society. Appropriating the XXX symbol representing the thirtieth anniversary of the People's Republic of Poland in 1974, which was used on postage stamps, coins, public monuments and posters, the stitched-together lips of Zieliński's painting, with their ironic, speechless smile, imply forced censorship and silencing. – LD

154
Joe Tilson
Page 19 He, She & It 1969–70
Screenprint and oil paint
on canvas on wood relief
186.7×125

155
Joe Tilson
Page 20 He, She & It 1969–70
Screenprint on canvas
on wood relief
186.7×125

156
Joe Tilson
*Page 7 Snow White and
the Black Dwarf* 1969
Screenprint on canvas
on wood relief
186.7×125

157
Joe Tilson
Page 9 Black Dwarf 1969
Screenprint on canvas
on wood relief
186.7×125

158
Mario Schifano
Comrades comrades 1968
Enamel and spray paint
on canvas and Perspex
140×140

242

159
Mario Schifano
Comrades comrades 1968
Enamel and spray paint
on canvas and Perspex
140×140

160
Peter Roehr
Film-Montages I–III (extract) 1965
16mm film, digitalised
1 min 39 sec

244

161
Peter Roehr
Film-Montages I–III (extract) 1965
16mm film, digitalised
1 min 04 sec

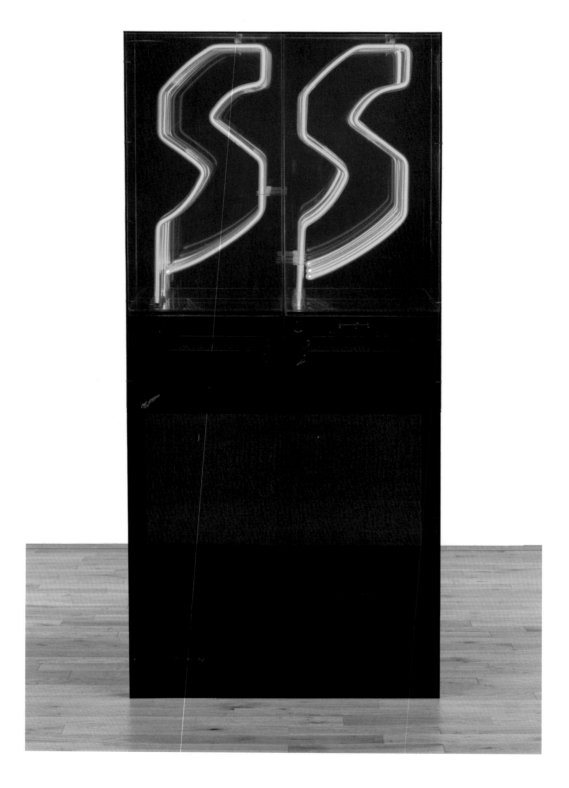

162
Chryssa Vardea
Study for Gates No.4 1967
Perspex, 8 neon lights and timer
109.2 × 88.3 × 70.2

NOTES

Political Pop: An Introduction
Jessica Morgan

1 In *University of Windsor Review*, vol.11, no.1, 1966, pp.1–10; reprinted in E. McLuhan and W.T. Gordon (eds.), *Marshall McLuhan Unbound* (4), California 2005, pp.7–8.

2 See, for example, chapter three of Midori Yamamura's thesis 'Yayoi Kusama: Biography and Cultural Confrontation, 1945–1969', PhD dissertation, The City University of New York, Graduate Center, 2012: '1960–1966 Objects into Art: The Canonization of American Pop and the Case of Kusama' on the gradual exclusion of Kusama from the New York galleries that defined pop art.

3 The connection to socialist realism, the other, often unacknowledged, realist movement of the time, is also in need of further examination.

4 This dual nature of the portrait is present throughout Warhol's oeuvre, as explored by Richard Meyer, among others, in terms of sexuality and Cold War politics.

5 See chapter 'Tito – the missing Pop icon' of Lina Džuverovic's PhD *Hybrid Practices: Inter-disciplinarity and Pop Art Sensibilities in Yugoslav Art from 1960 to 1985*, in which she analyses the surprising lack of imagery of Tito.

6 This subject has been addressed eloquently by the art historian Kalliopi Minoudaki in her essay 'Pop Proto-Feminisms: Beyond the Paradox of the Woman Pop Artist' in Sid Sachs and Kalliopi Minioudaki (eds.), *Seductive Subversion: Women Pop Artists, 1958–1968*, Philadelphia 2010, pp.90–141, and in Angela Stief (ed.) *Power up: Female Pop Art*, Vienna 2010.

Pop Effects in Eastern Europe under Communist Rule
David Crowley

1 See Laura J. Hoptman and Tomáš Pospiszyl (eds.), *Primary Documents: A Sourcebook for Eastern and Central European Art Since the 1950s*, New York 2002, pp.65–77.

2 Jutta Scherrer, '"To Catch Up and Overtake" the West: Soviet Discourse on Socialist Competition', in Katalin Miklóssy and Melanie Ilic (eds.), *Competition in Socialist Society*, London 2014, p.11.

3 See, for instance, Mikhail Alexandrovich Lifshitz and Lidija Jakovlevna Rejngardt, *Krizis bezobrazija. Ot kubizma k pop-art*, Moscow 1968; Viktor Sibirjakov, *Pop-art i paradoksy modernizma*, Moscow 1969; M. Kuz'mina, '"Pop-art"', *Modernizm*, Moscow 1973.

4 See, for instance, Iurii Gerchuk, 'The Aesthetics of Everyday Life in the Khrushchev Thaw in the USSR (1954–1964)', in David Crowley and Susan Reid (eds.), *Style and Socialism*, Oxford 2002, pp.81–96.

5 See Jindřich Chalupecký, *Umění dnes*, Prague 1966; Urszula Czartoryska, *Od Pop-Artu do Sztuki Konceptualnej*, Warsaw 1972.

6 Chalupecký 1966, p.126.

7 See Boris Kelemen (ed.), *Pop Art*, exh. cat., Galerija Suvremene Umjetnosti, Zagreb, March 1966.

8 Michael L. Krenn, *Fall-out Shelters for the Human Spirit: American Art and the Cold War*, Chapel Hill, North Carolina 2005.

9 Lakner described witnessing Rauschenberg's works in the American Pavilion at the Venice Biennial in 1964 as being like a blow to the head. Lakner cited by Péter Sinkovits, 'Progresszív álmok: beszélgetés Lakner Lászlóval', *Új művészet*, vol.16, no.4, 2005, pp.4–7.

10 See Sirji Helme, *Popkunst Forever. Eesti popkunst 1960. ja 1970. aastate vahetusel*, Tallinn 2010.

11 Piotr Piotrowski, *In the Shadow of Yalta: Art and the Avant-garde in Eastern Europe, 1945–1989*, London 2011, pp.61–105.

12 See Claus Groh, *Aktuelle Kunst in Osteuropa*, Koln 1972.

13 János Major cited by Anik Cs. Asztalos (Éva Körner), 'No isms in Hungary', *Studio International*, March 1974, pp.105–11.

14 Matthew Jesse Jackson, *The Experimental Group: Ilya Kabakov, Moscow Conceptualism, Soviet Avant-Gardes*, Chicago and London 2010, pp.69–70.

15 See David Crowley and Susan E. Reid, 'Introduction', in *Pleasures in Socialism. Leisure and Luxury in the Eastern Bloc*, Evanston, Illinois, pp.3–51.

16 Mieczysław Porębski, *Ikonosfera*, Warsaw 1972.

17 Raoul Vaneigem, *The Revolution of Everyday Life*, trans. John Fullerton and Paul Sieveking, London 1979, p.36.

18 Urszula Czartoryska, '"Kronika" Andy'ego Warhola' (1965), in (ed.) Leszek Brogowski *Fotografia – Mowa Ludzka: perspektywy historyczne*, Gdańsk 2006, p.155.

19 Czartoryska (1965) cited by Jerzy Kossak, in *Dylematy Kultury Masowej*, Warsaw 1966, p.97.

20 Václav Havel 'The Power of the Powerless' (1978), in John Keane (ed.), *The Power of the Powerless. Citizens Against the State in Central-Eastern Europe*, trans. Paul Wilson, London 2009, p.15.

21 Aleš Erjavec, 'Introduction', in *Postmodernism and the Postsocialist Condition: Politicized Art Under Late Socialism*, Berkeley, CA 2003, p.37.

22 Beke cited by Klara Kemp-Welch, in *Antipolitics in Central European Art: Reticence as Dissidence under Post-Totalitarian Rule 1956–1989*, London 2014, p.163.

23 See Branislav Dimitrijević, 'DIY POP: Artistic Craftsmanship of Dušan Otašević', in *Dušan Otašević – popmodernizam/popmodernism. Retrospektivna izložba 1965–2003*, exh. cat., Muzej savremene umetnosti, Belgrade October–December 2003, p.112.

24 Jean Baudrillard cited by Hal Foster, *The Return of the Real: The Avant-garde at the End of the Century*, Boston, MA 1996, p.128.

1966 in the World of Pop
Flavia Frigeri

1 Lucy R. Lippard, *Pop Art*, New York 1966, p.7.

2 Lippard, *Pop Art*, p.173.

3 'A Conversation between Anna Maria Maiolino and Helena Tatay' in Helena Tatay ed., *Anna Maria Maiolino*, Fundació Antoni Tàpies, Barcelona, 2010.

4 Vitaly Komar interviewed by Tate Modern 2014/2015.

Unfolding the 'Present': Some Notes on Brazilian 'Pop'
Giulia Lamoni

My ongoing reflections on Brazilian art of the 1960s have received important support from the Museu de Arte Contemporânea da Universidade de São Paulo, which granted me a travel fellowship in 2014, and from the Fundação para Ciência e Tecnologia, Portugal. I would like to thank the artists who agreed to be interviewed and helped me with my research, Maria do Carmo Secco, Regina Vater, Cybèle Varela, Anna Maria Maiolino, Judit Lauand, Anna Bella Geiger, Mona Gorovitz and her sister Gisela, Sonia von Brusky as well as Daisy Peccinini, Marília Andres Ribeiro, Ana Magalhães and Annalivia Cordeiro.

This title of this essay refers to Cybèle Varela's 1967 work *The Present*, which was withdrawn from the São Paulo Biennial in the same year and destroyed.

1 'foi um desastre formidável'. Mário Pedrosa in 'Bienal, GAM promove o debate', *GAM*, Vol. 9/10, 1967, p.61. All translations from Portuguese, unless indicated, are by the author. Original passages are quoted in the notes.

2 'foi uma verdadeira invasão de bárbaros'. Ibid.

3 Ibid.

4 'atitude contemplativa'. Ibid.

5 'um pouco impetuosamente demais'. Ibid. In some instances the audience consumed the artworks literally as well as metaphorically, in a sort of playful and unintentional act of cannibalism. As indicated by Pedrosa, in certain cases that he considers 'exceptional', the works were the object of aggressive and destructive behaviour. Ibid.

6 For a general view on the IX Biennial see Liliane de Oliveira, 'A Pop Art analisada através das representações dos Estados Unidos e do Brasil na IX Bienal Internacional de São Paulo, em 1967', Master's Dissertation, Universidade Estadual de Campinas 1993.

7 For instance, in spite of the importance he attributed to this Biennial, Mário Pedrosa regarded the number of selected works as 'excessive' and considered that the jury had been particularly generous in its choices. Mário Pedrosa, 'Bienal e participação ... do povo', *Correio da Manhã*, Quarto Caderno, Rio de Janeiro 8 October 1967, Arquivo Bienal, p.1. See also: José Geraldo Vieira, 'Pop Art', *Correio da Manhã*, Quarto Caderno, Rio de Janeiro 17 September 1967, p.6; Geraldo Ferraz, 'Reverso na secção brasileira', *O Estado de São Paulo*, Suplemento Literário, São Paulo 23 December 1967, p.6. Aracy de Amaral considered, in two texts published in *O Estado de São Paulo* in 1967, that many of the works exhibited by the youngest generation of Brazilian artists lacked quality and technique. She linked this to Brazil's weak art education system: Aracy de Amaral, 'Arte sem educação, ou/e o Brasil visto de fora', *O Estado de São Paulo*, Suplemento Literário, São Paulo 25 November 1967, p.5 and 'Diante do espelho', *O Estado de São Paulo*, Suplemento literário, São Paulo 2 December 1967, p.3. Also published in Aracy de Amaral, *Arte e meio artístico: entre a feijoada e o x-burger (1961–1981)*, São Paulo 1983, pp.133–44.

8 De Amaral, 'Arte sem educação', 1967, p.133.

9 Ibid.

10 'uma explosão de vitalidade criadora'. Mário Schenberg, 'A representação brasileira na IX Bienal de São Paulo', *Correio da Manhã*, Quarto Caderno, Rio de Janeiro 17 September, 1967, Arquivo Bienal, p.3.

11 'o momento revolucionário atual da arte brasileira'. Ibid.

12 'uma espécie de anarquia geral, a marca de uma transição, de uma fase de transição'. Pedrosa, 'Bienal, GAM promove o debate', 1967, p.61.

13 'o pavilhão mais bem montado'. Jayme Maurício, 'IX Bienal, A bandeira como motivação pictórica', *Correio da Manhã*, Segundo Caderno, Rio de Janeiro 2 November 1967, p.1. A similar remark was also made by Frederico Morais in 'Roteiro da IX Bienal: Como ver o melhor em pouco tempo', *Diário de Notícias*, Caderno 2, Rio de Janeiro 22 September 1967, p.1; Marc Berkowitz, 'A Bienal n°9',*GAM*, vol. 9/10, 1967, pp.50–4.

14 Mário Pedrosa, 'Pop-art e Norte-Americanos na Bienal', *Correio da Manhã*, Quarto Caderno , Rio de Janeiro 15 October 1967, p.3.

15 Frederico Morais, 'A mulher na Bienal de São Paulo', *Diário de Notícias*, Revista Feminina, Rio de Janeiro 1 October 1967, Arquivo MAC USP, unpag.

16 Interestingly, in March 1967, Sérgio Ferro wrote that 'opposing itself to the sophistication of Warhol or Rosenquist, our painting is 'gross'. Its technique has the country's underdevelopment'. 'Opondo-se ao requinte de um Warhol ou de um Rosenquist, nossa pintura é "grossa". Sua tecnica tem o subdesenvolvimento do país'. Sérgio Ferro, 'Os limites da denúncia', *Rex Time*, vol.4, March 1967, p.3.

17 See, for instance, De Amaral, 'Diante do Espelho', 1967, p.14; Sergio Ferro, 'IX Bienal, Mondrian, Op e nós', *Correio da Manhã*, Quarto Caderno, Rio de Janeiro 8 October 1967, Arquivo Bienal, p.3.

18 See, for instance, Frederico Morais, 'Pop: Arte quente ou fria', *Diário de Notícias*, Caderno 2, Rio de Janeiro 1 February 1967,p.3; Odacir Soares, 'Op e pop no Brasil: nem op nem pop', *Diário de Notícias*, Suplemento literário, Rio de Janeiro 3 April 1966, p.6.

19 See, for example, Ferro, 'IX Bienal, Mondrian, Op e nós', 1967, p.3. At the same time, this reading is not unanimous. For instance, in his article 'Pop: Arte quente ou fria', Frederico Morais criticises Roberto Teixeira Leite's view of pop as passive regarding its approach to reality. Morais considers that pop art is not totally devoid of criticism and in this sense is sometimes 'hot'.

20 Mário Schenberg, 'Um novo realismo', in *Proposta 65*, exh. cat., FAAP, São Paulo December 1965, unpag.

21 'What we do – and when I say "we" I refer to António Dias, Pedro Escosteguy, Roberto Magalhães and some other vanguard artists – is absolutely not pop art or new figuration. It is, yes, a critical realism'. 'O que nós fazemos, e quando digo nós, me refiro a António Dias, Pedro Escosteguy, Roberto Magalhães e alguns outros artistas de vanguarda, não é absolutamente pop-arte ou nova figuração, é, isto sim, um realismo crítico'. Rubens Gerchman in *A Cigarra*, São Paulo c.1966. Also, in Marisa Alvarez Lima, *Marginália, Arte e cultura na 'Idade da Pedrada'*, Rio de Janeiro 2002, p.58.

22 Sônia Salzstein, 'Pop as Crisis in the public Sphere', in Kobena Mercer (ed.), *Pop Art and Vernacular Cultures*, London and Cambridge MA 2007, p.96.

23 An exhibition of works by Argentinean artists Ernesto Deira, Romuló Macció, Luis Felipe Noé and Jorge De La Vega took place at the Bonino gallery in Rio de Janeiro in 1963. Daisy Peccinini insists on the impact that these artists had on a young generation of Brazilian artists such as Rubens Gerchman and António Dias. In Daisy Peccinini, *Figurações Brasil anos 60*, São Paulo 1999, p.99. In 1964 the Museum of Modern Art in Rio exhibited Enrico Baj, Mimmo Rotella, Emilio Vedova and Piero Dorazio, and the gallery Relevo organised an exhibition entitled *Nova Figuração: Escola de Paris*. See Frederico Morais, *Cronologia das artes plásticas no Rio de Janeiro*, Rio de Janeiro 1994.

24 I draw here on a well-established historiography of Brazilian art of the 1960s that includes: Peccinini 1999; Paulo Sérgio Duarte, *Anos 60, Transformações da Arte no Brasil*, Rio de Janeiro 1998; Otília B.F. Arantes, 'De Opinião 65 à 18a Bienal', *Novos Estudos CEBRAP*, São Paulo, no.15, July 1986, pp.69–84.

25 *Opinion 65*.

26 Ceres Franco, 'Apresentação de Opinião 65', 1965. Reprinted in Frederico Morais, *Opinião 65*, exh. cat., Cíclo de exposições sobre arte no Rio de Janeiro, Galeria BANERJ, Rio de Janeiro August 1985, unpag.

27 For a discussion on this connection, see Mário Pedrosa, 'Opinião ... Opinião ... Opinião', *Correio da Manhã*, Quarto Caderno, Rio de Janeiro 11 September 1966, p.3.

28 As recalled by Frederico Morais, some of the Brazilian works on display – such as *Vencedor?* by António Dias, *O general* by Carlos Vergara and *Campanha de Ouro para o bem do Brasil* by Wesley Duke Lee – explicitly evoked the country's social and political situation. Frederico Morais, *Opinião 65: ontem, hoje*, Rio de Janeiro, 1985, unpag.

29 As explored, for instance, in the work of Hélio Oiticica, Raymundo Colares or Waldemar Cordeiro.

30 Augusto de Campos, for instance, created the word 'popcreto' to qualify Waldemar Cordeiro's new production. 'It looked like those "paintings", structurally concrete, had swallowed, in a critic and anthropophagic way, in a Brazilian form, the experience of American pop art'. 'Pareceu-me que aqueles "quadros", estruturalmente concretos, haviam deglutido, crítica e antropofagicamente, à brasileira, a experiência da pop art americana'. In José Louzeiro, 'Poetas da vanguarda tomam posição', *Correio da Manhã*, Segundo Caderno, Rio de Janeiro 13 March 1965, p.1.

31 See, for instance, Mário Pedrosa, 'Quinquilharia e pop-art', *Correio da Manhã*, Quarto Caderno, Rio de Janeiro 13 August 1967, p.1. See also: Soares, 'Op e Pop no Brasil: nem Op nem Pop', 1966, p.6. Ferreira Gullar, for example, considered, that 'an art of opinion can, because of its own critical, objective, nature, become an international movement without eliminating the elements that are specific to each culture, country, region.' 'Uma arte de opinião pode, por sua própria natureza crítica, objetiva, tornar-se um movimento internacional sem eliminar os elementos particulares a cada cultura, a cada país, a cada região'. Ferreira Gullar, 'Opinião 65', *Revista Civilização Brasileira*, Rio de Janeiro, vol.I, no.4, September 1965, p.225. Digital Archive ICAA, Museum of Fine Arts, Houston.

32 Schenberg, 'Um novo realismo', 1965, unpag.

33 'definir uma posição específica'. Oiticica, 'Situação da vanguarda no Brasil', 1966, in Daisy Peccinini, *Objeto na arte: Brail anos 60*, exh. cat., FAAP, São Paulo 1978, p.69.

34 'Como artista integrante dessa vanguarda brasileira, e téorico, digo que o acervo de criações, ao qual podemos chamar de vanguarda brasileira, são um fenomeno novo no panorama internacional, independente dessas manifestações típicas americanas ou européias'. Ibid.

35 'deslocamento do que se designa como arte'. Ibid.

36 In two articles of the same year, Frederico Morais, while quoting the term 'new objectivity', described the relation with foreign cultural models by referring to Oswald de Andrade's idea of anthropophagy – their assimilation and transformation in local terms – and insisted on the importance of taking into account Brazil's oppressive situation in order to comprehend the vanguard's engagement with political and social questions. Frederico Morais, 'A institucionalização da vanguarda brasileira', *Diário de Notícias*, Caderno 2, Rio de Janeiro 14 December 1966, p.1; Frederico Morais, 'Nova objetividade brasileira', Caderno 2, *Diário de Notícias*, Rio de Janeiro 29 December 1966, p.3.

37 Morais, 'A institucionalização da vanguarda brasileira', Caderno 2, 14 December 1966, p.1.

38 Morais, 'Nova objectividade brasileira', 29 December 1966, p.3.

39 In fact, the exhibition presented works by a young generation of realists – António Dias, Rubens Gerchman, Anna Maria Maiolino, Marcelo Nietsche, Nelson Leirner and Maria do Carmo Secco – along with works by a generation previously engaged in neo-concrete art, such as Lygia Pape, Lygia Clark and Oiticica himself, or in concretism, such as Waldemar Cordeiro. See *Nova objectividade brasileira*, exh. cat., Museu de Arte Moderna de Rio de Janeiro April 1967.

40 'Abordagem e tomada de posição em relação a problemas politicos, sociais e éticos'. Ibid, unpag.

41 Although the ideas of Ferrera Gullar are particularly important in this sense, the author is not able to develop this text in that specific direction. Significantly, Oiticica also referred to cultural colonialism by Europe and the USA and invoked 'super-anthropophagy' as a strategy, a 'defense', against 'exterior domination'. 'a defesa que possuímos contra tal domínio exterior'. Ibid, unpag. In this sense, the environment presented by the artist in the exhibition – entitled *Tropicália* and displaying a sort of tropical 'chacara' (farmstead) with sand, plants and macaws – emphasised typically Brazilian elements, thus constituting 'a very ambitious attempt to create a language that was ours, characteristic, confronting the international pop and op imagery in which a large part of our artists was immersed'. 'uma tentativa ambiciosíssima de criar uma linguagem nossa, característica, que fizesse frente à imagética pop e op internacional, na qual mergulhava boa parte de nossos artistas'. Hélio Oiticica in Maria Ignez Corrêa da Costa, 'O tropicalismo por trás da imagem digerida', *O Jornal do Brasil*, Caderno b, Rio de Janeiro 23 March 1968, p.1.

42 Morais 1985, unpag.

43 For a challenging discussion of the 'popular' in this context, see Rodrigo Alonso, 'Un'arte di contraddizioni', in *Pop, realismi e politica: Brasile – Argentina, anni sessanta*, exh.cat., Bergamo 2012, pp.25–37.

44 'Foi a primeira vez que o povo entrou no museu'. Morais, 1985, unpag.

45 *Seeing Listening*.

46 For a very interesting reading of this film, see Sérgio B. Martins, *Constructing an Avant-Garde. Art in Brazil 1949–1979*, Cambridge MA and London 2013. See also Clarival do Prado Valladares, 'Cinema instrumento de crítica: Ver e ouvir', *Jornal do Brasil*, Rio de Janeiro, 9 December 1967, Caderno b, p.4. The film is accessible via YouTube.

47 Unfortunately, it is not possible to discuss or mention the work of many artists that the author considers key to a wider understanding of Brazilian 'pop', among them: Dileny Campos, Maurício Nogueira Lima, Flávio Imperio, Wanda Pimentel, Wilma Martins, Décio Noviello, Judit Lauand, Waldemar Cordeiro, Raymundo Colares, Geraldo de Barros, Pedro Escosteguy, Marcelo Nietsche, Roberto Magalhães, António Manuel and Wesley Duke Lee. Also, this text does not include the significant events that took place in Belo Horizonte. See: Marília Andres Ribeiro, *Neovanguardas: Belo Horizonte anos 60*, Belo Horizonte 1997.

48 *Multidão*.

49 *Beauty Contest*.

50 See José Carlos Oliveira, 'E aconteceu o happening', *Jornal do Brasil*, Caderno b, Rio de Janeiro 26 April 1966, p.1.

51 'Galeria fecha com exposição', *O Estado de São Paulo*, São Paulo, 19 May 1967, Arquivo Bienal, p.9.

52 José Carlos Oliveira, 'E aconteceu o happening', *Jornal do Brasil*, Caderno b, Rio de Janeiro 26 April 1966, p.1.

53 In this sense one should remember the film by Antonio Carlos Fontoura, *Ver Ouvir* (1966) in which Rubens Gerchman is filmed with his painting in the street, and also a 1968 work by Nelson Leirner in which the artist disseminated posters in the streets of São Paulo. It was, according to the artist, a critique of propaganda itself. In 'Ao encontro do povo', *Jornal do Brasil*, Caderno b, Rio de Janeiro, 24 June 1968, p.2.

54 See, for instance, Frederico Morais, 'Parangolé de Oiticica: da capa ao urbanismo', *Diário de Notícias*, Caderno 2, Rio de Janeiro 27 July 1968, p.1.

55 See Harry Laus, 'Quando os quadros são muitos, bons e baratos', *Jornal do Brasil*, Caderno b, Rio de Janeiro 12 April, 1966, p.5.

56 See Walmir Ayala, 'Dia das bandeiras', *Jornal do Brasil*, Caderno b, Rio de Janeiro, 17 February 1968, p.1.

57 'numa mostra improvisada, na esquina da avenida Brasil com a rua Augusta, defronte da Igreja N.S. do Brasil'. 'As bandeiras apreendidas', *Folha de São Paulo*, 26 December 1967, Arquivo Bienal, p.10.

58 Apparently the flags had previously been exhibited at the Atrium gallery in São Paulo. 'Os temas da cidade e os temas do Sertão', *Folha de São Paulo*, 2° Caderno, 16 December 1967, Arquivo Bienal, p.3. See also: Geraldo Ferraz, 'Popularização da arte em bandeira', *O Estado de São Paulo*, 22 December 1967, Arquivo Bienal, p.12.

59 'Bandeiras. Bandeiras na praça', *O Globo*, Matutina, Rio de Janeiro, 16 February 1968, Arquivo Bienal, p.4.

60 'Domingo de bandinha e bandeiras', *Jornal do Brasil*, Caderno b, Rio de Janeiro 20 February 1968, Arquivo Bienal, p.8.

61 In 1966–7, he managed, with the Rex Group, composed of Wesley Duke Lee and Geraldo de Barros, among others, the alternative gallery space, Rex Gallery and Sons, in São Paulo and edited the magazine *Rex Time*, a publication combining information and opinions with satire.

62 *Cockroach box*.

63 Lygia Pape, '*Caixa de baratas* and *Caixa de formigas*', (not dated), in *Lygia Pape, Magnetized Space*, exh. cat., Museu Reina Sofia, Madrid; Serpentine Gallery, London; Pinacoteca do Estado de São Paulo 2011, p.243.

64 To my knowledge, the role of women in Brazilian pop – at the core of my research – has not yet been the subject of an in-depth study. The question has been briefly discussed, though, in Peccinini 1999 and in Marília Andres Ribeiro, *Teresinha Soares*, Belo Horizonte 2011. An important study that tackles aspects of this question is Trizoli 2011. For studies on women and pop at large see Kalliopi Minioudaki's groundbreaking research work. For instance: 'Pop Ladies and Bad Girls: Axell, Pauline Boty and Rosalyn Drexler', *Oxford Art Journal*, vol.30, issue 3, 2007, pp.402–30.

65 In the early 1960s, Maiolino studied printmaking with António Dias, Roberto Magalhães and Rubens Gerchman at the Escola Nacional de Belas Artes. See 'A Conversation between Anna Maria Maiolino and Helena Taty', in Helena Tatay, *Anna Maria Maiolino*, exh. cat., Fundació Tàpies, Barcelona, London 2011 p.39.

66 Maiolino 2011, ibid.

67 See *Lotus Lobo*, Belo Horizonte, 2001; *Lotus Lobo, Marca Registada*, Belo Horizonte 2006. Introduction by Marília Andres Ribeiro.

68 'No dizer de Ceres Franco há muita pintora por aí. Mas são raras aquelas que se enquadram nos padrões da estética contemporânea, onde mandam e determinam os homens'. 'Ceres Franco explica a nova dimensão da arte', *Jornal do Brasil*, Rio de Janeiro 22 March 1965, Revista de domingo, p.2.

69 Frederico Morais, 'A mulher na Bienal de São Paulo', *Diário de Notícias*, Rio de Janeiro 1 October 1967, Revista Feminina, unpag.

70 'a mulher está se considerando como tema, se questionando'. Ibid. unpag.

71 The title plays with the polysemy of the word 'presente', meaning the 'present' in time and the 'gift'. The artist generously gave me a photograph of the work, which had been destroyed.

72 Author's e-mail correspondence with the artist, 23 February 2012.

73 See 'Polícia tomou objeto', *O Estado de São Paulo*, São Paulo, 23 September 1967, Arquivo Bienal, p.7.

74 *O Herói*.

75 *Masters*.

76 *Of everything that could have been and has not been.* MAC USP collection.

77 *Lovemaking Box*.

78 See Trizoli 2011.

79 I refer, in particular, to the impact of Simone de Beauvoir's presence in Rio de Janeiro, in August/September 1960, which coincided with the publication of *The Second Sex* in Brazil. At the end of August De Beauvoir gave a conference on the female condition at the National Faculty of Philosophy in Rio de Janeiro. See, for instance, Helena Solberg, 'Simone de Beauvoir: a condição da mulher', *Diário de Notícias*, Rio de Janeiro 28 August 1960, O Metropolitano (unpag.) and Leo Gilson Ribeiro, 'Simone de Beauvoir e a Mulher', *Diário de Notícias*, Rio de Janeiro 4 September 1960, Suplemento Literário, p.3. In 1966 writer Rose-Marie Muraro published her book *A mulher na construção do mundo futuro*, Petrópolis 1966. On this question see also Trizoli 2011. On the participation of women in political movements against the regime, see Cynthia Sarti, 'O início do feminismo sob a ditadura no Brasil: o que ficou escondido', XXI Congresso Internacional da LASA, Chicago, 24–26 September 1998: biblioteca.clacso.edu.ar/ar/libros/lasa98/Sart.pdf (last accessed 23 January 2015).

80 *Trademark*.

81 Lygia Pape, 'A mulher na iconografia de massa', Relatório, 10 December1978. CEDOC Archive, FUNARTE, Rio de Janeiro (accessed in Autumn 2011).

82 *Eat me - gluttony or lust?*

83 Pape 1978, p.15.

Feminist Eruptions in Pop, Beyond Borders
Kalliopi Minioudaki

1 Evelyne Axell, *Pop Art, Nieuwe Figuratie, Nouveau Réalisme: Néo Dada et Tendances Apparentées*, exh. cat., Casino Knokke, Knokke, 1970, unpag.

2 Martha Rosler, 'Benjamin Buchloh: A Conversation with Martha Rosler', in Catherine de Zegher (ed.), *Martha Rosler: Positions in the Life World*, Cambridge, MA and London 1998, p.28.

3 Barbara Kruger, 'No Progress in Pleasure', in Carole Vance (ed.), *Pleasure and Danger: Exploring Female Sexuality*, London 1992, p.210.

4 While this argument is supported in this essay by the work of many artists in this exhibition, it also applies to the work of a number of other female contributors to pop in its various contexts, such as Pauline Boty, Rosalyn Drexler, Marie Louise Ekman, Jann Haworth, Marisol, Niki de Saint Phalle, Dalila Puzzovio, Marjorie Strider, Idelle Weber etc.

5 *Seductive Subversion: Women Pop Artists 1958–1968*, which started at the Rosenwald Wolf Gallery, University of the Arts, in Philadelphia in 2010 and ended at the Brooklyn Museum of Art, in New York in 2011, and *Power Up: Female Pop Art* at the Vienna Kunsthalle in 2010.

6 Of course, there are factors that modify the contours of the neglect of women in each context, such as the left politics underpinning the theorisation of pop in Spain as a realism critical of the Franco regime that undermined the sexual politics, or double militancy of its female participants. In this exhibition there are also artists, such as Minujín and González, whose association with pop art has played an important role in their national and international reputations – an effect concomitant with the internationalising drives that shaped the art discourse of their national contexts in the 1960s. Yet this hardly belies the effect of the silencing of female artists' contributions to pop art by its discourses in its centres and peripheries. For the author's analyses of the reasons for the neglect of women pop artists, including the role of the sexism of the 1960s society and art world and, ironically, feminist criticism, see Kalliopi Minioudaki, 'Other's Pop: The Return of the Repressed of Two Discourses', in *Power Up* 2010, pp.134–41 and 'Pop Proto-Feminisms Beyond the Woman Pop Artist', in Sid Sachs and Kalliopi Minioudaki (eds.), *Seductive Subversion* 2010, pp.90–141. See also Sue Tate, 'A Transgression Too Far: Women Artists and the British Pop Art Movement', in *Seductive Subversion*, pp.200–21.

7 Marsha Meskimmon, 'Chronology Through Cartography: Mapping 1970s Feminist Art Globally', in Cornelia Butler (ed.), *WACK! Art and the Feminist Revolution*, Cambridge, MA, and London 2007, pp.322–36.

8 It is also proved by the exaltation of Saint Phalle in 'Why the Feminine', an essay published in São Paulo in 1965 by Mona Gorovitz, one of several female artists who employed pop art in Brazil in the late 1960s to address both patriarchal and political repression from an often radical feminist perspective – as discussed by Gulia Lamoni in 'Brazilian Babies Suck Coca Cola: Women Artists and the Brazilian New Figuration in the late 1960s', a talk delivered at the 2012 Feminist Art History Conference, American University, Washington, DC.

9 A practice that resonates with Pauline Boty's fanzine rendering of stars (such as Jean Paul Belmondo or Marilyn Monroe) into objects of female desire and models of transgressive identification respectively.

10 Nicola L's coats also echo the sensate awakening of the body sought as much by the genderless mattress environments as the multisensory happenings of Minujín's experienced-based pop.

11 Lucy Lippard, 'Household Images in Art', in *The Pink Glass Swan: Selected Feminist Essays on Art*, New York 1995, p.62, first published in *Ms.*, vol.1, no.9, 1973.

12 As manifested in early works by Teresa Burga and Maria Pinińska-Bereś for instance, or artists not included in this show, such as Jann Haworth, Marie Louise Ekman, and the filmmaker Guvnor Nelson.

13 Dalila Puzzovio's installation *La Esfera del Tiempo* 1965 and Mimi Smith's *Girdle* 1966, made from bathtub mats, constitute important comparative examples.

14 See Agata Jakubowska, 'Ambiguous Liberation: The Early Works of Maria Pinińska-Bereś', *Konsthistorisk Tidskrift/Journal of Art History*, vol.83, no.2, 2014, pp.168–82.

15 As observed by Ana Maria Reyes, in 'Art and the Limits of Modernization: The Artistic Production of Beatriz Gonzáles During the National Front in Colombia', PhD thesis, University of Chicago 2011.

16 This is also pointed out by Iveković's juxtaposition of photos of herself and public photos of models from various international women's and lifestyle magazines, or of Marilyn Monroe in *Double Life* and *Tragedy of a Venus*, both of 1975–6. With their 'retroactive perspective' they conduct a 'double investigation' both of the 'social condition of consumerism and its reflection in a socialist framework', as well as 'an investigation into her personal role as a woman in structuring social conditions', as put by Branislava Andjelcović in 'How "Persons and Objects" Become Political in Sanja Iveković's Art', in *Sanja Iveković: Selected Works*, exh. cat., Fundació Antoni Tàpies, Barcelona 2008, p.21. By exposing her participation in the media-dictated performativity of gender, Iveković also admits to its pleasures and the inescapability of the society of spectacle.

17 See Laura Mulvey, 'Visual Pleasure and Narrative Cinema', *Screen*, vol.16, no.3, 1975, pp.6–18 and Griselda Pollock, 'What's Wrong with Images of Women?', *Screen Education*, no.24, Fall 1977, pp.25–33.

18 Jacques Collard, 'Evelyne Axell: Harmonie et Couleur', *Pourquoi Pas?*, 20 February 1969, p.140.

19 Axell often portrayed herself as an artist in the nude, based many of her nudes on photographs in which she mimics mass culture's poses of sexualised femininity, occasionally using wigs, and posed in the nude with her work.

20 Amelia Jones, 'The Rhetoric of the Pose: Hannah Wilke and the Radical Narcissism of Feminist Body Art', *Body Art: Performing the Subject*, Minneapolis and London 1998, pp.151–98.

21 See Kalliopi Minioudaki, 'Pop's Ladies and Bad Girls: Axell, Boty and Drexler', *Oxford Art Journal*, vol.30, no.3, Winter 2007–8, pp.402–31, and 'Bad Girl or Sweden's Bad Feminist? Thoughts on Marie Louise Ekman's Intimate Revolution and

its Misunderstandings', in Tone Hansen and Maria Lind (eds.), *No is Not an Answer: On the Work of Marie Louise Ekman*, Berlin 2013, pp.56–95.

22 Agata Jakubowska, 'Transferring Feminism Across the Iron Curtain. The Case of Natalia LL', talk presented at the panel *Towards Transnational Feminisms in the Arts?*, CAA Conference, Chicago 2014, and 'Natalia Ist Sex', in *Natalia LL Opera Omnia*, Wrocław 2009. See also Izabela Kowalczyk, 'The Ambivalent Beauty', in Bojana Pejić (ed.), *Gender Check: Femininity and Masculinity in the Art of Eastern Europe*, exh. cat., Museum Moderner Kunst Stiftung Ludwig Wien, Cologne 2010, pp.38–45.

Oiran Goes Pop: Contemporary Japanese Artists Reinventing Icons
Reiko Tomii

Author's Note: In this text, in order to differentiate the art-historical and theoretical interpretation of Pop art and the proto-Pop phenomena and the popular culture aspect of 'pop' (as in pop star, pop music, etc.), Pop is capitalised where appropriate. Japanese names are given in traditional order, surname first (e.g. Yokoo Tadanori).Exceptions are made in the case of individuals who primarily reside outside their native countries and adopt the Western system (e.g. Ushio Shinohara). All translation from the Japanese sources is by the author.

1 For the significance of 'international contemporaneity' in world art history, see Reiko Tomii, *Radicalism in the Wilderness: International Contemporaneity and 1960s Art in Japan*, Cambridge, MA, forthcoming in 2016.

2 See Reiko Tomii, 'Concerning the Institution of Art: Conceptualism in Japan' and 'Artists' Biographies', in *Global Conceptualism: Points of Origin, 1950s–1980s*, exh. cat., Queens Museum of Art, New York 1999, pp.14–29; Mika Yoshitake (ed.), *Requiem for the Sun: The Art of Mono-ha*, exh. cat., Blum & Poe, Los Angeles 2012.

3 For Anti-Art, see Charles Merewether and Rika Iezumi Hiro, *Art, Anti-Art, Non-Art: Experimentations in the Public Sphere in Postwar Japan, 1950–1970*, exh. cat., Getty Research Institute, Los Angeles 2007.

4 For an overview of Pop in Japan and its conflicted relationship with American art and culture, see Hiroko Ikegami, '"Drink More?" "No, Thanks!"': The Spirit of Tokyo Pop', in *International Pop*, exh. cat., Walker Art Center, Minneapolis, 2015.

5 For Shinohara's work, including these three series, see Hiroko Ikegami and Reiko Tomii, *Shinohara Pops!: The Avant-Garde Road, Tokyo/New York*, exh. cat., Samuel Dorsky Museum of Art, SUNY New Paltz 2012.

6 Ushio Shinohara, *Zen'ei no michi* (Avant-garde road) (1968); excerpted and translated by Reiko Tomii in ibid., p.100.

7 For more on the significance of Shinohara's *Imitation Art*, see Hiroko Ikegami, *The Great Migrator: Robert Rauschenberg and the Global Rise of American Art*, Cambridge, MA 2010, pp.174–202.

8 For a contemporary depiction of the life of *oiran*, see *Sakuran* (meaning 'derangement'), originally a manga by Anno Moyoco (from 2001 to 2003), which was subsequently made into a film by the contemporary artist Ninagawa Mika in 2007.

9 Ushio Shinohara, interview with the author, 27 October 2014.

10 Ushio Shinohara, interview with the author, 15 February 2015.

11 Tateishi (Ichige) Fumiko, interview with the author, 15 October 2014.

12 Tiger Tateishi, as quoted in 'Tateishi Taigaa nenpu' (Tiger Tateishi chronology), *Metamorufōze Taigā/ Metamorphose Tiger*, exh. cat., O Art Museum, Tokyo 1999, p.88.

13 Although only three examples are extant, the series is well documented in 35mm slides.

14 See Tateishi 1999, p.87.

15 Tanaami Keiichi in Nagasawa Akio, 'Tanaami Keiichi intabyū' (Interview with Tanaami Keiichi), insert in *Eizō kairaku-shugi: Tanaami Keiichi 2/ Tanaamism 2*, Tokyo 2003.

16 Ikegami 2015.

17 This work is accessible at http://www.ubuweb.com/film/tanaami_crayon.html (accessed 29 October 2014).

18 The meaning of Tanaami's motifs are gathered from an Oral History Interview with Tanaami Keiichi, conducted by Ikegami Hiroko and Miyata Yūka, 1 and 15 August 2013, Oral History Archives of Japanese Art (URL: www.oralarthistory.org); Nanzuka Shinji, interview with the author, 15 October 2014.

19 Matsumoto Toshio, ''75', quoted in *Hakuchūmu: Matsumoto Toshio no sekai – Gensō no radikarizumu/ Phantom/Vertigo Produced by Matsumoto Toshio: Radicalism of Illusion*, exh. cat., Kuma Museum of Art, Ehime Prefecture 2012, p.85.

20 Ibid., p.88.

21 For the project's history, see Yamamoto Atsuo, '"Watashi no aidoru" kara "Kioku no enkinjutsu", soshite ...' (From *My Idols* to *Perspective of Memory*, and ...), in *Kioku no enkinjutsu: Shinoyama, Yokoo o toru/Yokoo by Kishin*, exh. cat., Geijutsu Shinbunsha, Tokyo 2014, unpag.

22 Mishima Yukio, quoted in ibid.

Pop Art in Argentina
Mercedes Trelles-Hernández

1 Oscar Masotta, 'Prologue', El Pop Art, Buenos Aires 1967.

2 The Instituto Torcuato di Tella was a privately funded initiative. In 1963 it opened a venue for the arts in Florida Street, named the Centro de Artes Visuales. It was designed in a modernist style by architect Clorindo Testa.

3 Pierre Restany, 'Buenos Aires y el Nuevo Humanismo', *Planeta*, no.5, 1965, pp.119–29. Author's translation.

4 *Informalismo* is the name given to large abstract paintings, heavily dependent on texture effects and influenced by French *Informel. Nueva figuración*, on the other hand, refers to the re-introduction of figurative elements within paintings that still use a gestural approach and texture as their formal basis.

5 Delia Cancela worked in conjunction with Pablo Mesejean, creating both installations and fashion designs. In 1971 she instituted a fashion label, Paul and Delia. Most of her work since the 1970s is dedicated to fashion.

6 Jacqueline Barnitz, 'A Latin Answer to Pop', *Arts Magazine*, vol.40, no.8, June 1966.

7 'La Menesunda' by Marta Minujín, Rubén Santantonín and Jorge Romero Brest, flyer distributed for the presentation of *La Menesunda* at the ITDT, Buenos Aires, 26 May – 13 June 1965. Reprinted in Inés Katzenstein, *Listen Here Now! Argentine Art of the 1960s*, New York 2004, pp.107–10.

8 Marta Minujín quoted in Marta Minujín, *Obras 1959–1989*, Buenos Aires 2010. Lawrence Alloway, who visited Buenos Aires in 1966, two years after Pierre Restany, wrote harshly about the public and its restrictive and conservative taste, which he called 'exaggerated, controlling and punctilious': *Primera Plana*, 4 October 1966, as quoted in María José Herrera, *Pop, la consagración de la primavera*, Buenos Aires 2010, p.7.

9 Edgardo Giménez had worked in advertising. Many of his works, as well as those of Dalila Puzzovio, play with the idea of art as circulation and self-portrait as advertising. Especially interesting in this respect are a group of three offset photographic posters in which the lettering emulates publicity messages while the image is that of the artist himself.

10 Multiples are works of art produced in limited editions and designed to improve the availability of art.

11 Author's unpublished interview with Dalila Puzzovio and Carlos Squirru, Summer 1998.

Children of Marx and Coca-Cola: Pop in a Divided World
Sarah Wilson

1 See Christoph Bourseiller, *Les Maöistes, La folle histoire des gardes rouges français*, Paris 1996.

2 See Josef Augusta, *Les hommes préhistoriques*, Paris 1966, illustrated by Zdeněk Burian.

3 Slavoj Žižek on Einstein's 1917 fascist mass performances: 'In other words there is no "Fascism *avant la lettre*" because it is *the letter itself, the "nomination"* which makes out of the bundle of elements Fascism proper'. Afterword to Jacques Rancière, *The Politics of Aesthetics: the Distribution of the Sensible*, London 2006, p.63.

4 See also Joel Selvin, *Summer of Love*, New York 1994, and Christoph Grunenberg (ed.), *Summer of Love: Art of the Psychedelic Era*, London 2005.

5 Gaston Diehl was director of the Institut Franco-Vénézuélien. He wrote in the Latin American and European art press, while facilitating artists' trips to Europe.

6 Dina Scoppetone, in 'The Salon de Mai in Cuba and the *Mural colectiva, 1967*', MA thesis, London, Courtauld Insitute, 1998, discusses its role as a riposte to American cultural exchange programmes including the Visual Arts Unit of the OAS (Organisation of American States), the Center for Inter-American Relations at the Solomon R. Guggenheim

Museum and the Center for Inter-American Relations in New York, funded by the Rockefellers. See also Frances Stonor Saunders, *Who Paid the Piper: The CIA and the Cultural Cold War*, London 2000.

7 *São Paulo 9. Edward Hopper. Environment U.S.A.: 1957–1967*, with essays by William C. Seitz and Lloyd Goodrich, 1967 (bilingual). Hilton Kramer confirmed US dominance in the *New York Times*, 20 September 1967.

8 Rex Group artists: Wesley Duke Lee, Nelson Leirner, Geraldo de Barros, Carlos Fajardo, José Resende, Carlos Vergara, Carlos Zilio, Claudio Tozzi, Sergio Sister, Luiz Paulo Baravelli, Rubens Gerchman and Manuel Antonio. See Giulia Lamoni's 'Unfolding the 'present': Some notes on Brazilian 'pop' – in this catalogue.

9 See Sarah Wilson, *Picasso/Marx and Socialist Realism in France*, Liverpool 2013.

10 See 'Saison de la Nouvelle Peinture Anglaise, Patrick Caulfield, Derek Boshier', 4th Biennale de Paris, Musée d'art moderne de la Ville de Paris, 1965; Galerie Aujourd'hui, Brussels 1966; and *United States of America V Paris Biennale*, Musée d'art moderne de la ville de Paris, Pasadena Art Museum, Pasadena, 1967 with Llyn Foulkes, Craig Kauffman, John McCracken and Edward Ruscha.

11 Peter Saul, Oral history interview, Archives of American Art, 3–4 November 2009, http://www.aaa.si.edu/collections/interviews/oral-history-interview-peter-saul-15737, accessed 16 February 2015.

12 *My darling Clementine* was shown in his 2015 retrospective; see Christian Briend (ed.), *Hervé Télémaque*, Paris 2015.

13 *Pop Por, Pop Corn, Corny*, Jean Lacarde, art contemporain, Paris 29 June–14 August 1965; see also Télémaque with Alexia Guggemos, *Confidence d'Hervé Télémaque*, Paris 2015.

14 François Pluchart, *Pop Art & Cie, 1960–1970*, luxury edition with César expansion in gilded bronze, Paris 1971.

15 See Amy Dempsey, 'The Friendship of America and France: a New Internationalism', PhD thesis, University of London, 1999, and Camille Morineau (ed.), *Niki de Saint Phalle*, Bilbao and New York, with a text by Sarah Wilson. (English edition).

16 See Clémence Bigel, 'Le Pop'Art à Paris, une histoire de la réception critique des avant-gardes américaines entre 1959 et 1978', Mémoire de Master 2, Université de Paris 1, Panthéon-Sorbonne, 2 vols., 2013, with installation diagrams and collected criticism.

17 See *Four germinal painters, Four younger artists*, New York, Jewish Museum for the 32nd Venice Biennale, American Pavilion, and Hiroko Ikegami, *The Great Migrator, Robert Rauschenberg and the Global Rise of American Art*, MA 2010.

18 See Laurent Gervereau and David Mellor (eds.), *Les Sixties: Great Britain-France, 1962–73, The Utopian Years*, London 1997.

19 Franz Fanon, *Les Damnés de la Terre* (The Wretched of the Earth), Paris 1961, with a preface by Jean-Paul Sartre.

20 See 'L'art nègre', *Paris Match*, 21 May 1966; the show *Art nègre: sources, évolution, expansion* travelled from the Musée Dynamique, Dakar, to Paris's Grand Palais in 1966.

21 Compare Isidore Isou's hand-drawn parodies in *Initiation à la haute volupté*, Paris 1960, with the outright appropriated material used by Guy Debord in the *Internationale Situationniste*, 1958–69, discussed as 'applied strategy' by Emmanuel Guy, in '"Par tous les moyens, même artistiques": Guy Debord, stratège', PhD thesis, Université Paris XIII, 2015.

22 F. Mathey et al., *Bande dessinée et figuration narrative, histoire esthétique, production et sociologie de la bande dessinée mondiale: procédés narratifs et structure de l'image dans la peinture contemporaine*, Musée des Arts Décoratifs, Paris 7 April – 5 June 1967, with an introuction by *Tarzan* creator Burne Hogarth.

23 See the separate chapters on Bernard Rancillac, Jacques Monory, Gérard Fromanger etc., in Sarah Wilson, *The Visual World of French Theory: Figurations*, New Haven and London 2010; literary and cinema parallels could be greatly developed.

24 I resurrected *Vivre et laisser mourir… Live and Let Die* for *Paris Capital of the Arts, 1900–1968*, Royal Academy of Arts, London 2001; subsequently Edouardo Arroyo has sold this series to the Reina Sofia Museum, Madrid.

25 Gilles Aillaud, Eduardo Arroyo and Antonio Recalcati, *Une passion dans le désert, d'après une nouvelle de Honoré de Balzac*, Paris January 1965.

26 *F-111* was shown at Leo Castelli, New York, 17 April – 13 May 1965, then in the Jewish Museum; the European tour incuded the Moderna Museet, Stockholm; the Louisana Museum of Modern Art; the Stedelijk Museum, Amsterdam; the Städliche Kunsthalle, Baden Baden; the Kunsthalle, Bern; the Galerie d'Art Moderna, Rome and the Musée des arts décoratifs, Paris (7 April – 5 June 1967) prior to the showing at the São Paolo Biennale in September 1967 and finally the Metropolitan Museum, New York, April 1968.

27 See Vincent Chambariac, Amélie Lavin and Bertrand Tiller (eds.), *Les Malassis, une cooperative des peintres toxiques, 1968–1981*, Museé des Beaux-Arts, Dole 2014. Painters Lucien Fleury, Jean-Claude Latil, Michel Parré and Gérard Tisserand joined Cueco.

28 Fromanger's *Album The Red*, prefaced by Alain Jouffroy, was shown in 1970 at the Galerie Bama, Paris; at the Tokyo Print Biennial and at the Galerie Carmine Siniscalco, Rome in 1971; in Sarajevo and Mostar and at the Stedelijk Museum, Amsterdam in 1973; in 1976, in Bordeaux. See Serge July, *Gérard Fromanger*, Paris 2002, p.282.

29 'Ces oeuvres ne célèbrent pas franchement les manifestations et n'invitent à rien? … Elles prennent acte, énergiquement, d'une force en marche … L'ensemble est épique, gai et terrifiant … Des corps horrifiés et magnifiés par la rencontre avec leur destin historique.' Henri Cueco, in Gérard Gassiot Talabot (ed.), *Henri Cueco*, Paris 1995, pp.31–2.

30 See *Vladimir Ilitch Lénine, 1820–1924*, Grand Palais, Paris, May–June 1970.

31 See *Kunst und Politik*, Kustverein Karlsruhe, curated by Georg Bussman, June–September 1970; (then to the Frankfurter Kunstverein), and Herbert Marcuse, *One Dimensional Man, Studies in the Ideology of Advanced Industrial Society*, New York 1964, p.7.

32 Bernd Bücking, 'Karl Marx und die Kinder von Coca-Cola', *Tendenzen*, no.66, May–June 1970, pp.45–52.

33 Arroyo's *Miró Refait*, Galerie André Weil, Paris 15 February–3 March 1969, anticipated American 'appropriation art'.

34 See Simon Martin and Marco Livingstone, *Colin Self, Art in a Post-Nuclear Age*, Pallant House Gallery, Chichester 2008, pp.24, 42, etc.

35 For example, *Buste étincelant, Glowing Bust* 1967; see Sarah Wilson, 'Alina Szapocznikow in Paris: worlds in action and in retrospect', in Agata Jabubowska (ed.), *Alina Szapocznikow Awkward Objects*, Museum of Modern Art, Warsaw 2001, pp.211–28.

36 See Laura Cottingham, *Vraiment, féminisme et art, Le Magazin*, Centre National d'Art Contemporain de Grenoble 1997; Aline Dallier-Popper, *Art, féminisme, post-féminisme, un parcours de critique d'art*, Paris 2009; Kalliopi Minioudaki and Sid Sachs, *Seductive Subversion, Women Pop Artstis 1958–1968*, New York, 2010; Fabienne Dumont, *Artistes et féministes en France des années 1970*, Presses Universitaires de Rennes 2014.

37 Jean-François Lyotard, *Histoire de Ruth*, Paris 1983 and 'La Brûlure de silence', written for *Ruth Francken, Mirrorical Returns, Hostages, Wittgenstein Variations*, Musée des Beaux-Arts, La Cour d'Or, Metz 1991.

38 *Douze ans d'art contemporain en France, 1960–1972*, Grand Palais, Paris, Éditions des Musées Nationaux 1972

39 See Carole Hanish, 'The Personal is Political' 'Notes from the Second Year: Women's Liberation', 1970, www.carolehanisch.org /Chwritings/PEP.html (accessed 14 July 2015).

40 See Sarah Wilson, 'Rites of Passage, Myriam Bat-Josef and Performance', in *Myriam Bat-Josef, Paintings, Objects, Performances*, Paris 2005, pp.92–107.

41 Jean-Clarence Lambert, '1967, l'époque post-moderne est déjà commencé, *Opus International*, vol. 50, May 1974, p.26. Alain Touraine's *La societé postindustrielle*, Paris 1969, is the first reference in Lyotard (see note 42).

42 In *La Condition postmoderne. Rapport sur le savoir*, Paris 1979, Jean-François Lyotard speaks of 'l'incrédulité à l'égard des métarécits'. He relates this 'collapse of faith in grand narratives' to a crisis in metaphysical philosophy and its university institutions and the loss of heroes and aims (pp.7–8).

FURTHER READING

L. Alloway, R. Banham, D. Lewis, *This is Tomorrow*, exh. cat., Whitechapel Gallery, London 1956.

Mario Amaya, *Pop as Art: A Survey of the New Super-Realism*, Studio Vista, London 1965.

Mario Amaya, *The Obsessive Image*, exh. cat., Institute of Contemporary Arts, London 1968.

Aproximações do Espírito Pop: 1963–1968. Waldemar Cordeiro, Antonio Dias, Wesley Duke Lee, Nelson Leirner, exh. cat., Museu de Arte Moderna de São Paulo, 2003.

Stéphane Aquin (ed.), *Global Village: The 1960s*, exh. cat., The Montreal Museum of Fine Arts, 2003.

Arte de contradicciones. Pop, realismos y política. Brasil-Argentina 1960, exh. cat., Fundación PROA, Buenos Aires 2012.

J. Ashbery and P. Restany, *International Exhibition of the New Realists*, exh. cat., Sidney Janis Gallery, New York 1962.

T. Bezzola and F. Lentzsch (eds.), *Europop*, exh. cat., Kunsthaus Zürich, 2008.

Johanna Burton, *Pop Art: Contemporary Perspectives*, exh. cat., Princeton University Art Museum, Yale University Press, New Haven 2007.

Georg Bussmann (ed.), *Kunst und Politik*, exh. cat., Frankfurter Kunstverein, Karlsruhe 1970.

Jean-Luc Chalumeau, *La nouvelle figuration. Une histoire, de 1953 à nos jours*, Éditions Cercle d'art, Paris 2003.

Thomas Crow, *Long March of Pop Art – Art, Music and Design 1930–1995*, Yale Press 2015.

Thomas Crow, *Rise of The 1960s: American and European Art in the Era of Dissent, 1955–69*, Laurence King, London 1996.

S. Diederich and L. Pilz (eds.), *Ludwig Goes Pop*, exh. cat., Museum Ludwig, Köln, Cologne, 2014.

P. Dornacher, L. R. Hartl and S. Niggl (eds.), *Gruppe Geflecht. Arbeiten von 1965–1968*, exh. cat., Rathausgalerie der Landeshauptstadt München, Munich 2007.

Paulo Sergio Duarte, *The '60s: Transformations of Art in Brazil*, Campos Gerais, Rio de Janeiro 1998.

La figuration narrative dans les collections publiques, 1964–1977, exh. cat., Musée des Beaux-Arts d'Orléans, Paris 2005.

Mark Francis (ed.), *Les années pop 1956–1968*, exh. cat., Centre Pompidou, Paris, 2001.

Russell Ferguson (ed.), *Hand-Painted Pop American Art in Transition 1955–62*, exh. cat., The Museum of Contemporary Art, Los Angeles and New York 1992.

Hal Foster, *The First Pop Age: Painting and Subjectivity in the Art of Hamilton, Lichtenstein, Warhol, Richter, and Ruscha*, Princeton 2011.

Yuriko Furuhata, *Cinema of Actuality: Japanese Avant-Garde Filmmaking in the Season of Image Politics*, Durham and London 2013.

G. Gassiot-Talabot and O. Plassard, *Figurations critiques. 11 artistes des figurations critiques 1965 – 1975*, Espace Lyonnais de l'art contemporain (ELAC) 1992.

German Pop, exh. cat., Schirn Kunsthalle Frankfurt, Cologne 2014.

Christian Gether, *Europop: A dialogue with the US*, exh. cat., Arken Museum of Modern Art 1999.

C. Grunenberg and M. Hollein (eds.), exh. cat., *Shopping. A Century of Art and Consumer Culture*, Schirn Kunsthalle, Frankfurt 2002.

Barbara Haskell, *Blam! The Explosion of Pop, Minimalism and Performance 1958–1964*, exh. cat., Whitney Museum of American Art, New York 1984.

L. J. Hoptman and T. Pospiszyl (eds.), *Primary Documents: A Sourcebook for Eastern and Central European Art Since the 1950s*, The Museum of Modern Art, New York 2002.

Hiroko Ikegami, *The Great Migrator: Robert Rauschenberg and the Global Rise of American Art*, Cambridge, Mass. 2010.

I. Katzenstein and A. Giunta (eds.), *Listen, Here, Now! Argentine Art in the 1960s: Writings of the Avant-Garde*, The Museum of Modern Art, New York 2004.

Kunst und Politik, exh. cat., Kunsthalle Basel, Badischer Kunstverein 1969.

Lucy Lippard, *Pop Art*, New York 1966.

Marco Livingstone (ed.), *Pop Art*, exh. cat., The Royal Academy of Arts, London 1991.

Steven Henry Madoff, *Pop Art: A Critical History*, Berkeley 1997.

Magnet: New York. Argentine Art from the '60s, exh. cat., Fundación PROA, Buenos Aires 2010.

Kobena Mercer (ed.), *Pop Art and Vernacular Cultures*, Iniva, London and Cambridge, Mass. 2007.

Susan Martin (ed.), *Decade of Protest: Political posters from the United States, Vietnam, Cuba 1965–1975*, exh. cat., Track 16 Gallery, Santa Monica and Center for the Study of Political Graphics, Los Angeles 1996.

David Mellor, *The Sixties Art Scene in London*, exh. cat., Barbican Art Gallery, London 1993.

Mythologies Quotidiennes, exh. cat., Musée d'Art Moderne de la Ville de Paris, Paris 1964.

Piotr Piotrowski, *In the Shadow of Yalta: Art and the Avant-garde in Eastern Europe, 1945–1989*, London 2011.

Pop Art 1956–1968, exh. cat., Scuderie del Quirinale, Rome, Milan 2007.

Pop Art in Europa, exh. cat., Museum Het Valkof Nijmegen 2012.

Pop Art Myths, exh. cat., Museo Thyssen-Bornemisza, Madrid 2014.

Ł. Ronduda and P. Uklański, *Polish Art of the 1970s*, Ujazdowski Castle Centre for Contemporary Art, Warszaw 2009.

Pierre Restany, *Les Nouveaux Réalistes*, Galleria Apollinaire, Milan 1960.

J. Russel and S. Galik, *Pop Art Redefined*, London 1969.

S. Sachs and K. Minioudaki (eds.), *Seductive Subversion: Women Pop Artists, 1958–1968*, Philadelphia 2010.

Gabriele Shor (ed.), *Donna: Avanguardia femminista negli anni '70 dalla Sammlung Verbund di Vienna*, exh. cat., Sammlung Verbund, Vienna 2010.

Angela Stief (ed.), *Power Up – Female Pop Art*, exh. cat., Kunsthalle Wien, Cologne 2010.

Timo Valjakka (ed.), *SuperPop! Finnish and International Pop Art Then and Now*, exh. cat., Serlachius Museum Gösta, Julkaisija 2014.

Witness: Art and Civil Rights in the Sixties, exh. cat., Brooklyn Museum, New York 2014.

Evelyne Axell

Licensed in Both Ways
Permis dans les deux sens
1965
Oil paint on canvas
120×120
Private collection, London
(no.55)

Valentine
1966
Oil paint on canvas,
zipper and helmet
133×83
Collection of Philippe Axell
(no.35)

The Pretty Month of May
Le joli mois de mai
1970
Triptych, enamel
paint on Plexiglas
245.5×344.5×4.5
Mu.Zee Oostende
(no.58)

Joav BarEl

Kennedy Assassination
ידנק חצר
1968
Acrylic paint on canvas
80×60
Collection of Anke Kempkes,
BROADWAY 1602,
New York
(no.10)

Thomas Bayrle

The Laughing Cow
(Blue) Wallpaper
La Vache qui rit (blau)
Tapete
1967/2015
Wallpaper, silkscreen on paper
330×5 (each sheet)
Courtesy the artist, Air de Paris
and Groupe Bel, Paris
(endpapers/inside
cover of this book)

Renate Bertlmann

Exhibitionism
Exhibitionismus
1973
Wood, tempera, graphite,
Styrofoam and acrylic paint
Each 70.8×50×10
Tate Collection. Partial
gift of the artist and
partial purchase with funds
provided by Tate Members
2014
(no.134)

Cornel Brudaşcu

Composition
Compoziţie
1970
Oil paint on canvas
118×165×2.5
The Art Museum
of Cluj-Napoca, Romania
(no.146)

Group Portrait
Portret de grup
1970
Oil paint on canvas
161×180
Collection of the artist
(no.150)

Guitarist
Chitarist
1970
Oil paint on canvas
130×93
The Museum of
Visual Arts of Galati
(no.12)

Portrait (Ion Munteanu)
Portret (Ion Munteanu)
1970
Oil paint on canvas
120×91
Private collection,
The Netherlands
(no.13)

Youth on the building yard
Tineri pe şantier
1970
Oil paint on canvas
149.5×157×2
The Art Museum
of Cluj-Napoca, Romania
(no.147)

Boris Bućan

Bucan Art:
(according to Swissair)
1972
Acrylic paint on canvas
50×70
Courtesy Museum of
Contemporary Art Zagreb
(no.27 A)

Bucan Art:
(according to Pepsi)
1972
Acrylic paint on canvas
50×70
Marinko Sudac Collection
(no.27 B)

Bucan Art:
(according to Avis)
1972
Acrylic paint on canvas
50×70
Marinko Sudac Collection
(no.27 C)

Bucan Art:
(according to JAT)
1972
Acrylic paint on canvas
50×70
Marinko Sudac Collection
(no.27 D)

Bucan Art:
(according to Pan Am)
1972
Acrylic paint on canvas
50×70
Atlantic Grupa Collection
(no.27 E)

Bucan Art:
(according to Dunhill)
1972
Acrylic paint on canvas
50×70
Marinko Sudac Collection
(no.27 F)

Bucan Art:
(according to KLM)
1972
Acrylic paint on canvas
50×70
Atlantic Grupa Collection
(no.27 G)

Bucan Art:
(according to Coca-Cola)
1972
Acrylic paint on canvas
50×70
Marinko Sudac Collection
(no.27 H)

Bucan Art:
(according to IBM)
1972
Acrylic paint on canvas
50×70
Atlantic Grupa Collection
(no.27 I)

Bucan Art:
(according to ELF)
1972
Acrylic paint on canvas
50×70
Marinko Sudac Collection
(no.27 J)

Bucan Art:
(according to Nivea)
1972
Acrylic paint on canvas
50×70
Marinko Sudac Collection
(no.27 K)

Bucan Art:
(according to a No
Parking traffic sign)
1972
Acrylic paint on canvas
50×70
Marinko Sudac Collection
(no.27 L)

Bucan Art:
(according to Marlboro)
1972
Acrylic paint on canvas
50×70
Courtesy Museum of
Contemporary Art Zagreb
(no.27 M)

Bucan Art:
(according to Esso)
1972
Acrylic paint on canvas
50×70
Marinko Sudac Collection
(no.27 N)

Bucan Art:
(according to Life Magazine)
1972
Acrylic paint on canvas
50×70
Marinko Sudac Collection
(no.27 O)

Bucan Art:
(according to Agfa)
1972
Acrylic paint on canvas
50×70
Courtesy Museum of
Contemporary Art Zagreb
(no.27 P)

Bucan Art:
(according to Polydor)
1972
Acrylic paint on canvas
50×70
Marinko Sudac Collection
(no.27 Q)

Bucan Art:
(according to INA)
1972
Acrylic paint on canvas
50×70×2 cm
Marinko Sudac Collection
(no.27 R)

Bucan Art:
(according to a
500m traffic sign)
1972
Acrylic paint on canvas
50×70×2 cm
Courtesy Museum of
Contemporary Art Zagreb
(no.27 S)

Bucan Art:
(according to BMW)
1972
Acrylic paint on canvas
50×70×2 cm
Marinko Sudac Collection
(no.27 T)

Teresa Burga

Cubes
Cubos
1968
6 objects, painted plywood
Each 40×40×40
Mr. Eduardo
Hochschild Collection
(no.99)

Delia Cancela

Broken Heart
Corazón destrozado
1964
Oil paint on canvas,
lace and painted
wood panels
150×100
Collection
Mauro Herlitzka
(no.91)

Rafael Canogar

The Punishment
El castigo
1969
Polyester and wood
195×151×70
Private collection
(no.107)

Judy Chicago

Bigamy Hood
1965–2011
Sprayed automotive
lacquer on car hood
109×109×10.9
Courtesy Judy Chicago
/ Riflemaker London
(no.115)

Birth Hood
1965/2011
Sprayed automotive
lacquer on car hood
109×109×10.9
Courtesy Judy Chicago
/ Riflemaker London
(no.116)

Flight Hood
1965/2011
Sprayed automotive
lacquer on car hood
109×109×10.9
Courtesy Judy Chicago
/ Riflemaker London
(no.56)

Mari Chordà

The Great Vagina
La gran vagina
Enamel and oil paint
on canvas
1966
82.1×99.7
Private collection
(no.133)

Coitus Pop
1968
Enamel paint on wood
50×60
Collection of the artist
(no.132)

Raymundo Colares

Untitled
Sem Titulo
1969
Enamel paint on
folded aluminium plate
100×231×15
Coleção João Sattamini,
loaned to Museu de Arte
Contemporânea de Niterói
(no.44)

Equipo Crónica

Concentration or
Quantity becomes Quality
Concentración o La cantidad
se transforma en calidad
1966
Acrylic paint on canvas
160×160
Francisco Fandos
(no.39)

Socialist Realism and
Pop Art in the Battlefield
El realismo socialista y el
Pop Art en el campo de batalla
1969
Acrylic paint on canvas
200×200
Museo Nacional Centro
de Arte Reina Sofía, Madrid.
Depósito Temporal Colección
de Manolo Valdés, 2010
(no.1)

Henri Cueco

Large Protest
Grande manifestation
1969
Fixed black iron tubes
structure, 8 cut up plywood
figures lacquered in white,
black, and red with cold
enamel glycerophtallic paint
400×600×400
Collection of the artist
(no.6)

The Red Men, bas-relief
Les Hommes rouges, bas-relief
1969
Cold enamel glycerophtallic
paint on plywood
260×310×21
Collection of the artist
(no.106)

Antonio Dias

Accident at the Game
Acidente no Jogo
1964
Acrylic paint and oil paint
and vinyl on wood and
padded fabric
103×77×55
Collection of the artist
(no.45)

Note on the
Unforeseen Death
Nota sobre a morte
imprevista
1965
Acrylic paint on wood,
padded fabric,
Plexiglass and Duratex
195×176×63 cm
Collection of the artist
(no.5)

Romanita Disconzi

Interpretation Totem
Totem da Interpretação
1969
Duco paint on plywood
Each 40×40×40
Collection Museu de Arte
do Rio Grande do Sul
Ado Malagoli
(no.118)

Wesley Duke Lee

Trapeze or a Confession
O Trapézio
ou Uma Confissão
1966
One panel in aluminium,
cloth and plastic, two panels
in aluminium and plastic,
four paintings in graphite
and oil paint on canvas,
steel cable and cloth rope
Each panel 200×200
Roger Wright Collection,
on long-term loan to
the Pinacoteca do Estado
de São Paulo
(no.15)

Erró

Big Tears for Two
1963
Oil paint on canvas
130×195
Private collection, Paris
(no.102)

American Interior No 1
1968
Glycerophtalic paint
on blended fabric
130×162×2.5
museum moderner
kunst stiftung ludwig wien
(no.100)

American Interior No 5
1968
Glycerophtalic paint
on blended fabric
130×162×2.5
museum moderner kunst
stiftung ludwig wien
(no.130)

American Interior No 9
1968
Glycerophtalic paint
on blended fabric
130×162×2.5
museum moderner
kunst stiftung ludwig wien
(no.131)

Öyvind Fahlström

Mao-Hope March
1966
16 mm film, black and
white, sound, 4 min 30 sec
Sharon Avery-Fahlström,
The Öyvind Fahlström
Foundation
(no.40)

Ruth Francken

Man Chair
Siège Homme
1971
Polyurethane foam,
white lacquered epoxy
102.5
ADAM Art & Design
Atomium Museum
(Atomium, Brussels)
(no.81)

Gérard Fromanger

Album The Red
Album Le Rouge
1968–70
21 serigraphies
Each 60×90 cm
Collection of the artist
(no.139)

Film-tract n° : 1968
1968
In collaboration
with Jean Luc Godard
16mm film digitalised,
colour silent 2 min 49 sec
Collection of the artist
(no.140)

Àngela García

Breathing Out
(From the series *Morphologies*)
Respirando
(serie Morfologías)
1973
Acrylic paint on
canvas and wood
165×110×1.5
Collection of the artist
(no.110)

Divertimento
(From the series *Morphologies*)
Divertimento
(serie Morfologías)
1973
Acrylic paint on
canvas and wood
150×100×1.5
Collection of the artist
(no.109)

Self-Distraction
(From the series
Morphologies)
Yomisma (serie Morfologías)
1973
Acrylic paint on
canvas and wood
100×100×1.5
Collection of the artist
(no.108)

Beatriz González

The Suicides of Sisga I
The suicides of Sisga I
1965
Oil paint on canvas
120×100
Private collection
(no.78)

The Suicides of Sisga II
Los suicidas del Sisga II
1965
Oil paint on canvas
120×100
Museo La Tertulia
(no.79)

The Suicides of Sisga III
Los suicidas del Sisga III
1965
Oil paint on canvas
100×80
Colección Museo
Nacional de Colombia
(no.80)

The Last Table
La última mesa
1970
Enamel on metal plate
mounted within metal furniture
105×205×75
Tate Collection. Presented
by the American Fund for
the Tate Gallery, courtesy
of the Latin American
Acquisitions Committee 2013
(nos.135, 136)

Eulàlia Grau

Rich and Famous
(Ethnography)
Rics i famosos
(Etnografia)
1972
Photographic emulsion
and aniline on canvas
120.5×124.5
Private collection
(no.144)

Chicks and Cops
(Ethnography)
Donetes i polis
(Etnografia)
1973
Photographic emulsion,
aniline and acrylic paint
on canvas
170.5×120.5
Private Collection
(no.142)

Miss and Gangsters
(Ethnography)
Misses i gàngsters
(Etnografia)
1973
Photographic emulsion
and paint on canvas
108.5×115.8
MACBA Collection.
MACBA Consortium
(no.143)

Nixon (Ethnography)
Nixon (Etnografia)
1973
Photographic emulsion
on canvas
112.5×57
Private collection
(no.138)

Office (Ethnography)
Oficina (Etnografia)
1973
Photographic emulsion
and aniline on canvas
163.5×102.5
Private collection
(no.137)

Panic (Ethnography)
Pànic (Etnografia)
1973
Photographic emulsion,
aniline and acrylic paint
on canvas
98.5×120
Private collection
(no.141)

Vacuum cleaner
(Ethnography)
Aspiradora
(Etnografia)
1973
Photographic emulsion
and paint on canvas
164×110 cm
MACBA Collection. MACBA
Consortium
(no.73)

Sanja Iveković

Sweet Violence
Slatko nasilje
1974
Video, black and white,
sound, 5 min 39 sec
Courtesy of the artist
and espaivisor gallery.
(no.23)

Jozef Jankovič

Private Manifestation
Súkromná manifestácia
1968
Wood, plaster, fabric
and polyester
241×90×50
Meulensteen Collection
(no.111)

Kiki Kogelnik

Bombs in Love
1962
Mixed media with
Plexiglas and acrylic
paint on bomb casings
122×63×25
Kiki Kogelnik Foundation
Vienna / New York
(no.14)

Fallout
c.1964
Mixed media with oil
paintand acrylic paint
and sheet vinyl on canvas
137×183
Kiki Kogelnik Foundation
Vienna / New York
(no.57)

Hanging
1970
Mixed media with acrylic
paint, sheet vinyl and
hangers on canvas
168×137
Kiki Kogelnik Foundation
Vienna / New York
(no.54)

Friends
1971
Oil paint and acrylic
paint on canvas
170×680×43
Kiki Kogelnik Foundation
Vienna / New York
(no.41)

Komar and Melamid

Post Art No 1 (Warhol)
1973
Oil paint on canvas
121.9×91.4×3.8
Courtesy Ronald Feldman
Fine Arts, New York
(no.16)

Post Art No 2 (Lichtenstein)
1973
Oil paint on canvas
107×107
Courtesy The Boxer
Collection London
(no.17)

Post Art No 3 (Indiana)
1973
Oil paint on canvas
107×107
Courtesy The Boxer
Collection London
(no.18)

Nicola L

Woman Sofa
Femme-canapé
1968
Vinyl
31×208×85
ADAM Art & Design
Atomium Museum
(Atomium, Brussels)
(no.101)

Little TV Woman:
'I Am the Last Woman Object'
1969
Vinyl, wood and a television
111.5×50×45
Collection Xavier Gellier
(no.123)

Red Coat
1969
Vinyl, eleven slits and
eleven nodded jackets
Dimensions variable
Collection of the artist
(no.153)

Red Coat
1969–1970s
Super 8 film digitalised
12 min 39 sec
Collection of the artist

Uwe Lausen

Geometer
1965
Acrylic paint on canvas
180.5×221
DASMAXIMUM, Traunreut
(no.104)

Pilot
1966
Coloured, reinforced plaster
160×60×45
Private collection
(no.38)

Natalia LL

Consumer Art, excerpts
Sztuka konsumpeyjna,
fragmenty
1972, 1974, 1975
16mm film, digitalised
15 min 47 sec
Natalia LL and
lokal_30 gallery Warsaw
(no.24)

Sergio Lombardo

John F. Kennedy
1962
Enamel paint on canvas
170×200
Private collection
(no.151)

Nikita Krusciov
1962
Enamel paint on canvas
190×250
Private collection
(no.152)

Anna Maria Maiolino

Glu Glu Glu
1966
Acrylic paint on
quilted fabric
110×59×13
Gilberto Chateaubriand
MAMRJ Collection
(no.36)

Marisol

My Mum and I
Mi Mama y Yo
1968
Painted bronze and aluminium
185.4×142.2×142.2
Collection of the artist
(no.2)

Raúl Martínez

Listen America
Oye América
c.1967
Oil paint on canvas
292×256
Colección Museo Nacional
de Bellas Artes, Cuba
(no.105)

Toshio Matsumoto

Mona Lisa
1973
16 mm film transferred
to digital file 3 min 50 sec
Toshio Matsumoto
(no.82)

Marta Minujín

Mattress
Colchón
1962
Painted mattress
220×70×20
Collection of the artist
(no.95)

La Menesunda
1965
16mm film, digitalised
8 min 09 sec
Marta Minujín
Collection of the artist
(no.96)

Marcello Nitsche

I Want You
Eu quero você
1966
Cotton padded plastic
and acrylic paint on PVC
127×106×11.6
Coleção Museu de Arte
Moderna de São Paulo,
Fundo para aquisição
de obras para o acervo
MAM – Pirelli
(no.33)

Kill Fly
Mata mosca
1967
Plastic pipe, paint on
polystyrene and paint
on fiberglass and resin
68.5×312.5×58.7
Roger Wright Collection,
on long-term loan to the
Pinacoteca do Estado
de São Paulo
(no.46)

Isabel Oliver

Beauty Products (from
the series *The Woman*)
Cosmética (serie La Mujer)
1970–3
Acrylic paint on canvas
98×98×2
Collection of the artist
(no.69)

Happy Reunion (from the
series *The Woman*)
Reunión feliz (serie La Mujer)
1970–3
Acrylic paint on canvas
98×98×2
Collection of the artist
(no.72)

It is a Girl (from the
series *The Woman*)
Es niña (serie La Mujer)
1970–3
Acrylic paint on canvas
98×98×2
Collection of the artist
(no.71)

The Family (from the
series *The Woman*)
La Familia (serie La Mujer)
1970–3
Acrylic paint on canvas
98×98×2 cm
Collection of the artist
(no.64)

Surgery (from the
series *The Woman*)
Cirugía (serie La Mujer)
1970–3
Acrylic paint on canvas
98×98×2
Collection of the artist
(no.70)

Dušan Otašević

Towards Communism
on Lenin's Course
К коммунизму ленинским
курсом (*K kommunizmu
leninskim kursom*)
1967
Painted wood
Each 95×95
Collection of the artist
(no.112)

Ulrike Ottinger

Female Mannequin –
Legs Under Water
Femme Mannequin –
Les Jambes sous l'eau
1966
Mannequin, wood
and acrylic paint
180×42×62
Collection of the artist
(no.7)

God of War
Dieu de guerre
1967–8
Triptych. Acrylic paint
on wood
190×260×60 (open)
190×130×60 (closed)
Collection of the artist
(no.126)

Joe Overstreet

The New Jemima
1964, 1970
Acrylic paint on fabric
over plywood construction
260×154.3×43.8
The Menil Collection, Houston
(no.117)

Maria Pinińska-Bereś

Love Machine
Maszynka milosci
1969
Wood, plywood, papier
mâché, metal handle,
tempera, assemblage
94×63.5×71
Muzeum Narodowe we
Wroclawiu (The National
Museum in Wroclaw)
(no.76)

Screen
Parawan
1973
Plywood, canvas,
tempera, assemblage
194×132×63
Muzeum Narodowe we
Wroclawiu (The National
Museum in Wroclaw)
(no.77)

Joan Rabascall

Atomic Kiss
1968
Acrylic paint on canvas
162×97
MACBA Collection.
Barcelona City Council Fund
(no.113)

Bernard Rancillac

*At Last, a Silhouette
Slimmed to the Waist
Enfin silhouette affinée
jusqu'à la taille*
1966
Vinyl paint on canvas
195×130
Musée de Grenoble
(no.28)

*Dinner-Party of
the Head-Hunters
Le dîner des
collectionneurs de têtes*
1966
Vinyl paint on wood,
3 sections
170×150
Genevieve and
Jean Boghici collection
(no.103)

*Pilules Capsules
Conciliabules*
1966
Vinyl paint on canvas
146×228
Collection Marie-Claude
Rancillac
(no.37)

Equipo Realidad

*Divine Proportion
La divina proporción*
1967
Acrylic paint on board
131.5×114
Museo Nacional Centro
de Arte Reina Sofía, Madrid
(no.114)

Raimo Reinikainen

*Sketch 1 for the U.S. Flag
Luonnos 1. Yhdysvaltain lipuksi*
1966
Oil paint on paper with
newspaper, collage
36×65
The Museum of Contemporary
Art Kiasma, Finnish National
Gallery, Helsinki, Finland
(no.29)

*Sketch 2 for the U.S. Flag
Luonnos 2. Yhdysvaltain lipuksi*
1966
Oil paint on canvas with
newspaper, collage
40×65
Helsinki Art Museum
(no.31)

*Sketch 3 for the U.S. Flag
Luonnos 3. Yhdysvaltain lipuksi*
1966
Oil paint on canvas with
newspaper, collage
40×65
Helsinki Art Museum
(no.30)

*Sketch 4 for the U.S. Flag
Luonnos 4. Yhdysvaltain lipuksi*
1966
Oil paint on canvas with
newspaper, collage
40×65
Turku Art Museum
(no.32)

Glauco Rodrigues

*The Song of Solomon –
Concha Shell,* from the
series *Concha Shell
Cântico dos Cânticos –
Concha Shell –
série Concha Shell*
1967
Ink self-propelled on acrylic paint
and 3D glasses
127×136×16
Gilberto Chateaubriand
MAMRJ Collection
(no.43)

Peter Roehr

Film-Montages I–III
(extracts)
1965
16mm film, digitalised
9 min 47 sec (extracts)
Copyright The Estate
of Peter Roehr; Courtesy Mehdi
Chouakri, Berlin
(nos. 160, 161)

Sound-Montages I + III
(extracts)
1966
Audio CD
5 min 2 sec (extracts)
Copyright The Estate
of Peter Roehr; Courtesy
Mehdi Chouakri, Berlin

Martha Rosler

All works from the series
*Body Beautiful, or Beauty
Knows No Pain*

Cold Meat I
c.1966–72
Photomontage
The artist and Galerie Nagel
Draxler, Berlin / Cologne
(no.61)

Cold Meat II, or Kitchen II
c.1966–72
Photomontage
The artist and Galerie Nagel
Draxler, Berlin / Cologne
(no.62)

Damp Meat
c.1966–72
Photomontage
The artist and Galerie Nagel
Draxler, Berlin / Cologne
(no.59)

Kitchen I, or Hot Meat
c.1966–72
Photomontage
The artist and Galerie Nagel
Draxler, Berlin / Cologne
(no.60)

Pop Art, or Wallpaper
c.1966–72
Photomontage
The artist and Galerie Nagel
Draxler, Berlin / Cologne
(no.125)

*Woman With Vacuum,
or Vacuuming Pop Art*
c.1966–72
Photomontage
The artist and Galerie Nagel
Draxler, Berlin / Cologne
(no.63)

Mario Schifano

*Comrades comrades
Compagni compagni*
1968
Enamel and spray paint
on canvas and Perspex
140×140
Private collection, Courtesy
Fondazione Marconi
(no.4)

*Comrades comrades
Compagni compagni*
1968
Enamel and spray paint
on canvas and Perspex
140×140
Private collection, Courtesy
Fondazione Marconi
(no.158)

*Comrades comrades
Compagni compagni*
1968
Enamel and spray paint
on canvas and Perspex
140×140
Private collection, Courtesy
Fondazione Marconi
(no.159)

Colin Self

*Leopardskin Nuclear
Bomber No.2*
1963
Wood, aluminium,
steel and fabric
9.5×80×42
Tate Collection. Purchased 1993
(no.124)

Dorothée Selz

*Relative Mimetism –
Panther Woman
Mimétisme relatif -
Femme panthère*
1973
Gelatine silver print and
coloured mortar on wood
30×36×3
MACBA Collection.
MACBA Consortium
(no.128)

*Relative Mimetism – 'The
Vargas Girl' Woman After Vargas
Mimétisme relatif – Femme
'The Vargas Girl' d'après Vargas*
1973
Gelatine silver print and
coloured mortar on wood
36×30×3
MACBA Collection.
MACBA Consortium
(no.129)

*Relative Mimetism –
Woman with Boots and Lamp
Mimétisme relatif – Femme
avec bottes et lampadaire*
1973
Gelatine silver print and
coloured mortar on wood
30×36×3
MACBA Collection.
MACBA Consortium
(no.127)

Ushio Shinohara

*Doll Festival
女の祭り (Onna no Matsuri)*
1966
Fluorescent paint, oil paint,
plastic board on plywood
196.1×399.7
Hyogo Prefectural Museum of
Art, The Yamamura Collection
(no.83)

Teresinha Soares

*Die Wearing the Legitimate
Espadrille* (from the series
Vietnam)
*Morra usando a legítima
alpargata (Série Vietnã)*
1968
Mixed media
116×152.8×2.5
Collection of the artist
(no.51)

*So Many Men Die and
I Am Here So Lonely*
(from the series *Vietnam*)
*Morrem tantos homens
e eu aqui tão só (Série Vietnã)*
1968
Mixed media
117.5×152.5
Collection Universidade
Federal de Minas Gerais (UFMG)
(no.50)

Shinkichi Tajiri

Machine No.7
1967–8
Steel, aluminium,
Plexiglas and chromed iron
175×225×78
Museum Het Valkhof, Nijmegen,
The Netherlands, loan Cultural
Heritage Agency of the
Netherlands (RCE)
(no.11)

Keiichi Tanaami

Commercial War
1971
Animation film 4 min 30 sec
Courtesy of the artist
and NANZUKA
(no.145)

Crayon Angel
1975
Animation film 2 min 50 sec
Courtesy of the artist and
NANZUKA
(no.89)

Parviz Tanavoli

*The Poet and the Beloved
of the King*
1964–6
Wood, tin-plate, copper,
steel, fluorescent light,
Perspex and oil paint
189.7×108×107
Tate Collection. Purchased
with funds provided by
Edward and Maryam
Eisler 2012
(no.34)

Disciples of Sheikh San'an
1974
Screenprint on paper
100×69.8 cm
Tate Collection. Purchased
with funds provided by the
Middle East North Africa
Acquisitions Committee 2012
(no.122)

Nightingale
1974
Screenprint on paper
50×70
Tate Collection. Presented
by the artist 2012

Poet and Bird
1974
Screenprint on paper
50×70
Tate Collection. Purchased
with funds provided by the
Middle East North Africa
Acquisitions Committee 2012

Poet and Nightingale
1974
Screenprint on paper
76×60
Tate Collection. Purchased
with funds provided by the
Middle East North Africa
Acquisitions Committee 2012
(no.120)

Poet Squeezing Lemon
1974
Screenprint on paper
69.8×49.1
Tate Collection. Purchased
with funds provided by the
Middle East North Africa
Acquisitions Committee 2012
(no.119)

Three Lovers
1974
Screenprint on paper
49.7×70
Tate Collection. Purchased
with funds provided by
the Middle East North
Africa Acquisitions
Committee 2012

*Disciples of
Sheikh San'an*
1975
Wool
206×155×1.2
Tate Collection. Purchased
with funds provided by the
Middle East North Africa
Acquisitions Committee 2012
(no.121)

Joe Tilson

*Page 7 Snow White
and the Black Dwarf*
1969
Screenprint on canvas
on wood relief
186.7×125
Collection Museu
Coleção Berardo
(no.156)

Page 9 Black Dwarf
1969
Screenprint on canvas
on wood relief
186.7×125
Private collection
(no.157)

Page 18 Muhammad Speaks
1969–70
Screenprint and oil paint
on canvas on wood relief
186.7×125
Courtesy Galleria Tega,
Milano, Italy
(no.3)

Page 19 He, She & It
1969–70
Screenprint and oil paint
on canvas on wood relief
186.7×125
Museum Het Valkhof,
Nijmegen, The Netherlands
(no.154)

Page 20 He She & It
1969–70
Screenprint on canvas
on wood relief
186.7×125
Marlborough Fine Art, London
(no.155)

Claudio Tozzi

*Multitude
Multidão*
1968
Acrylic paint on agglomerate
199×120×4.5
Coleção Museu de Arte
Moderna de São Paulo, Fundo
para aquisição de obras para
o acervo MAM – Pirelli
(no.42)

Chryssa Vardea

Study for Gates No.4
1967
Perspex, 8 neon lights
and timer
109.2×88.3×70.2
Tate Collection. Presented
by S. Herbert Meller through
the American Federation of
Arts 1968
(no.162)

Tadanori Yokoo

KISS KISS KISS
1964
Animation film, 2 min 05 sec
Courtesy of the artist
(no.87)

Jana Želibská

*Breasts
Prsia*
1967
Diptych. Plywood
and mixed media
Each 120×70
Považká Galéria umenia,
Žilina / Museum of Art Žilina
(no.149)

*Nose I–II.
Nos I.–II.*
1967
Diptych. Plywood and
mixed media
Each 120×70
Linea Collection, Bratislava
(no.148)

*Object II
Objekt II*
1967
Mixed media, glass, metal
pelmet, textiles, lace, wood
148×70×50
Slovenská Národná Galéria,
Slovak National Gallery
(no.75)

Kandarya-Mahadeva
1969/2010–2012
Environment, mixed
media, plastic, mirrors,
paper, neon lights
Dimensions variable.
Column: 159×159×310
Linea Collection, Bratislava
(no.8)

Jerzy Ryszard 'Jurry' Zieliński

*Without Rebellion
Bez Buntu*
1970
Oil paint on canvas with
pillow, fabric and nail
150×200×4 Tongue approx.
45×80×130
Private collection, Courtesy
Luxembourg & Dayan
(no.26)

*The Smile, or
Thirty Years, Ha, Ha, Ha
Uśmiech, Czyli 'Trzydziesci'
– lac. 'Cha Cha Cha'*
1974
Oil paint on canvas
58.5×70
Piotr Nowicki Collection,
Courtesy of Polish Modern
Art Foundation, Warsaw
(no.25)

CREDITS

INDEX

SUPPORTING TATE

Tate relies on a large number of supporters – individuals, foundations, companies and public sector sources – to enable it to deliver its programme of activities, both on and off its gallery sites. This support is essential in order for Tate to acquire works of art for the Collection, run education, outreach and exhibition programmes, care for the Collection in storage and enable art to be displayed, both digitally and physically, inside and outside Tate.

Tate Foundation Trustees and Honorary Members
Abigail Baratta
Joseph P Baratta II*
Victoria Barnsley, OBE
John Botts, CBE*
Mrs James Brice
The Lord Browne of
    Madingley, FRS, FREng
Susan Burns
Christina Chandris
Melanie Clore
Sir Howard Davies
Dame Vivien Duffield
George Economou
Edward Eisler*
Maryam Eisler
Sasan Ghandehari
Noam Gottesman
Oliver Haarmann
Peter Kellner
The Hon Mrs Rita McAulay
Ronald McAulay
Scott Mead*
Mandy Moross
Elisabeth Murdoch
Lord Myners of Truro, CBE
Marilyn Ofer
Franck Petitgas (Chairman)*
Simon Palley*
John Porter
Lady Ritblat
Sir John Ritblat
Emmanuel Roman*
Dame Theresa Sackler
The Rt Hon Sir Timothy
    Sainsbury
Sir Anthony Salz*
Sir Nicholas Serota*
Peter Simon
Jon Snow
Lord Stevenson of
    Coddenham, CBE*
Mercedes Stoutzker
John Studzinski, CBE
Ian Taylor
Lance Uggla
Viktor Vekselberg

Sir David Verey, CBE
Anita Zabludowicz

*Executive Committee

Tate Members Council
Brian Chadwick
Chris Chinaloy
Hannah Collins
Dominic Harris
Suwin Lee
Rachel Lloyd
Amanda Pinto
Miranda Sawyer
Neil Scott
Jon Snow (Chair)
Simon Wilson
Alan Yates

**Tate Americas
Foundation Trustees**
Frances Bowes
Estrellita Brodsky
James Chanos
Henry Christensen III
Tiqui Atencio Demirdjian
    (Ex-officio)
Jeanne Donovan Fisher (Chair)
Ella Fontanals-Cisneros
Glenn Fuhrman
Noam Gottesman
Robert Rennie (Ex-officio)
John Studzinski, CBE
Marjorie Susman
Juan Carlos Verme

**Tate Modern Donors to the
Founding Capital Campaign**
29th May 1961 Charitable Trust
AMP
The Annenberg Foundation
Arts Council England
The Asprey Family Charitable
    Foundation
Lord and Lady Attenborough
The Baring Foundation
Ron Beller and Jennifer Moses
Alex and Angela Bernstein
David and Janice Blackburn
Mr and Mrs Anthony Bloom
BNP Paribas
Mr and Mrs Pontus Bonnier
Lauren and Mark Booth
Mr and Mrs John Botts
Frances and John Bowes
Ivor Braka
Mr and Mrs James Brice
The British Land Company plc
Donald L Bryant Jr Family
Melva Bucksbaum
Cazenove & Co
The Clore Duffield Foundation
CGU plc
Clifford Chance

Edwin C Cohen
The John S. Cohen Foundation
Ronald and Sharon Cohen
Sadie Coles
Carole and Neville Conrad
Giles and Sonia Coode-Adams
Douglas Cramer
Alan Cristea Gallery
Thomas Dane
Michel and Hélène David-Weill
Julia W Dayton
Gilbert de Botton
Pauline Denyer-Smith and
    Paul Smith
Sir Harry and Lady Djanogly
The Drapers' Company
Energis Communications
English Heritage
English Partnerships
The Eranda Foundation
Esmée Fairbairn Charitable Trust
Donald and Doris Fisher
Richard B. and Jeanne
    Donovan Fisher
The Fishmongers' Company
Freshfields Bruckhaus Deringer
Friends of the Tate Gallery
Bob and Kate Gavron
Giancarlo Giammetti
Alan Gibbs
Mr and Mrs Edward Gilhuly
GKR
GLG Partners
Helyn and Ralph Goldenberg
Goldman Sachs
The Horace W Goldsmith
    Foundation
The Worshipful Company
    of Goldsmiths
Lydia and Manfred Gorvy
Noam and Geraldine Gottesman
Pehr and Christina
    Gyllenhammar
Mimi and Peter Haas
The Worshipful Company
    of Haberdashers
Hanover Acceptances Limited
The Headley Trust
Mr and Mrs André Hoffmann
Anthony and Evelyn Jacobs
Jay Jopling
Mr and Mrs Karpidas
Howard and Lynda Karshan
Peter and Maria Kellner
Madeleine Kleinwort
Brian and Lesley Knox
Pamela and C Richard Kramlich
Mr and Mrs Henry R Kravis
Irene and Hyman Kreitman
The Kresge Foundation
Catherine and Pierre Lagrange
The Lauder Foundation –
    Leonard and Evelyn
    Lauder Fund
Lazard Brothers & Co., Limited

Leathersellers' Company
    Charitable Fund
Edward and Agnès Lee
Lex Service Plc
Lehman Brothers
Ruth and Stuart Lipton
Anders and Ulla Ljungh
The Frank Lloyd Family Trusts
London & Cambridge
    Properties Limited
London Electricity plc,
    EDF Group
Mr and Mrs George Loudon
Mayer, Brown, Rowe & Maw
Viviane and James Mayor
Ronald and Rita McAulay
The Mercers' Company
The Meyer Foundation
The Millennium Commission
Anthony and Deirdre Montagu
The Monument Trust
Mori Building, Ltd
Mr and Mrs M D Moross
Guy and Marion Naggar
Peter and Eileen Norton,
    The Peter Norton Family
    Foundation
Maja Oeri and Hans Bodenmann
Sir Peter and Lady Osborne
William A Palmer
Mr Frederik Paulsen
Pearson plc
The Pet Shop Boys
The Nyda and Oliver
    Prenn Foundation
Prudential plc
Railtrack plc
The Rayne Foundation
Reuters
Sir John and Lady Ritblat
Rolls-Royce plc
Barrie and Emmanuel Roman
Lord and Lady Rothschild
The Dr Mortimer and Theresa
    Sackler Foundation
J. Sainsbury plc
Ruth and Stephan Schmidheiny
Schroders
Mr and Mrs Charles Schwab
David and Sophie Shalit
Belle Shenkman Estate
William Sieghart
Peter Simon
Mr and Mrs Sven Skarendahl
London Borough of Southwark
The Foundation for Sports
    and the Arts
Mr and Mrs Nicholas Stanley
The Starr Foundation
The Jack Steinberg
    Charitable Trust
Charlotte Stevenson

267

Hugh and Catherine Stevenson
John J Studzinski, CBE
David and Linda Supino
The Government of Switzerland
Carter and Mary Thacher
Insinger Townsley
UBS
UBS Warburg
David and Emma Verey
Dinah Verey
The Vintners' Company
Clodagh and Leslie Waddington
Robert and Felicity
  Waley-Cohen
Wasserstein, Perella & Co., Inc.
Gordon D Watson
The Weston Family
Mr and Mrs Stephen Wilberding
Michael S Wilson
Poju and Anita Zabludowicz
and those who wish to
* remain anonymous*

Donors to The
Tate Modern Project
Abigail and Joesph Baratta
Blavatnik Family Foundation
Lauren and Mark Booth
The Deborah Loeb Brice
  Foundation
The Lord Browne of
  Madingley, FRS, FREng
John and Christina Chandris
James Chanos
Paul Cooke
The Roger De Haan Charitable
  Trust
Ago Demirdjian and Tiqui
  Atencio Demirdjian
Department for Culture,
  Media and Sport
George Economou
Edward and Maryam Eisler
English Partnerships
Mrs Donald B. Fisher
Jeanne Donovan Fisher
Mala Gaonkar
The Ghandehari Foundation
Thomas Gibson in memory of
  Anthea Gibson
Lydia and Manfred Gorvy
Noam Gottesman
The Hayden Family Foundation
Maja Hoffmann/LUMA
  Foundation
Peter and Maria Kellner
Madeleine Kleinwort
Catherine Lagrange
Pierre Lagrange
London Development Agency
Allison and Howard W. Lutnick
Donald B. Marron
Anthony and Deirdre Montagu
Elisabeth Murdoch
Eyal Ofer Family Foundation
Maureen Paley
Midge and Simon Palley
Daniel and Elizabeth Peltz
Catherine and Franck Petitgas
Barrie and Emmanuel Roman
The Dr Mortimer and Theresa
  Sackler Foundation
John J Studzinski, CBE

Tate Americas Foundation
Tate Members
The Uggla Family
Viktor Vekselberg
Nina and Graham Williams
The Wolfson Foundation
and those who wish to
* remain anonymous*

Tate Modern Benefactors
and Major Donors
Sirine and Ahmad Abu Ghazaleh
Ghazwa and Walid Abu-Suud
Carolyn Alexander
Basil and Raghida
  Al-Rahim Art Fund
Abdullah Al-Turki
Fernando Luis Alvarez
The Ampersand Foundation
Gregory Annenberg Weingarten
  and the Annenberg Foundation
The Fagus Anstruther
  Memorial Trust
Art Fund
Art Mentor Foundation Lucerne
Arts & Humanities Research
  Council
Arts Council England
Artworkers Retirement Society
Charles Asprey
Marwan T Assaf
The Estate of Mr Edgar Astaire
averda
Gillian Ayres
John Baldessari
Lionel Barber
The Barker-Mill Foundation
The Estate of Peter and
  Caroline Barker-Mill
The Barns-Graham
  Charitable Trust
Corinne Bellow Charity
Rosamond Bernier
Dorothy Berwin and
  Dominique Levy
Big Lottery Fund
Blavatnik Family Foundation
Pontus Bonnier
John C Botts, CBE
Louise Bourgeois
Frances Bowes
Frank Bowling, Rachel Scott,
  Benjamin and Sacha Bowling,
  Marcia and Iona Scott
Sir Alan and Lady Bowness
Pierre Brahm
Ivor Braka
The Estate of Dr Marcella
  Louis Brenner
British Council
Rory and Elizabeth
  Brooks Foundation
The Estate of Mrs Rachel Caro
Mr and Mrs Nicolas Cattelain
Roger Cazalet
The Trustees of the
  Chantrey Bequest
Henry Christensen III
Clore Duffield Foundation
The Clothworkers' Foundation
Borja Coca
Robert T. Coffland
R and S Cohen Foundation
Steven Cohen
Sadie Coles Gallery

Contemporary Art Society
Isabelle and John Corbani
Corvi-Mora
Douglas S Cramer
Thomas Dane Gallery
Thomas Dane Ltd
Dimitris Daskalopoulos
Tiqui Atencio Demirdjian
  and Ago Demirdjian
Department for Business,
  Innovation and Skills
Department for Culture,
  Media and Sport
Paul Dodds
Anthony and Anne d'Offay
Peter Doig
Joe and Marie Donnelly
Jeanne Donovan Fisher
Jytte Dresing, The Merla
  Art Foundation, Dresing
  Collection
Stephen Edge
EDP - Energias de Portugal, S.A.
Tony Edwards
The John Ellerman Foundation
Ibrahim El-Salahi
Carla Emil and Rich Silverstein
Tracey Emin
Stefan Edlis and Gael Neeson
European Union
Eykyn Maclean
Esmée Fairbairn
  Collections Fund
The Estate of Maurice
  Farquharson
Ronald and Frayda Feldman
HRH Princess Firyal of Jordan
Wendy Fisher
The Fischinger Trust,
  Long Beach, CA
Dr Kira and Neil Flanzraich
Eric and Louise Franck
Jay Franke and David Herro
The Estate of Lucian Freud
Erica and Alex Friedman
Frith Street Gallery
Froehlich Foundation, Stuttgart
Anna Fudge and Matthew Fudge
Glenn and Amanda Fuhrman
Gagosian Gallery
Mala Gaonkar
Garcia Family Foundation
Johanna and Leslie J. Garfield
Victoria Gelfand Magalhães and
  Pedro Magalhães
The Getty Foundation
The Hon HMT Gibson's
  Charity Trust
Thomas Gibson
Liam Gillick
Milly and Arne Glimcher
Goethe-Institut
Nicholas and Judith Goodison
Marian Goodman Gallery
Douglas Gordon and Artangel
Lydia and Manfred Gorvy
Noam Gottesman
The Granville-Grossman Bequest
Sarah and Gerard Griffin
Guaranty Trust Bank Plc
Calouste Gulbenkian Foundation
Agnes Gund
The Estate of Mr John Haggart

Nigel Hall
Paul Hamlyn Foundation
Mark Hannam
Noriyuki Haraguchi
Hauser & Wirth
Bowness, Hepworth Estate
Heritage Lottery Fund
Mauro Herlizka
The Estate of Miss Grace
  Patricia Hills
Roger Hiorns
Damien Hirst
David Hockney
The Estate of Mrs Mimi Hodgkin
Karin und Uwe Hollweg Stiftung
Michael Hue-Williams
Vicky Hughes and John A Smith
Huo Family Foundation (UK)
Leili Huth and Reza Asfar
  Kharaghan
Institut Françias
Iran Heritage Foundation
Amrita Jhaveri
Karpidas Family
Dr Martin Kenig
J. Patrick Kennedy and
  Patricia A. Kennedy
Anne Simone Kleinman
  and Thomas Wong
Leon Kossoff
Tomio Koyama Gallery
The Kreitman Foundation
Samuel H. Kress Foundation,
  administered by the
  Foundation of the American
  Institute for Conservation
Andreas Kurtz
Kirby Laing Foundation
The Estate of Jay and Fran
  Landesman
The Leathersellers' Company
  Charitable Fund
Agnès and Edward Lee
Legacy Trust UK
The Leverhulme Trust
Ruben Levi
Gemma Levine
Harris Lieberman
Timothy Llewellyn
London Organising Committee
  of the Olympic Games and
  Paralympic Games
The Loveday Charitable Trust
The Henry Luce Foundation
Luhring Augustine
LUMA Foundation
The Estate of Sir Edwin Manton
The Manton Foundation
Lord McAlpine of West Green
Fergus McCaffery
The Andrew W Mellon
  Foundation
The Paul Mellon Centre
  for Studies in British Art
Sir Geoffroy Millais
Mondriaan Fund, Amsterdam
The Henry Moore Foundation
Simon and Catriona Mordant
Daido Moriyama
Elisabeth Murdoch
The Estate of Mrs Jenifer
  Ann Murray
National Heritage Memorial Fund
Stefan Edlis and Gael Neeson

269

Martyn Gregory
Mrs Kate Grimond
Richard and Odile Grogan
Mrs Helene Guerin-Llamas
Louise Hallett
Arthur Hanna
Mark Harris
Michael and Morven Heller
James Holland-Hibbert
Lady Hollick, OBE
Holtermann Fine Art
Jeff Horne
John Huntingford
Maxine Isaacs
Helen Janecek
Sarah Jennings
Mr Haydn John
Mr Michael Johnson
Mike Jones
Jay Jopling
Mrs Brenda Josephs
Tracey Josephs
Mr Joseph Kaempfer
Andrew Kalman
Ghislaine Kane
Ivan Katzen
Dr Martin Kenig
Mr David Ker
Nicola Kerr
Mr and Mrs Simon Keswick
Richard and Helen Keys
Sadru Kheraj
Mrs Mae Khouri
David Killick
Mr and Mrs James Kirkman
Brian and Lesley Knox
Tatiana Kovylina
Kowitz Trust
Mr and Mrs Herbert Kretzmer
Linda Lakhdhir
Ms Anna Lapshina
Simon Lee
Mr Gerald Levin
Leonard Lewis
Sophia and Mark Lewisohn
Mr Gilbert Lloyd
George Loudon
Mrs Elizabeth Louis
Mark and Liza Loveday
Catherine Lovell
Jeff Lowe
Alison Loyd
Daniella Luxembourg Art
Mrs Ailsa Macalister
Kate MacGarry
Anthony Mackintosh
Eykyn Maclean LLC
The Mactaggart Third Fund
Mrs Jane Maitland Hudson
Lord and Lady Marks
Marsh Christian Trust
Ms Fiona Mellish
Mrs R W P Mellish
Professor Rob Melville
Mr Alfred Mignano
Victoria Miro
Jan Mol
Lulette Monbiot
Mrs Bona Montagu
Mrs William Morrison
Ms Deborah Norton
Julian Opie
Pilar Ordovás
Desmond Page

Maureen Paley
Dominic Palfreyman
Michael Palin
Mrs Adelaida Palm
Stephen and Clare Pardy
Mrs Véronique Parke
Frans Pettinga
Trevor Pickett
Mr Alexander Platon
Mr Oliver Prenn
Susan Prevezer QC
Mr and Mrs Ryan Prince
James Pyner
Ivetta Rabinovich
Patricia Ranken
Bernadette Rankine
Mrs Phyllis Rapp
Dr Laurence Reed
The Reuben Foundation
Lady Ritblat
Ms Chao Roberts
David Rocklin
Frankie Rossi
Mr David V Rouch
Mr James Roundell
Mr Charles Roxburgh
Naomi Russell
Mr Alex Sainsbury and
    Ms Elinor Jansz
Mr Richard Saltoun
Mrs Cecilia Scarpa
Cherrill and Ian Scheer
Sylvia Scheuer
Mrs Cara Schulze
Hakon Runer and Ulrike
    Schwarz-Runer
Ellen Shaprio
The Hon Richard Sharp
Neville Shulman, CBE
Ms Julia Simmonds
Paul and Marcia Soldatos
Mr Vagn Sørensen
Louise Spence
Mr Nicos Steratzias
Stacie Styles and Ken
    McCracken
Ayse Suleyman
Mrs Patricia Swannell
Mr James Swartz
The Lady Juliet Tadgell
Elaine Thomas
Anthony Thornton
Britt Tidelius
Mr Henry Tinsley
Ian Tollett
Karen Townshend
Monica Tross
Andrew Tseng
Melissa Ulfane
Mrs and Mrs Petri Vainio
Mrs Cecilia Versteegh
Gisela von Sanden
Michelle Wafa
Audrey Wallrock
Sam Walsh AO
Stephen and Linda Waterhouse
Offer Waterman
Miss Cheyenne Westphal
Walter H. White, Jnr.
Mr David Wood
Mr Douglas Woolf
and those who wish to
    remain anonymous

Young Patrons
HH Princess Nauf AlBendar
    Al-Saud
Miss Noor Al-Rahim
Fahad Alrashid
HRH Princess Alia Al-Senussi
    (Chair, Young Patrons
    Ambassador Group)
Miss Sharifa Alsudairi
Miss Katharine Arnold
Ms Mila Askarova
Miss Olivia Aubry
Flavie Audi
Daniel Axmer
Katrina Beechey
Sarah Bejerano
Athena Bersimis
William Bertagna
Roberto Boghossian
Georgina Borthwick
Johan Bryssinck
Miss Verena Butt
Sarah Calodney
The Hon Nicholas Campbell
Miss Livia Carpeggiani
Francesca Castelli
Cecile Champy
Alexandra and Kabir Chhatwani
Yoojin Choi
Arthur Chow
Aidan Christofferson
Bianca Chu
Adam Clay
Niamh Coghlan
Caroline Cole
Thamara Corm
Tara Wilson Craig
Sadrine Currimjee Debacker
Mr Theo Danjuma
Henry Danowski
Mr Joshua Davis
Ms Lora de Felice
Countess Charlotte de la
    Rochefoucauld
Agnes de Royere
Federico Martin Castro
    Debernardi
Carine Decroi
Sue Deveci
Suzana Diamond
Mira Dimitrova
Ms Michelle D'Souza
Guillaume Duval
Indira Dyussebayeva
Alexandra Economou
Miss Roxanna Farboud
Anaïs Ferrier
Ottavia Fontana
Jane and Richard Found
Jessica L. Frey
Magdalena Gabriel
Mr Andreas Gegner
Benedetta Ghione
Nicolas Gitton
David Green
Lise Grendene
Judith Greve
Antonella Grevers
Georgia Griffiths
Mr Nick Hackworth
Alex Haidas
Angus Haldane
Ms Michelle Harari
Sara Harrison

Andrew Honan
Simona Houldsworth
Hus Gallery
Kamel Jaber
Scott Jacobson
Ms Melek Huma Kabakci
Sophie Kainradl
Miss Meruyert Kaliyeva
Mrs Vasilisa Kameneva
Miss Tamila Kerimova
Ms Chloe Kinsman
Sadie Kirshman
Daniel Klier
Berrak Kocaoglu
Ellie Konstantilieri
Anastasia Koreleva
Maria Korolevskaya
Stephen Kovalcik
Mr Jimmy Lahoud
Isabella Lauder-Frost
Miss MC Llamas
Alex Logsdail
Wei-Lyn Loh
Lindsey Love
Ms Sonia Mak
Dr Christina Makris
Mr Jean-David Malat
Kamiar Maleki
Daria Manganelli
Zoe Marden
Krzysztof Maruszewski
Dr. F. Mattison Thompson
Charles-Henri McDermott
Fiona McGovern
Amanda Mead
Miss Nina Moaddel
Mr Fernando Moncho Lobo
Erin Morris
Ali Munir
Nina Neuhaus
Katia Nounou
Heline Odqvist
Erendira Old
Berkay Oncel
Andrew Paradis
Christine Chungwon Park
William Pelham
Anna Pennink
Sonata Persson
Alexander V. Petalas
The Piper Gallery
Courtney Plummer
Victoria Poniatowski
Radhika Radia
Asta Ramonaite
Mr Eugenio Re Rebaudengo
Elise Roberts
Louisa Robertson
Katharina Sailer
Mr Simon Sakhai
Miss Tatiana Sapegina
Paola Saracino Fendi
Natasha Maria Sareen
Franz Schwarz
Alex Seddon
Lea Sednaoui
Count Indoo Sella
    Di Monteluce
Jelena Seng
Robert Sheffield
Henrietta Shields
Ms Marie-Anya Shriro
Jag Singh
Tammy Smulders

Gemma Stewart-Richardson
Dominic Stolerman
Mr Edward Tang
Nayrouz Tatanaki
Dr Kafui Tay
Miss Inge Theron
Soren S K Tholstrup
Mr Giancarlo Trinca
Mr Philippos Tsangrides
Ms Navann Ty
Celine Valligny
Alexandra Warder
Mr Neil Wenman
Kim Williams
Ms Seda Yalcinkaya
Reza Yazdi
Daniel Zarchan
Olivia Zarka
and those who wish to
remain anonymous

International Council Members
Mr Segun Agbaje
Staffan Ahrenberg, Editions
    Cahiers d'Art
Mr Geoff Ainsworth AM
Dilyara Allakhverdova
Doris Ammann
Mr Plácido Arango
Gabrielle Bacon
Anne H Bass
Cristina Bechtler
Nicolas Berggruen
Olivier and Desiree Berggruen
Mr Pontus Bonnier
Frances Bowes
Ivor Braka
The Deborah Loeb Brice
    Foundation
The Broad Art Foundation
Melva Bucksbaum and
    Raymond Learsy
Andrew Cameron AM
Fondation Cartier pour l'art
    contemporain
Nicolas and Celia Cattelain
Trudy and Paul Cejas
Mrs Christina Chandris
Richard Chang (Vice Chair)
Pierre TM Chen, Yageo
    Foundation, Taiwan
Adrian Cheng
Lord Cholmondeley
Mr Kemal Has Cingillioglu
Mr and Mrs Attilio Codognato
Sir Ronald Cohen and Lady
    Sharon Harel-Cohen
Mr Douglas S Cramer and
    Mr Hubert S Bush III
Mr Dimitris Daskalopoulos
Mr and Mrs Michel David-Weill
Julia W Dayton
Ms Miel de Botton
Tiqui Atencio Demirdjian
    and Ago Demirdjian
Joseph and Marie Donnelly
Mrs Olga Dreesmann
Barney A Ebsworth
Füsun and Faruk Eczacibaşi
Mr and Mrs Edward Eisler
Stefan Edlis and Gael Neeson
Carla Emil and Rich Silverstein
Fares and Tania Fares
HRH Princess Firyal of Jordan
Mrs Doris Fisher

Mrs Wendy Fisher
Dr Kira Flanzraich
Dr Corinne M Flick
Amanda and Glenn Fuhrman
Candida and Zak Gertler
Mrs Yassmin Ghandehari
Mr Giancarlo Giammetti
Alan Gibbs
Lydia and Manfred Gorvy
Mr Laurence Graff
Ms Esther Grether
Konstantin Grigorishin
Mr Xavier Guerrand-Hermès
Mimi and Peter Haas Fund
Margrit and Paul Hahnloser
Andy and Christine Hall
Paul Harris
Mrs Susan Hayden
Jorge and Sylvie Helft
Ms Ydessa Hendeles
Marlene Hess and James D. Zirin
André and Rosalie Hoffmann
Ms Maja Hoffmann (Chair)
Vicky Hughes
ITYS, Athens
Dakis and Lietta Joannou
Sir Elton John and Mr David
    Furnish
Pamela J. Joyner
Mr Chang-Il Kim
Jack Kirkland
C Richard and Pamela Kramlich
Bert Kreuk
Mrs Grażyna Kulczyk
Andreas and Ulrike Kurtz
Catherine Lagrange
Mr Pierre Lagrange
Baroness Lambert
Bernard Lambilliotte
Agnès and Edward Lee
Mme RaHee Hong Lee
Jacqueline and Marc Leland
Mr and Mrs Sylvain Levy
Mrs Fatima Maleki
Panos and Sandra Marinopoulos
Mr and Mrs Donald B Marron
Mr Ronald and The Hon
    Mrs McAulay
Mark McCain and Caro
    MacDonald
Angela Westwater and
    David Meitus
Mr Leonid Mikhelson
Aditya and Megha Mittal
Mr Donald Moore
Simon and Catriona Mordant
Mrs Yoshiko Mori
Mr Guy and The Hon
    Mrs Naggar
Fayeeza Naqvi
Mr and Mrs Takeo Obayashi
Hideyuki Osawa
Irene Panagopoulos
Young-Ju Park
Ms Lisa Paulsen
Yana and Stephen Peel
Daniel and Elizabeth Peltz
Andrea and José Olympio Pereira
Catherine Petitgas
Sydney Picasso
Mr and Mrs Jürgen Pierburg
Jean Pigozzi

Lekha Poddar
Miss Dee Poon
Ms Miuccia Prada and
    Mr Patrizio Bertelli
Laura Rapp and Jay Smith
Maya and Ramzy Rasamny
Patrizia Sandretto Re
    Rebaudengo and Agostino
    Re Rebaudengo
Robert Rennie and Carey Fouks
Sir John Richardson
Michael Ringier
Lady Ritblat
Ms Hanneli M Rupert
Ms Güler Sabanci
Dame Theresa Sackler, DBE
Mrs Lily Safra
Muriel and Freddy Salem
Rajeeb and Nadia Samdani
Dasha Shenkman, OBE
Uli and Rita Sigg
Norah and Norman Stone
Julia Stoschek
John J Studzinski, CBE
Maria and Malek Sukkar
Mrs Marjorie Susman
Mr Budi Tek, The Yuz
    Foundation
Mr Robert Tomei
The Hon Robert H Tuttle and
    Mrs Maria Hummer-Tuttle
Mr and Mrs Guy Ullens
Mrs Ninetta Vafeia
Corinne and Alexandre
    Van Damme
Paulo A W Vieira
Robert and Felicity Waley-Cohen
Diana Widmaier Picasso
Christen and Derek Wilson
Michael G Wilson
Mrs Sylvie Winckler
The Hon Dame Janet Wolfson
    de Botton, DBE
Anita and Poju Zabludowicz
Michael Zilkha
and those who wish to
remain anonymous

Africa Acquisitions Committee
Kathy Ackerman Robins
Tutu Agyare (Co-Chair)
Anshu Bahanda
Mrs Nwakaego Boyo
Priti Chandaria Shah
Mrs Kavita Chellaram
Colin Coleman
Salim Currimjee
Harry G. David
Mr and Mrs Michel David-Weill
Robert Devereux (Co-Chair)
Hamish Dewar
Robert and Renee Drake
Mrs Wendy Fisher
Andrea Kerzner
Samallie Kiyingi
Matthias and Gervanne Leridon
Caro Macdonald
Dominick Maia-Tanner
Dale Mathias
Professor Oba Nsugbe QC
Pascale Revert Wheeler
Emile Stipp
Ana Luiza and Luiz Augusto
    Teixeira de Freitas
Mr Varnavas A. Varnava

Burkhard Varnholt
Mercedes Vilardell
and those who wish to
remain anonymous

Asia-Pacific
Acquisitions Committee
Matthias Arndt
Bonnie and R Derek Bandeen
Andrew Cameron AM
Mr and Mrs John Carrafiell
Richard Chang
Pierre TM Chen, Yageo
    Foundation, Taiwan
Adrian Cheng
Mr Yan d'Auriol
Katie de Tilly
Mr Hyung-Teh Do
Elaine Forsgate Marden
Ms Mareva Grabowski
Reade and Elizabeth Griffith
Cees Hendrikse
Philippa Hornby
Mr Yongsoo Huh
Mrs Natalie Kadoorie González
Shareen Khattar Harrison
Mr Chang-Il Kim
Ms Yung Hee Kim
Alan Lau (Co-Chair)
Woong-Yeul Lee
Mr William Lim
Ms Dina Liu
Juliette Liu
Ms Kai-Yin Lo
Anne Louis-Dreyfus
Elisabetta Marzetti Mallinson
Marleen Molenaar
John Porter
The Red Mansion Foundation
Dr Gene Sherman (Co-Chair)
Leo Shih
Sir David Tang
Mr Budi Tek, The Yuz
    Foundation
Neil Wenman
Yang Bin
and those who wish to
remain anonymous

Latin American Acquisitions
Committee
Ghazwa Abu-Soud
Monica and Robert Aguirre
Karen and Leon Amitai
Luis Benshimol
Celia Birbragher
Estrellita and Daniel Brodsky
Carmen Busquets
Trudy and Paul Cejas
David Cohen Sitton
HSH the Prince Pierre d'Arenberg
Tiqui Atencio Demirdjian (Chair)
Andrea Dreesmann
Patricia Druck
Angelica Fuentes de Vergara
Ronald Harrar
Barbara Hemmerle-Gollust
Rocio and Boris Hirmas Said
Marta Regina Fernandez Holman
Julian Iragorri
Anne Marie and Geoffrey Isaac
Nicole Junkermann
José Luis Lorenzo
Milagros Maldonado

Fatima and Eskander Maleki
Francisca Mancini
Fernanda Marques
Denise and Felipe Nahas Mattar
Veronica Nutting
Victoria and Isaac Oberfeld
Paulina and Alfonso
  Otero-Zamora
Catherine Petitgas
Claudio Federico Porcel
Frances Reynolds
Erica Roberts
Judko Rosenstock and
  Oscar Hernandez
Lilly Scarpetta
Norma Smith
Juan Carlos Verme
Tania and Arnoldo Wald
Juan Yarur Torres
and those who wish to
  remain anonymous

Middle East and North Africa Acquisitions Committee
HRH Princess Alia Al-Senussi
Abdullah Al Turki
Mehves Ariburnu
Sule Arinc
Marwan T Assaf
Niloufar Bakhtiar Clignet
Perihan Bassatne
Foundation Boghossian
Ms Isabelle de la Bruyère
Füsun Eczacibaşi
Maryam Eisler (Co-Chair)
Shirley Elghanian
Delfina Entrecanales, CBE
Noor Fares
Raghida Ghandour Al Rahim
Taymour Grahne
Maha and Kasim Kutay
Mrs Fatima Maleki
Fayeeza Naqvi
Dina Nasser-Khadivi
Shulamit Nazarian
Ebru Özdemir
Mrs Edwina Özyegin
Mr Moshe Peterburg
Charlotte Philipps
Ramzy and Maya Rasamny
  (Co-Chair)
Mrs Madhu Ruia
Mrs Karen Ruimy
Dania Debs-Sakka
Shihab Shobokshi
Miss Yassi Sohrabi
Maria and Malek Sukkar
Faisal Tamer
Ana Luiza and Luiz Augusto
  Teixeira de Freitas
Tsukanov Family Foundation
Berna Tuglular
Yesim Turanli
Mahdi Yahya
Roxane Zand
and those who wish to
  remain anonymous

North American Acquisitions Committee
Carol and David Appel
Jacqueline Appel and
  Alexander Malmaeus
Abigail Baratta

Dorothy Berwin and
  Dominique Levy
Paul Britton
Many Cawthorn Argenio
Dillon Cohen
Matt Cohler
Michael Corman and Kevin Fink
Theo Danjuma
James Diner
Wendy Fisher
Glenn Fuhrman
Victoria Gelfand-Magalhaes
Amy Gold
Nina and Dan Gross
Pamela Joyner
Monica Kalpakian
Elisabeth and Panos Karpidas
Christian Keese
Anne Simone Kleinman and
  Thomas Wong
Rachelli Mishori and Leon
  Koffler
Marjorie and Michael Levine
James Lindon
Rebecca Marks
Lillian and Billy Mauer
Liza Mauer and Andrew Sheiner
Nancy McCain
Stavros Merjos
Gregory R. Miller
Megha Mittal
Shabin and Nadir Mohamed
Jenny Mullen
Elisa Nuyten and David Dime
Amy and John Phelan
Nathalie Pratte
Melinda B and Paul Pressler
Liz Gerring Radke and Kirk
  Radke
Laura Rapp and Jay Smith
Robert Rennie (Chair) and Carey
  Fouks
Kimberly Richter and Jon Shirley
Carolin Scharpff-Striebich
Komal Shah
Dasha Shenkman
Donald R Sobey
Robert Sobey
Beth Swofford
Laurie Thomson and Andy
  Chisholm
Dr. Diane Vachon
Christen and Derek Wilson
and those who wish to remain
  anonymous

Photography Acquisitions Committee
Her Highness Sheikha Fatima
  Bint Hazza' Bin Zayed Al
  Nahyan
Ryan Allen
Artworkers Retirement Society
Nicholas Barker
Cynthia Lewis Beck
Marisa Bellani
Pierre Brahm (Co-Chair)
Mrs. William Shaw Broeksmit
Elizabeth and Rory Brooks
Marcel and Gabrielle Cassard
Nicolas (Co-Chair) and Celia
  Cattelain
Mr and Mrs Michel David-Weill
Charlie Fellowes and Jeremy
  Epstein, Edel Assanti

Nikki Fennell
David Fitzsimons
Lisa Garrison
Ms Emily Goldner and Mr
  Michael Humphries
Margot and George Greig
Alexandra Hess
Bernard Huppert
Dede Johnston
Jack Kirkland
David Knaus
Mr Scott Mead
Sebastien Montabonel
Mr Donald Moore
Alexandra Nash
Saadi Soudavar
Nicholas Stanley
Maria and Malek Sukkar
Mrs Caroline Trausch
Michael and Jane Wilson
and those who wish to
  remain anonymous

Russia Eastern Europe Acquisitions Committee
Dmitry Aksenov
Dilyara Allakhverdova
Maria Baibakova
Razvan BANESCU
David Birnbaum
Maria Bukhtoyarova
Mark Čuček
Elena Evstafieva
Dr Kira Flanzraich (Chair)
Lyuba Galkina
Suad Garayeva
Dr Dr Joana Grevers
Konstantin Grigorishin
Cees Hendrikse
Mr. Vilius Kavaliauskas
Carl Kostyál
Arina Kowner
Mrs Grażyna Kulczyk
Peter Kulloi
Krzysztof Madelski
Eduard Maták
Teresa Mavica
Luba Michailova
Maarja Oviir-Neivelt
Lorenzo Paini
Neil K. Rector
Valeria Rodnyansky
Robert Runták
Maria Rus Bojan
Ovidiu Şandor
Zsolt Somlói
Elena Sudakova
Mrs Elena Todorova
The Tretyakov Family Collection
Miroslav Trnka
Mrs Alina Uspenskaya
Jo Vickery
Georgi Voynov
Veronika Zonabend
Mr Janis Zuzans
and those who wish to
  remain anonymous

South Asia Acquisitions Committee
Maya Barolo-Rizvi
Krishna Bhupal
Akshay Chudasama
Anjali and Gaurav Grover
Zahida Habib

Dr Amin Jaffer
Aparajita Jain
Yamini Mehta
Mr Rohan Mirchandani
Shalini Misra
Amna and Ali Naqvi
Fayeeza Naqvi
Mrs.Chandrika Pathak
Puja and Uday Patnaik
Lekha Poddar (Co-Chair)
Mr Raj and Mrs Reshma Ruia
Nadia Samdani
Rajeeb Samdani (Co-Chair)
Mrs Tarana Sawhney
Sanjiv Singhal
Osman Khalid Waheed
Manuela and Iwan Wirth
and those who wish to
  remain anonymous

Tate Modern Corporate Supporters
Amsterdam Trade Bank
Bank of America Merrill Lynch
Bloomberg
BMW
BP
Christie's
Credit Suisse
Deutsche Bank AG
EY
Hanjin Shipping
Hildon Ltd
Hyundai Card
Hyundai Motor
Laurent Perrier
Le Méridien
Markit
Sotheby's
and those who wish to
  remain anonymous

Tate Modern Corporate Members
AIG
Bank of America Merrill Lynch
BCS Consulting
Citi
Clifford Chance LLP
CREATIVE HEAD
The Cultivist
Deutsche Bank
EY
Finsbury
GAM (UK) Limited
HSBC
Hyundai Card
JATO Dynamics
Kingfisher plc
Linklaters
McGuirewoods London LLP
The Moody's Foundation
Morgan Stanley
Pearson
Saatchi & Saatchi
Siegel + Gale
Slaughter and May
The Brooklyn Brothers
Tishman Speyer
Unilever
Wolff Olins
and those who wish to
  remain anonymous